Planning Your Qualitative Research Thesis and Project

The new edition of *Planning Your Qualitative Research Thesis and Project* provides easily accessible worked examples and valuable models which can be used as guides for plans and proposals. By demonstrating the thought and forward planning that is required when proposing a credible interpretivist study, this book provides the reader with all the theory and practical understanding necessary to conduct a successful qualitative research project.

This new edition provides examples of contemporary topics related to a range of countries across the developed and developing world, and new chapters which include:

- An example of a 'prospectives' study
- Policy studies and the interpretivist paradigm
- Life history studies
- Interactionist historical studies
- The interpretivist paradigm and research based on 'problem focused' ideas

With chapters and studies providing contemporary and relevant examples, this new edition is the perfect introductory guide for students looking to complete their first qualitative thesis project. Bridging the gap between theory and practice, it is an accessible introduction, and an invaluable resource for early stage doctoral students, and for students undertaking research and enquiry.

Tom O'Donoghue is Professor of Education in the Graduate School of Education, The University of Western Australia.

Planning Your Qualitative Research Thesis and Project

An Introduction to Interpretivist Research in Education and the Social Sciences

Second Edition

Tom O'Donoghue

Routledge
Taylor & Francis Group
LONDON AND NEW YORK

Second edition published 2019
by Routledge
2 Park Square, Milton Park, Abingdon, Oxon OX14 4RN

and by Routledge
711 Third Avenue, New York, NY 10017

Routledge is an imprint of the Taylor & Francis Group, an informa business

First edition published by Routledge 2006

British Library Cataloguing in Publication Data
A catalogue record for this book is available from the British Library

Library of Congress Cataloging in Publication Data
A catalog record for this book has been requested

ISBN: 978-0-8153-4902-0 (hbk)
ISBN: 978-0-8153-4903-7 (pbk)
ISBN: 978-1-351-16556-3 (ebk)

Typeset in Galliard
by Taylor & Francis Books

I dedicate this book to Adjunct Professor Judith Chapman AM for her mentoring, generosity and kindness when most needed

Contents

Tables

Preface

Over the last 40 years qualitative research has emerged to rival quantitative research as a serious approach to inquiry in a variety of social science areas, including education. I pointed out in the 2007 edition of this book (O'Donoghue, 2007) that this has been a welcome development, as has been the acceptance over the last decade that, far from being oppositional, these two broad approaches are complementary. At the same time, however, there is still wide scope for providing a series of guides for beginning researchers on how to go about planning qualitative research projects. This is not to argue that there is a shortage of works on various aspects of qualitative research; on the contrary, a great number of texts already exist. A particular group of such texts consists of works laying out the epistemological foundations of the approach. Another group consists of texts which elaborate on the great number of theoretical positions derived from such epistemological foundations in response to the desire to pursue particular research avenues. And then there is the large body of work detailing approaches to the gathering and analysis of qualitative data. Nevertheless, there are very few books which attempt to tie all these orientations together in the form of primers or guides to assist beginning researchers in planning their qualitative research projects. This book is a contribution to filling this lacuna.

One of the difficulties faced by new researchers due to a lack of books like this one is that many of the texts within the various groups outlined above stress that qualitative research is interdisciplinary, drawing from academic disciplines as wide ranging as psychology, sociology, anthropology and linguistics. The position adopted here is that while some approaches to qualitative research can be interdisciplinary, qualitative research does not always have to be so. Also, to seek to plan research projects within an interdisciplinary framework necessitates an academic training of both great depth and breadth, since to achieve competence in the central concepts of any one of the academic disciplines mentioned above takes years of sustained and concentrated study. Yet, many conscientious students approaching a qualitative research project for the first time, particularly in order to produce a thesis as part of the requirements of a university degree, often do not have this position made clear to them. Consequently, they regularly embark on an unsystematic dredge through a wealth of material, driven by a belief that they have, somehow, to master not only the central concepts and methods of investigation of a number of disciplines, but also those of the sub-schools within them, some of which are diametrically opposed to one another. Also, because of the emphasis on the interdisciplinary nature of qualitative research, students often seem to think that their task is to reconcile competing positions, develop their own eclectic stance and then defend it as being suitable to undergird their chosen research questions.

This is not to argue that it is a waste of time to engage in the latter exercise; indeed, cognitive dissonance has long been considered to be a valuable learning experience. On the other hand, the enormity of the task of constructing an eclectic theoretical framework for one's qualitative research project is often not appreciated by new students. Consequently, they dig deeper and deeper, often only to find that they have simply wandered into a swamp from which, without expert guidance, they find it extremely difficult to extricate themselves. I regularly have students come to me after engaging in various introductory programmes desperately trying to disentangle, compartmentalise and connect together such strange bedfellows as discourse analysis, positivism, case study research, telephone interviewing techniques, dilemma analysis, post-structuralism, auto-ethnography and non-participant observation.

I find with many students that one way forward is to take a particular structured approach. I also ask students to keep in mind that I do not dismiss the possibility that after they have worked through this approach a number of times they may eventually, and quite legitimately, reject it and embark, this time with confidence, on developing once again their own eclectic conceptual frameworks. Nevertheless, I hold that without a structured approach as initial scaffolding when they embark on planning their initial research projects, many are unlikely to ever come out of the swamp of confusion. The structured approach I promote requires students to consider how their chosen area of research connects to:

a an underlying research paradigm;
b a specific theoretical position within the paradigm;
c a specific methodology consistent with the paradigm and the theoretical position; and
d a set of methods for data gathering and analysis consistent with the specific methodology.

This book follows the logic of the above approach. It is specifically concerned with planning qualitative research projects where the research paradigm is interpretivism, the specific theoretical position is symbolic interactionism, the specific methodology is grounded theory and the research methods are semi-structured interviewing, participant and non-participant observation, and document analysis.

Finally, it needs to be re-emphasised that this is a book about planning research projects. It is not another book dealing specifically with any one of the four parts of the structured approach outlined above, although reference is made throughout to significant positions and to various specialised texts to help students in their planning. The early chapters provide in expository form the scaffolding referred to already. This is followed by examples of the write-up of two research projects of the central types addressed by this book. As before in the first edition of this book, a number of research proposals are then outlined in separate chapters. In all, there are seven proposals, only one of which appeared in the 2007 edition. The purpose of including these proposals is to illustrate some products of working through the planning process advocated, with some extension to the basic ideas central to the book's focus. Finally, most of the examples used throughout this book relate to projects with which the author and his students have been engaged at The University of Western Australia over the past decade. These, however, are also projects which could just as easily have been undertaken, with minor variations, in most of the English-speaking world.

Part I

An overview of the research process

Chapter 1

Introduction

For many years it has been common to place the process of engaging in research alongside experiencing and reasoning as the principal ways in which people attempt to understand their environments (Cohen and Manion 1985). While many of us have been socialised into assuming that such engagement is the most sophisticated of the three activities, Candy (1989: 1) has argued that it 'seems to be as much a natural human function as breathing'. On this he quoted Emery (1986: 1) as follows:

> Research ... is an ancient and ubiquitous activity. Curiosity about others and the worlds in which they live has always been displayed through conversation, asking questions, working together to see what happens after different kinds of actions are performed, talking or gossiping about others to tease out intentions and other reasons for behaviour, clarifying and understanding circumstances; all are fundamental research functions.

Candy (1989: 1) concluded his consideration of this point by arguing that it is upon such slender foundations that 'the whole massive superstructure of "research" is based'.

Notwithstanding the basic foundations of the research process, however, an important challenge for anyone contemplating engaging in it is to try to find a pathway from one's 'natural' research inclination into this 'massive superstructure' which Candy talks about. One way of proceeding is to view the initial stage in the research process as consisting of two major steps. The first step has its origins in an observation one makes. This observation may arise from viewing something on TV, reading something in the newspaper, hearing something on the radio, becoming cognisant of a particular policy issue, or being faced with some difficult decision to make. What may quickly follow is some curiosity, perplexity, confusion or doubt on one's part. This curiosity, perplexity, confusion or doubt, in turn, prompts one to want to know something. The result is that one begins to engage in research.

The second major step in the initial stage of the research process often follows quite rapidly. Here the practice, as Bouma (2000: 25) has put it, involves 'moving from an ordinary everyday question to a researchable question by focusing on one aspect of the issue arousing your interest'. Bouma further argues that the goal in this step is to produce a clear statement of the problem to be studied. Such a statement of a problem must explicitly identify the issues on which the researcher has chosen to focus. This, as he sees it, requires one to 'clarify the issues' and narrow the 'focus of concern' (Bouma 2000: 36).

Harry Wolcott, the famous anthropologist of education, suggested a way of thinking to help one engage in these related processes of clarifying the issue and narrowing the focus. His position is that as inquiry proceeds, the idea that prompted it should become both better formed and better informed (Wolcott 1992: 7). To this end, he suggested three categories which 'form a modest typology' of the ideas that guide inquiry: reform-driven ideas, concept-driven ideas and 'big' theory-driven ideas. This can be represented diagrammatically as shown in Table 1.1. Also, each of these positions is spelt out in recent work by Bhattacharya (2017) in a suitable manner that is helpful for beginning researchers.

It is arguable that most research in education and the social sciences has its origin in reform-driven ideas. On this, it is important to keep in mind that Wolcott uses 'reform' as a blanket term to include 'problem-oriented' and 'decision-oriented' research. What underlies all research questions articulated within the category, however, is an 'assumption on the part of the researcher that things are not right as they are or, most certainly, are not as good as they might be' (Wolcott 1992: 15). Examples of research questions which could be posed in this vein include the following:

- What is the most effective leadership style to adopt in schools?
- Does smoking affect academic performance?
- What is the extent of truancy in inner-city high schools?
- Does a concurrent programme of teacher education where students engage in teaching practice throughout their years of undergraduate study produce better-skilled teachers than a consecutive programme where students first study for a degree in a substantive subject-area and then undertake a one-year teacher preparation programme?

The researcher who poses questions such as these usually feels that all is not well with current practice and is prompted to bring about change directed at trying to improve the situation.

Wolcott's second category of ideas that guide inquiry are those identified as 'concepts'. These come in all shapes and sizes: 'Concepts point in an orienting

Table 1.1 A typology of ideas that guide inquiry

Inquiry based on reform-driven ideas	Inquiry based on concept-driven ideas	Inquiry based on 'big' theory-driven ideas

consciousness-raising, but saucily independent manner' (Wolcott 1992: 11). He went on to state that working at this level with, for example, a concept like 'culture', 'can provide a focus without allowing the seeming absence of theoretical structure to become overbearing' (Wolcott 1992: 11). The main concern of those adopting such an approach is with attempting to describe aspects of culture, an activity often referred to as ethnography. Goetz and Le Compte (1984: 17) described the activity thus:

> The purpose of educational ethnography is to provide rich, descriptive data about the contexts, activities, and beliefs of participants in educational settings. Typically, such data represent educational processes as they occur. The result of these processes is examined within the whole phenomenon; isolation of outcomes is rarely considered.

Researchers who are informed by a cultural perspective in their investigations are said to succeed if their research reports enable readers to behave appropriately in the particular cultural settings they purport to describe (Bogdan and Biklen 1984: 38).

LeCompte and Preissle (1993: 137–8) have provided a number of other examples to illustrate how research can be concept-guided. They pointed out that Sindell (1974) developed research questions in his study of the socialization of Mistassini Cree children from factors identified as important in Bandura's social learning theory. They also pointed out that Spindler's examination of the impact of the school on perspectives on urbanization among inhabitants of a rural German village drew explicitly from assimilation theory (Spindler 1974). Another trend they highlighted was a tendency in much research on adolescent alienation from school to draw heavily on the concepts of hegemony, symbolic violence and the political context of knowledge and meaning (LeCompte and Preissle 1993: 138).

Wolcott's third category of ideas that guide inquiry encompass those ideas that relate to an overall 'grand' or 'big theory'. He quoted the sociologist Robert Merton in this regard, where Merton spoke of 'the all-inclusive systematic effort' to develop a unified theory that explains 'all the observed uniformities of social behaviour, social organization and social change' (Merton 1968: 39). Wolcott argued that those who 'think theory' in this 'grand' sense are attempting to 'link up in someone's – perhaps even their own – Big Theory, everything that matters to everyone' (Wolcott 1992: 7).

This book is about undertaking a particular type of research from the point of view of Wolcott's third category of ideas that guide inquiry, namely, that of 'big theory'. The argument running throughout is that research in education and the social sciences can, in fact, be underpinned by one of four major 'big' theories, namely, positivism, interpretivism, critical theory, and postmodernism. Also, it is held that each of these 'big theories' can, in turn, be broken down into a number of related theoretical perspectives. For example, the interpretivist 'big theory' embraces such theoretical positions as hermeneutics, ethnomethodology, symbolic interactionism, and phenomenology. This categorization of 'big' theory can be represented as shown in Table 1.2.

The specific aim of this book is to provide new researchers with a guide to planning qualitative research projects based upon interpretivism as the 'big theory' and upon symbolic interactionism within it. At the same time, as readers progress through the work they should come to recognise that all research, including that guided by concept-driven ideas and problem-focused ideas, can ultimately be mapped back to show that it has 'grand theory' or 'big theory' foundations. Yet, this is not a book which explicitly seeks to engage readers in such a backward-mapping exercise. Instead, in setting out to demonstrate how research projects can be planned by adopting interpretivism as one's 'big theory' – and adopting within it the theoretical position of 'symbolic interactionism' – it is recognised that one can also plan research projects based upon one of the other 'big theories'.

Before moving directly to such planning issues, however, it is necessary to clarify a number of central ideas so that the theoretical foundations of the remainder of this book are clearly established. The rest of this chapter provides such clarification. First, consideration is given to the position that the idea of research as being guided by 'big theory' is more usually talked and written about as being research which is 'paradigm guided'. To this end, the notion of a research paradigm is explained and the four major 'big theories' already outlined are considered in terms of how each constitutes a research paradigm. Consideration is also given to the matter of how research questions are posed differently, depending upon the research paradigm one adopts.

The chapter then moves on to argue that a paradigm's approach to research requires us to adopt a view of the process as involving much more than simply rushing headlong into selecting appropriate methods for the investigation of a problem. Certainly, examining any problem or hypothesis requires the use of methods in the form of techniques to gather and analyse data. However, once we have grasped the

Table 1.2 Interpretivist paradigm and related theoretical perspectives

'Big' theories	*Four major theoretical perspectives within the interpretivist 'big' theory*
Positivism	
Interpretivism	• Hermeneutics • Ethnomethodology • Phenomenology • Symbolic interactionism
Critical theory	
Postmodernism	

notion of what is involved in a paradigm-guided approach to research, we quickly come to recognise the need for a strategy, plan of action, process or design to link our paradigm-guided questions with particular methods. This is what is referred to when we argue for the need for an appropriate methodology. A wide variety of such methodologies exist, ranging from survey research to ethnography, from experimental research to grounded theory, and from discourse analysis to heuristic inquiry.

Overall, then, the intention of the remainder of this chapter is to provide an overview of:

- the idea of paradigms;
- the basic ideas of the four major paradigms;
- the distinction between methodology and research methods.

Such an overview should provide appropriate scaffolding for an understanding of *why* one particular type of qualitative research project can be planned where:

- the paradigm is interpretivism;
- the specific theoretical position adopted within the paradigm is symbolic interactionism;
- the methodology is grounded theory;
- the research methods are semi-structured interviewing, participant and non-participant observation, and document study.

This understanding should, in turn, place one in a better position to understand the remaining chapters of the book, where the emphasis is very much on *how* research projects based on such a framework can be planned.

Research paradigms

At this point it is important to once again recall Wolcott's (1992) third type of research, namely, that of 'grand theory' or 'big theory'. As has already been pointed out, the more sophisticated term used when referring to such research is to talk about it as being 'paradigm guided'. In considering what is meant by this it is important to recognise from the outset the point made by Punch (1998: 28) that paradigm is a complex term. He elaborates as follows:

> As used in social science it [paradigm] means a set of assumptions about the social world, and about what constitutes proper techniques and topics for inquiry. In short, it means a view of how science should be done. It is a very broad term, encompassing elements of epistemology, theory and philosophy, along with methods. Paradigms have been the subject of vigorous debate.
>
> (Punch 1998: 28)

Usher (1996) is helpful in developing this point. He proceeds by highlighting some aspects of the thinking of Thomas Kuhn whose major work, *The Structure of Scientific Revolutions* (1970), played a significant part in 'changing our understanding of science, research and scientific method' (Usher 1996: 14).

In Kuhn's work the concept of the paradigm is defined both as 'the entire constellation of beliefs, values, techniques, shared by members of a given scientific community' (Kuhn 1970: 75) and 'as an exemplar or exemplary way of working that functions as a model for what and how to do research, what problems to focus on and work on' (Usher 1996: 15). On this, Usher states:

> Paradigms are frameworks that function as maps or guides for scientific communities, determining important problems or issues for its members to address and defining acceptable theories or explanations, methods and techniques to solve defined problems. When a paradigm becomes settled and dominant within a scientific community, Kuhn calls the research carried out 'normal science'. This way of doing research is largely characterised by routine, problem-solving discontinuities (which Kuhn calls 'scientific revolutions'). Here a paradigm shift occurs, dominant paradigms are overthrown and new paradigms take their place.
>
> (Usher 1996: 15)

He concludes by saying that a paradigm shift involves a new way of looking at the world, and hence new ways of working, or new ways of doing 'normal' science.

Over the past 30 years or so there has been much talk and debate about the various major paradigms which exist and which influence the production of research in education and the social sciences. Some researchers and theorists have produced 'typological charts listing the principal schools of contemporary research methodology along with some definitive statements for each' (Bhattacharya 2017: 2; Carspecken 1996: 1). These include charts where paradigms are compared according to their ontological and epistemological assumptions. Such charts, of which that of Guba and Lincoln (1994: 109) is probably the best known, are invaluable in that they illustrate a range of frameworks which are of help in locating and clarifying the paradigm within which we might wish to locate our research. Also, they help to remind us that all research in education and the social sciences is either implicitly or explicitly conducted within a framework of theoretical assumptions.

One could engage in a review of the various charts which exist. To do so, however, would be to confuse many readers from the outset. In order to make sense of them one would need quite a background in philosophy in general, and philosophy of science in particular. The contention is that a more practical way to proceed is to commence by outlining a simple typology of paradigms. To such an end, the particular typology chosen here is that developed by Connole et al. (1993: 38–9), with its four paradigms – positivist, interpretivist, critical and postmodernist. This is much simpler than the typologies of Guba and Lincoln and much more valuable as an initial heuristic device or scaffolding. Overall, it lays the foundation for the main body of the text, which considers in detail how to engage in research based on the second of the major paradigms identified, namely, the interpretivist paradigm, with the theoretical position being that of symbolic interactionism – about which much more will be said in Chapter T; the methodology being grounded theory – about which much more will be said in Chapter 4; and the research methods being semi-structured interviewing, participant and non-participant observation, and document study.

Four major paradigms

Connole et al. (1993: 38–9), as stated above, argue that research methodologies can be grouped according to four main paradigms: positivism, interpretivism, critical, and postmodernism. Each paradigm is based upon sharply different assumptions about epistemology – the study of how knowledge is generated and accepted as valid – and about the purposes of research. A useful starting point in elaborating on this is to consider the position of the philosopher Jurgen Habermas (1972), who contended that those who adopt the research approach associated with the positivist research paradigm are pursuing one of three human 'cognitive interests', namely, the interest in technical control. It is this interest which leads us to want to know all the facts and figures associated with an area of interest, and the answers are provided by empirical-analytic knowledge. The basis of such knowledge, it is claimed, involves careful and controlled observation, where the observer takes a dispassionate position independent of the object of observation.

Smith and Lovatt (1991: 57), in elaborating on what is involved in pursuing technical knowledge, focus on the practices associated with both the behaviourist form of psychology and the functionalist form of sociology. These disciplines, they argue, which are based on fairly specific ideas about human behaviour and human society respectively, have developed precise research approaches with positivist foundations. The typical initial strategy is that of formulating hypotheses, setting up a clinical observation, and recording observations. The latter are regarded as objective devices and, hence, reliable. The next step is to quantify the data and present the findings by means of statistics. The final set of statistics is seen as providing knowledge that is both objective and generalizable, and which, it is held, can be used to predict and control events.

The second major research approach is that based upon the interpretivist paradigm. This approach emphasises social interaction as the basis for knowledge. The researcher uses his or her skills as a social being to try to understand how others understand their world. Knowledge, in this view, is constructed by mutual negotiation and is specific to the situation being investigated.

Habermas contends that those engaged in research within the interpretivist paradigm are pursuing the second human cognitive interest, namely, the interest in understanding the meaning behind something. This contrasts sharply with the positivist's interest in prediction and control. Also, a very different notion of how one knows something is emphasised. Again, the nature of what is involved is addressed by Smith and Lovatt. They argue that this second way in which one knows something can be seen in the method used in attempting to convey understanding through textbooks like the present one. In such situations, the writer uses words to convey ideas and meanings to the reader. Smith and Lovatt (1991: 75) clarify this point:

> The only way that you can prove to us (or we can know) that you have understood my ideas with the meaning that we intended, is for you to paraphrase in your own words, the meaning that you have gained from my words. In other words, a very important way that we come to know something is through a negotiation of meaning through communication.

They conclude by saying that the way one proves one knows these things is through either a verbal or written account, although often the meanings of such accounts still need to be negotiated between the speaker and the listener, or the writer and the reader.

Habermas holds that those who engage in research within the third paradigm, namely, the critical paradigm, operate on an assumption that knowledge is problematic and capable of systematic distortion. The contention is that it can never be value free, but always represents the interests of some group within society. Consequently, it is argued, knowledge has the potential to be either oppressive or emancipatory. The purpose of the researcher working within the critical paradigm is to unmask the ideologies which maintain the status quo 'by restricting the access of groups to the means of gaining knowledge' and by raising their 'consciousness or awareness about the material conditions that oppress or restrict them' (Usher 1996: 22). Emphasis is placed on understanding the causes of 'powerlessness, recognising systemic oppressive forces and acting individually and collectively to change the conditions of life' (Usher 1996: 22). Equally stressed alongside an emphasis on social critique is, however, the importance of being guided by this critique in taking social action to improve the quality of human life. Denzin and Giardina's recent book entitled *Qualitative Inquiry Through a Critical Lens* is a useful guide for engaging in this practice (Denzin and Giardina 2016).

The fourth research paradigm is that of postmodernism. A particular position underpinning this fourth paradigm is that 'knowledge claims are governed by privileged sets of rules and social relations' (Connole et al. 1993: 12). Overall, as Usher puts it, what the fourth paradigm does is challenge 'the powerful view that there is a determinate world which can be definitively known and explained' (Usher 1996: 23). Also, the various theoretical approaches associated with it do not relate to Habermas' three cognitive interests. Rather, collectively they represent an epistemological break with other research paradigms. Thus, they seek to challenge our understandings of knowledge as being based on truth.

Research paradigms and the posing of research questions

From considerations thus far it should be clear that what differentiates one paradigm from another is that each offers a rationale for its choice, for the kinds of research questions it can address, for the varieties of research design it uses and for an introduction to its methods. Husén (1988: 18) elaborates on this as follows:

> The paradigm determines how a problem is formulated and methodologically tackled. According to the traditional positivist conception, problems that relate, for example, to classroom behaviour should be investigated primarily in terms of the individual actor, wither the pupils, who might be neurotic, or the teacher, who might be ill-prepared for his or her job.

LeCompte and Preissle (1993: 139) illustrated this notion by focusing in particular on how research questions are posed differently, depending upon the paradigm which one is adopting. The problem they chose in order to illustrate this is that of the 'at-risk' student, or potential dropout. They demonstrated that if one adopts the positivist position known as 'functionalism' then the research questions which can be asked are as follows:

1 What are the characteristics of the dropout population?
2 What role do dropouts, as a group, play in the social system of the school?
3 To what extent does dropping out serve to remove from schools those students for whom formal schooling is inappropriate or wasteful of public resources?

To pose these questions is to approach students as conscious 'dropouts' who choose to leave school prematurely. This is to view the issue as a person-centred one, with an emphasis on the self-esteem, family background, motivation, and intelligence of the student. However, if one favours the 'critical' approach one poses questions like the following:

1 What patterns of resistance do students – and teachers – employ to resist the hegemony of the dominant order in schools?
2 What processes operate within the school to push students out?

Such questions arise when one shifts one's focus to viewing students as 'push outs' who are actively encouraged in their departure by school practices which require investigation focusing on such issues as 'the bureaucratic organization of schools and the time schedule, the behaviour of students and staff, the structure of the curriculum, and the general relationship between schools and the structure of opportunity in the larger society' (LeCompte and Preissle 1993: 140).

LeCompte and Preissle (1993: 139) go on to illustrate how different sets of questions can be raised yet again within other paradigms and, indeed, within sub-positions within these paradigms. For example, still staying with the same issue, they state that if one favours the 'postructuralist' approach one can pose questions like the following:

1 Which students' or other school participants' experiences are ignored by contemporary researchers?
2 How do such students define and structure the school experience?

To summarise, then, on this matter of different 'types' of research questions, the argument is that the adoption of a different paradigm can predispose a researcher to approach a research problem differently in terms of the questions asked. This situation will, in turn, lead the researcher to choose different research methodologies and research methods.

Methodology and research methods

To argue along lines like those above is to argue that research needs to be thought of as being about much more than simply choosing a *method*, or 'a program or set of procedures for designing, conducting and reporting research' (Lancy 1993: 8). As Crotty (1998: 3) puts it, methods are 'the techniques or processes used to gather and analyse data related to some research question or hypothesis', while the notion of 'methodology' constitutes the link between the paradigm-related questions and the methods. The latter is so in the sense that methodology is 'the strategy, plan of action, process or design lying behind the choice and use of particular methods and linking the choice and use of methods to the desired outcomes' (Crotty 1998: 3).

Crotty elaborates on this when he argues that 'in developing a research proposal, while we need to put considerable effort into answering what methodologies and methods will be employed in the research we propose to do, we also need to ask how we justify this choice and use of methodologies and methods' (Crotty 1998: 2). He goes on to argue that the answer to the second of these questions lies with the purposes of our research – in other words, with the research question that our piece of inquiry is seeking to answer. However, he also holds that there is more to it than that: 'Justification of our choice and particular use of methodology and methods is something that reaches into the assumptions about reality that we bring to our work' (Crotty 1998: 2). This is to once again highlight the importance of how one positions oneself from a paradigm's perspective.

I find it helpful to bring all of this together by rearranging and paraphrasing Crotty's (1998: 2) outline where he argues that when we view research through this lens we ask ourselves four questions. My rearrangement and paraphrasing of these questions is as follows:

1 What research paradigm informs our approach to our research area of interest?
2 What theoretical perspective do we choose within this paradigm regarding our research area of interest?
3 What methodology do we choose as a result of our location of the research area of interest within a particular theoretical perspective derived from a particular paradigm?
4 What methods are most appropriate to use in light of our chosen methodology?

The remaining chapters of this book are concerned with outlining an approach to developing research proposals where the paradigm is interpretivism, the specific theoretical position is symbolic interactionism, the methodology is grounded theory, and the research methods are semi-structured interviewing, participant and non-participant observation, and document study.

The chapters which go to make up the book were outlined in the Preface. It is now important to note that they are organised into two parts. Part I consists of this chapter and five others. Chapter 2 details some basic principles of interpretivism and outlines how the theoretical position of 'symbolic interactionism' is located within it as one of a number of related theoretical positions. Chapter 3 is based on the contention that there are two basic types of studies which can be developed from the symbolic interactionist view of the individual, namely, studies aimed at generating theory regarding the perspectives which participants hold with regards to something and studies aimed at generating theory regarding how participants 'manage', 'deal with', or 'cope with' situations. The focus is on considering how to develop appropriate research questions for engaging in these two basic types of theory-generation studies.

Chapter 4 goes on to provide an exposition on what is meant by 'theory' in the sense in which the term is used with regards to the types of studies being promoted in this book. It also considers the types of populations with which it is 'normal' to work when generating such theory. Furthermore, it provides an overview of the range of arguments which are used as a justification for the value of engaging in studies aimed at theory generation. Finally, Chapters 5 and 6 are exemplars of the two main types of theory-generation studies considered to this point.

Part II consists of seven proposals indicating various types of studies that can be based on the considerations of the previous chapters. Chapter 7 is a proposal for a 'frozen in time' study and Chapter 8 a proposal for a 'deal with' study. The next three chapters relate to 'policy studies', 'life history studies', and 'interactionist historical studies', respectively. Chapters 12 and Chapter 13 relate to the 'problem-focused' variety. A point not to lose sight of, however, is that while studies with terms such as 'policy', 'life history', and 'problem-focused' in their titles can be underpinned by a variety of foundations other than those of interpretivism and symbolic interactionism, the concern in Part II is with studies where interpretivism and symbolic interactionism are chosen as the central foundations. Each chapter makes this very clear, illustrating what is involved through the outline of a series of research proposals.

It is in these proposals that one is also brought face-to-face for the first time with details on research methods, or techniques for the gathering of qualitative data. The emphasis throughout is on three main types of data-gathering approaches, namely, semi-structured interviewing, participant and non-participant observation, and document study. Furthermore, the approaches recommended are those which have been standard since qualitative research approaches gained popularity within education studies over the past 25 to 30 years. There are some excellent texts which provide overviews on these approaches, including the recent works of Punch (2005), Silverman (2005), and Woods (2005). There has also been an increase in recent years in works which illustrate the potential of computers for speeding up access to documentary material (McCulloch 2004) and for using widely available internet technology in conducting interviews with participants at a distance when we are unable to meet with them in person (Mann and Stewart 2002).

Finally, it should not be assumed that this book champions the interpretivist paradigm over other paradigms, or symbolic interactionism over other interpretivist theoretical positions. Instead, it is strongly influenced by the adage, 'be guided by the question'. In adopting this position it is also held that it is not helpful for the new researcher to spend too much time attempting to reconcile a number of paradigms in order to develop an eclectic position to guide a research project. At this stage of one's career, where one is faced with a complex research area which seems to have affinities with various paradigms, one would be better employed breaking it up into a number of sub-projects, each grounded in the appropriate paradigm. After completing this process, the new researcher, if interested in pursuing the research approach outlined in this book, can select an interpretivist sub-project for investigation. This is a view which sees that the sub-projects could then be collated, perhaps by an overall project director, in a work which would present them as a series of discrete, but complementary studies leading to some overall conclusions for theory, practice, and future research. This allows for a variety of possibilities, not least that of engaging in what we might call a 'second level of analysis' of the theory generated. For example, those attracted by the critical theory paradigm might usefully interrogate their newly-generated theory with symbolic interactionist underpinnings by drawing upon some of the central political concepts utilised by critical theorists. It should be stressed, however, that this is not the same as developing an empirical study from the outset based upon the central assumptions of the critical theory paradigm. For some excellent primers on the latter approach one has to look at works like those of Carspecken (1996) which continue to be very helpful to researchers (Hardcastle et al. 2018).

The thinking behind this book also does not favour the view that symbolic interactionism, phenomenology, and other theoretical positions within the interpretivist paradigm can be combined loosely to underpin an eclectic research approach. This is not to argue against eclectic research approaches in principle; rather, it is to maintain that they need to be supported by rigorous logical arguments which make crystal clear what is involved. And here I return again to the ideas of Wolcott. In a consideration of the wide variety of research approaches available, he has states that 'in the real world of science, the most seasoned veterans probably are conversant with no more than one or two different approaches' (Wolcott 1992: 18). My understanding of the point he was making here is that it is better, particularly when starting out on one's early research projects, to base them upon an in-depth command of one research approach rather than a superficial grasp of many. It is in such a spirit that this book has been conceptualised and written.

Chapter 2

The general background

Introduction

This chapter is an exposition of issues which need to be considered by way of a general background to understanding the interpretivist paradigm and the place of the symbolic interactionist theoretical position within it. The chapter opens by first detailing some basic foundation principles of interpretivism. A brief historical account of interpretivism as it unfolded in the form of symbolic interactionism is then outlined. Third, the chapter provides an exposition on the concept of 'perspectives', a central concept within symbolic interactionism. Finally, three important distinctions which many tend to blur in developing eclectic approaches to interpretivist research of the sort discouraged in the previous chapter are clarified: the distinction between behaviour and action; the distinction between 'perspectives' and 'perceptions', and the distinction between 'perspectives' and 'attitudes'.

Foundation principles

For the interpretivist, the individual and society are inseparable units. From this, it follows that a complete understanding of one is not possible without a complete understanding of the other. Also, society is to be understood in terms of the individuals making it up, and the individuals are to be understood in terms of the societies of which they are a members. In other words, the individual and society are inseparable; the relationship is a mutually interdependent one rather than a one-sided deterministic one. That said, it is possible to separate the two units for the sake of analysis. This book does so by concentrating on the individual or, more correctly, on individuals and groups of individuals, while never overlooking the societal dimension.

One of the most basic ideas of interpretivism regarding the individual is that all human action is meaningful and hence 'has to be interpreted and understood within the context of social practices' (Usher 1996: 18). It follows from this that an understanding of the meanings that create, and are created by, interaction between human beings is essential to an understanding of the social world and the myriad phenomena which it contains. Consistent with this view, interpretivists examine the meanings that phenomena have for people in their everyday settings. The concern is with the study of 'how people define events or reality' and 'how they act in relation to their beliefs' (Chenitz and Swanson 1986: 4).

A number of assumptions underpin the interpretivist approach to research. In particular, these assumptions involve everyday activity, freedom, meaning, interaction, and negotiation. Blackledge and Hunt (1985: 234) are very helpful in developing this position through an elaboration on four of the major assumptions. First, they state that everyday activity is the building block of society. As they see it, every aspect of society can be traced back to the way people act in everyday life. They illustrate this by pointing out that what keeps the educational system together is the day-to-day activity of teachers, learners, administrators, inspectors, and other educational professionals. Furthermore, any changes in education or society are brought about by changes in such activity. Thus, the argument goes, if we want to understand education we must begin by looking at everyday activity in the different education sectors.

The second assumption highlighted by Blackledge and Hunt reiterates that of Blumer (1969: 2) when he stated that everyday activity is never totally imposed; there is always some autonomy and freedom (Blumer 1969: 2). This, as it is put, 'is not to say that there are no constraints on the way people act; nor does it imply that people are uninfluenced by their background' (Blackledge and Hunt 1985: 236). Rather, as Blackledge and Hunt (1985: 235) conclude, 'what is insisted upon is that people can and do create their own activity to some extent; everyday life is produced by people employed within the system acting together and producing their own roles and patterns of action'.

The third assumption highlighted by Blackledge and Hunt is that everyday activity nearly always involves a person interacting with other people rather than acting in isolation. As a result, individuals not only give meaning to their own actions, they also give meaning to the actions of others. Put differently, it is contended that 'people mutually interpret the behaviour of other people with whom we interact. It follows from this that subsequent action depends on our interpretation' (Blackledge and Hunt 1985: 236). Also, the argument is that our interpretation of other people's activity is influenced by what we currently consider we know about them, including our knowledge of their age, race, intelligence, and motivation.

A fourth assumption highlighted by Blackledge and Hunt is that everyday activity involves a process of 'negotiation' of meaning and, through this we come to modify our understandings and views. They go on as follows:

> It is important to note that the analysis of action must include a study of the participants' meanings and interpretations. However, it would be incorrect to think that meanings and interpretations remain static and unchanging. It is clear, for example, that people do modify their views. Also, over time, participants in various circumstances tend to come to have shared understandings and interpretations. The sharing is brought about through a process of

> 'negotiation' of meaning. Negotiation is seen as a continuous process, not something that happens once and is finished. It occurs in subtle ways, with modification to the participants' understanding of what is going on. Shared assumptions develop.
>
> (Blackledge and Hunt 1985: 236)

They conclude by stressing that the term negotiation does not imply that all parties have the same power at their disposal.

Each of the four assumptions of interpretivism outlined apply specifically in the case of symbolic interactionism which, as has been stated repeatedly, is a major theoretical position within the interpretivist paradigm. This position, as the historical exposition in the next part of the chapter points out, derives from the Chicago School of Sociology of the 1920s and 1930s, particularly the ideas of its chief exponent, George Herbert Mead, whose work was popularised by Herbert Blumer. Indeed, it is Blumer who is attributed with having first coined the term 'symbolic interactionism'. Key concepts which have been developed to articulate this particular theoretical approach within interpretivism are 'self', 'interaction', 'self-interaction', 'voluntarism', and 'common symbolic language'. Of these, the concept of 'self' is of primary importance to the understanding of the symbolic interactionist approach to research.

Mead (1934) postulated that the individual develops a sense of self through interaction with others. As such, the self is created in childhood when a person begins to make judgements about the way he or she is perceived by others. The process continues through life and involves individuals taking the role of others as a means of looking back at themselves from the perspectives of the people with whom they interact. In this regard, one constructs an image of how one believes one is seen by others. Furthermore, this image changes throughout life because of social interaction.

The significance of the concept of 'self' lies in its potential for facilitating each individual in the engagement of self-interaction. The self becomes an object for the individual to consider, assess, communicate with, and act towards. This ongoing interplay between an individual (subject) and self (object) enables individuals to anticipate the reaction they may receive if deciding to act in a particular way. On this, Schwartz and Jacobs (1979: 23) observe that self-interaction allows the person to 'really "see" others' reactions to his *[sic]* own actions before these reactions occur'. For Mead (1934), and for his successors who operate within the symbolic interactionist theoretical approach, the concept of self relates directly to the way people attach meaning to, and act towards, particular objects and phenomena.

In an elaboration on Mead's ideas, Blumer (1969: 2) formulated three principles. First, he stated that 'human beings act towards things on the basis of the meanings they have for them'. On this, Woods (1992) has argued that, unlike approaches which hold that human behaviour is determined by structural societal forces, or is the product of internal psychological drives, the view of the symbolic interactionist is that individuals attach their own meanings to 'things', for example, material objects, people, institutions, concepts, in their environment and then act towards them on the basis of these meanings. In other words, people are volitional rather than organisms which merely respond. They are organisms who have to manage by constructing and directing their line of action. Here we are back to the notion that meanings influence actions.

Blumer's second principle is that social interaction is the source from which meanings are derived. Thus, the meanings that a person has for a thing in his or her world are created by the actions of other people. This principle asserts that 'the meaning of a thing for a person grows out of the ways in which other persons act towards the person with regards to the thing' (Taylor and Bogdan 1989: 9). In other words, people learn how to see the world from other people. What is also implied is that the meaning each person has for a thing may be constantly adjusted by the actions of other people. This new meaning also has its effect on human actions. Another way of putting it is that meaning is acquired from one's experience of the world and because one is constantly interacting with the world that meaning may be confirmed, modified, reinforced, or changed.

Blumer's third principle is that meanings are 'handled in, and modified through, an interpretive process used by the person in dealing with the things he [*sic*] encounters' (Blumer 1969: 2). He goes on to say that there are two steps in this process. First, one points out to oneself the things that have meaning. One then selects, checks, suspends, regroups, and transforms the meaning in the light of the situation in which one is placed and the direction of one's action. This process, which is an essential component of social life, is the means by which individuals align their actions with others and with groups. It is through this interpretive process that shared meanings are attributed to the full range of objects that comprise the human experience. This is to reject a view of human action as deriving from such internal forces as instincts, drives, and needs, and also to reject the concept of 'attitude' as an internal tendency – a matter taken up in some detail in the fourth part of this chapter. It is also to reject those theories which view the actions of an individual as determined by such large-scale external forces as '"social system", "social structure", "culture", "status position", "social role", "custom", "institution", "collective representation", "social situation", "social norm" and "values"' (Ritzer 1994: 301). Rather, human action, as Meltzer, Petras and Reynolds (1975: 2) have put it, is seen as arising out of 'a reflective and socially derived interpretation of the internal and external stimuli that are present'.

By now astute readers may be a little unsettled by the way in which the terms 'understandings', 'meanings', 'beliefs', and 'perspectives' have been used so far. They have good reason to be, as the exposition to this point has been allowed to proceed in a manner which mirrors the practice in much of the literature, namely, to use these terms interchangeably. What is important to note here is that to engage in this practice is not technically incorrect and the terms largely mean the same thing. Rather, the contention is that it is a confusing practice. To deal with this situation, the term which has been selected for use consistently from this point onwards is that of 'perspectives'. An elaboration on what is meant by the term is presented in the third part of this chapter. For the moment, however, it is sufficient to keep in mind the definition by Woods (1983: 7) of perspectives as 'frameworks through which people make sense of the world'. Charon (2001: 4) puts it similarly when he states that perspectives are made up of words which are used by the observer to make sense out of situations. He goes on to state that 'the best definition of perspectives is a *conceptual framework*, which emphasises that perspectives are really interrelated sets of words used to order physical reality'.

To recap then in light of the position taken above, it is held that the value of adopting an interpretivist approach to research, and of the symbolic interactionist theoretical approach within it, is that it can uncover people's perspectives on a phenomenon. The important reality, it is argued, is what people perceive it to be. This reflects a tradition in social science that fundamentally depends on observations taken in people's natural settings and interacting with them in their own language and on their terms (Kirk and Miller 1986: 9). This is the point Matza (1969) was making when he argued that research methods should respect the nature of the empirical world. The emphasis, as Woods (1992) puts it, should be on 'naturalism' and on 'unobtrusive methods'. In this way, the issues which are focused upon for study are those which are issues for the participants being investigated, rather than those which might exist from the outset as problems in the mind of the researcher which he or she deems worthy of investigation.

In summary, a researcher adopting a symbolic interactionist theoretical approach when conducting research within the interpretivist paradigm is concerned with revealing the perspectives behind empirical observations, the actions people take in the light of their perspectives, and the patterns which develop through the interaction of perspectives and actions over particular periods of time. In such an approach, the researcher is the primary data-gathering instrument, using guiding questions aimed at understanding a phenomenon through semi-structured or open-ended interviews with the people involved and in their own surroundings.

Other important means of gathering data are through an examination of documents and other records, and on-site observations. These methods rely on the interactional, adaptive, and judgemental abilities of the human inquirer. Also, they can lead to the production of a vast amount of data about a small number of people. In later chapters, examples of how data can be gathered and analysed are outlined and expositions are presented on what the product of analyses could look like and the value of such products to the academic, the professional, and the general community. At this point, however, it is considered appropriate to give the reader a greater understanding of the historical background to the interpretivist paradigm, with particular reference to the symbolic interactionist theoretical approach within it as espoused by the Chicago School of Sociology

The historical background

Interpretivism, as should be clear from discussions so far, is not a homogenous position, although the various theoretical positions within it do tend to share the four major assumptions identified by Blackledge and Hunt (1985) outlined in the previous section. Also, some of these theoretical positions are very prominent. In tracing the origins of a number of them, Husén (1988: 17) opened by focusing on that tradition within educational research where the concern is with modelling the activity of those working in the natural sciences, with an emphasis on 'empirical quantifiable observations which lend themselves to analyses by means of mathematical tools'. The task within this tradition is to establish causal relationships in order to provide an explanation. Also, it is a tradition deemed valuable because of the contention that it allows for the prediction of future behaviour on the basis of present action.

The interpretivist paradigm is based on different assumptions. On this, Husén highlights the distinction made by Wilhelm Dilthey (1833–1911) in the 1890s between '*erklaren*' and '*verstehen*'. The former refers to 'explanation' and is associated with positivism, while the latter refers to 'understanding' and is associated with interpretivism. Furthermore, in making this distinction, Dilthey maintained that the humanities have their own logic of research, pointing out that the difference between the natural sciences and humanities is that the former tries to explain, while the latter tries to understand. He also maintained that there are two kinds of psychology, 'the one which by means of experimental methods attempts to generalise and predict, and the one that tries to understand the unique individual in its entire, concrete setting' (Husén 1988: 18). Husén draws our attention to the emergence of similar positions in the same period, such as that espoused by Henri Bergson (1859–1941) in France, 'who maintained that the intellect was unable to grasp the living reality which could only be approached by means of intuition' and that of John Landquist in Sweden who 'advanced the epistemology of human knowledge about human affairs' (Husén 1988: 18).

Various other interpretivist positions also emerged around the same time. Among the most well-known of these within the discipline of philosophy was the phenomenological philosophy of the German, Edmund Husserl (1859–1938). Again, Husén (1988: 18) offers a good summary of the basic assumptions of this position:

> It [Husserl's phenomenology] emphasised the importance of taking a widened perspective and of trying to 'get to the roots' of human activity. The phenomenological and later the hermeneutic approach is holistic. It tries by means of empathy ('*Einfuhlung*') to understand the motive behind human reactions. By widening the perspective and to understand human beings as individuals in their entirety and in their proper context, it tries also to avoid the fragmentation caused by the positivistic and experimental approach that takes out a small slice which it subjects to closer scrutiny.

Symbolic interactionism constitutes another theoretical position yet again within the interpretivist paradigm. Also, it is an approach which can be subdivided into a number of schools. The notion of a school, as used here, is that offered by Ritzer (1994: 66) who defines it as 'a group of academics who share a common time and place, have a high degree of interaction with one another, and have a common way of doing their subject'. The most well-known of the symbolic interactionist schools is that of the Chicago School of Sociology which was established in 1892, which went into decline around 1935, and which has re-emerged with various degrees of force at different periods in time up to the present day.

Ritzer (1994) has provided us with a very scholarly overview of the development of the Chicago School, and it is this overview which provides the basis of the account throughout the remainder of this section of the chapter. He starts off by noting that the city of Chicago grew dramatically between the 1840s and 1892, the year of the establishment of the school of sociology at the University, while also reminding us it constituted an 'openair laboratory' with 'its neighbourhoods; its racial and ethnic diversity; its problems, such as stockyards; and its occupations, even deviant occupations such as prostitution' (Ritzer 1994: 69). He concludes that 'the youth and dynamism of both the city and the University made them conducive to new and important developments in many domains, including academic fields' (Ritzer 1994: 69). The University responded by encouraging its departments and faculty members to do original thinking and research regarding the city, to publish their results and to become involved in public service. The hope was that all this activity would be of assistance in coping with the city's social problems.

A significant lead was given in pursuit of the University's mission by the philosophy department under the direction of the world-famous thinker, John Dewey, himself a key figure in a new school of philosophy which came to be termed 'pragmatism' and which was primarily an American response to the modern world. When Dewey came to Chicago in 1894, he brought George Herbert Mead (1863–1931) with him. While Mead was a professor in the philosophy department, he attracted a lot of students from the sociology department to his courses, and particularly to a course entitled 'advanced social psychology'. Through this and other activities, Mead played a very major role both in the development of sociology at the University and also in its development as a distinctive academic discipline. While he wrote very little during his academic life, his lecture notes were copiously documented by his students who published them posthumously in a book entitled *Mind, Self and Society* (Mead 1934). The concern in the book is with Mead's central ideas, namely, the emergence of mind and self in the process of social interaction.

The key figures located within the Chicago sociology department in those early years were Albion Small, who became head of the department in 1892, and W.I. Thomas. Of these two individuals, Thomas made by far the greatest contribution to academic scholarship. In terms of contributing to social theory, he was responsible for promoting the notion of subjects' 'definition of the situation' as a central idea within the Chicago School. Ritzer (1994: 82) has summarised this notion as follows:

> This means that what matters most is the way in which people, not sociologists, define their social lives. Additionally, it means that people's definitions matter as much as or more than the actual situation. If people define a given situation in a particular way, then that is what matters. This kind of subjective orientation leads the sociological researcher in the direction of ethnography and away from the kinds of studies that are easily analysed statistically.

Thomas is also well-known for pioneering two research approaches, namely, the 'self-reported life history' and what we now term 'document study'. The use of these two approaches in the collection of empirical data was a major departure from the armchair theorizing and library-study approaches dominant up until then. The product of Thomas' labour along these lines is best exemplified in the five-volume work published between 1918 and 1920, *The Polish Peasant in Europe and America* (Thomas and Znaniecki 1918–20) which he co-authored with a Polish peasant, Florian Znaniecki. This is a work based partly on letters, newspaper accounts, records of court trials, sermons, pamphlets, and other documentary sources, and partly on a self-reported life history. Interestingly also, Ritzer notes that Thomas did not use those specific methods that were to come to dominate later Chicago research, namely, face-to-face observation and interviewing.

The other important member of the Chicago school of sociology at the time, Robert Park (1864–1944), favoured the use of participant observation – participating directly in the lives of the people being studied – in his research aimed at writing about 'city life in vivid detail' (Ritzer 1994: 77). He would, as Ritzer (1994: 77) puts it, 'go into the field, observe and analyze, and finally wrap up his observations'. On the other hand, he was opposed to the statistical analysis of data, dismissing the approach cynically as 'parlor magic' because, as he saw it, its use 'prevented sociologists from analysing not only subjectivity, but also the idiosyncratic and the peculiar'. For Park, all these things 'tended to be washed away when the researcher was dealing only with a sea of numbers' (Ritzer 1994: 77). The dominance of this view resulted, for a while, in the marginalisation of the important work in quantitative methods that was being undertaken at the time by William Fielding Ogburn and others within the sociology department at the University of Chicago. On the other hand, it did not hinder the emergence of an alternative school of symbolic interactionism at the University of Iowa. While not of concern within this book, it is instructive to realise that the Iowa School was also centred on such concepts as the 'nature of self' and 'interaction', yet was associated with positivism in working from the assumption that 'it is possible to obtain knowledge of the social world through detached study and the application of quantitative techniques' (Layder 1995: 63).

During its heyday, researchers associated with the Chicago School produced a major corpus of work, most of which consisted of participant observation studies of urban life. These included *The Hobo* (Anderson 1923), *The Taxi Dance Hall* (Cressey 1932), *The Gang* (Thrasher 1927), *The Ghetto* (Wirth 1928) and *The Gold Coast and the Slum* (Zorbaugh 1929). A related set of studies was conducted on the life histories of juvenile delinquents and criminals. Included in this set were *The Natural History of a Delinquent Career* (Shaw 1931), *The Professional Thief* (Sutherland, 1937) and *The Jack Roller* (Shaw 1966).

The Chicago School went into decline in the 1930s. Thomas and Small had, by now, left the University, Park had retired and Mead had died. Also, there was a major move to positivist science in sociology within the University of Chicago sociology department and to the accompanying use of advanced modes of statistical analyses. Two major scholars, Herbert Blumer and Everett Hughes, however, continued to work within the department and laid the basis for a renewal of the interpretivist thrust in the late 1940s and early 1950s. Among the best-known members of the resultant Second Chicago School were Erving Goffman, Howard Becker and Eliot Friedson. Since then also, symbolic interactionism within the tradition of the Chicago School has continued to be promoted in various textbooks, including those of Rose (1962) in the 1960s, Meltzer et al. (1975) in the 1970s, Ritzer (1983) in the 1980s, and Ritzer (1994) and Layder (1995) in the 1990s. More recently, Prus (1996) produced a text aimed at highlighting once again the importance of symbolic interactionism of the Chicago School type in investigating what he sees as central in social life, namely, intersubjective experience and meaning. It is also arguable that this position permeates such very influential texts as Hage and Powers (1992) *Post-industrial Lives* and Castells (2000) *The Rise of the Network Society*. In addition, Atkinson and Housley (2003: xiv), speaking as sociologists, hold that 'we are all interactionists now … in the sense that many of the key *ideas* of interactionism have become part of the contemporary mainstream of sociological thought'.

The engagement in symbolic interactionist research within the field of education took off in earnest in the USA in the 1970s, at a time when a host of other research approaches involving the use of qualitative research methods were also gaining in popularity. As would be expected, the symbolic interactionists 'held to the basic and optimistic assumption' (Bogdan and Biklen 1992: 24) that participants would grant access to a research site if they could. They also had an 'empathic' perspective; that is, 'they called for sympathy and understanding towards those whom they studied' (Bogdan and Biklen 1992: 24). Such assumptions and approaches led to quite a degree of conflict between themselves and other researchers, and not just those committed to the use of quantitative research methods. Nevertheless, a significant number of books and papers emerged on various aspects of life in educational settings which were underpinned by the symbolic interactionist theoretical approach and which were the product of the use of in-depth interviewing, participant and non-participant observation, and the study of primary-source documents.

Woods (1992: 339) notes that there was a similar development in the United Kingdom. Catalysts, he argues, were provided by the collection edited by Young

(1971), *Knowledge and Control*, and the Open University (1972) course, *School and Society*. Works from such key symbolic interactionists in the Chicago School tradition as Blumer, Becker and Hughes, were reproduced, although other theoretical approaches, and not only from the interpretivist paradigm, were also represented. Out of this, Woods has observed, emerged two scholarly movements, namely, one adopting a more deterministic Marxist-oriented line and the other a more interactionist one. The main thrust of the latter has been summarised in the following words:

> British interactionists (more or less) used the school as a social laboratory, opening up the 'black box' that hitherto had been impervious to the 'input-output' studies that had prevailed hitherto. Here was a fascinating new world, where action did not simply take place as a product of external structural and cultural forces but, rather, was constructed within classrooms. How this occurred and with what consequences seemed a crucial question, not only for sociology but also for education. Sociology of education in Britain had only really begun in the 1950s, and while important work was done on background factors and their relationship to achievement, the standard survey approaches gave no assistance with understanding the processes of what actually went on in schools, how it was experienced by teachers and pupils, what different perspectives they brought to bear, how they related together, and how conflict was resolved if that was a consequence.
>
> (Woods 1992: 340)

Out of this movement emerged a large number of symbolic interactionist studies on various aspects of education and focusing on the various participants in the educational process (Blackledge and Hunt 1985: 231–89; Woods 1983). A number of methodological commentaries also emerged in order to provide guidance for other researchers (Finch 1986; Hammersley and Atkinson 1983; Woods 1986).

The remainder of this chapter clarifies some of the central concepts within symbolic interactionism not considered so far; concepts which have the potential to cause confusion. Such clarification is necessary before proceeding in the remaining chapters to outline an approach aimed at providing beginning researchers with a systematic approach for engaging in some basic symbolic interactionist-type research on educational topics. It is also important to realise at this point that the approach which will be outlined does not attempt to relate symbolic interactionism to the other interpretivist positions already mentioned, or to such other well-known positions as phenomenological psychology and ethnomethodology. This is to eschew the temptation to argue that a beginning researcher should spend a significant amount of time trying to construct some grand synthesis of interpretivist positions to underpin a research project. Such a stance is taken on the grounds that while the different interpretivist positions are underpinned by the same general foundation principles, they nevertheless developed out of an interest in addressing different, even if related, research questions. In other words, the stance is that one should 'be guided by the research question' *within* paradigms as well as *between* paradigms. Thus, one needs to look elsewhere to get an understanding of what is involved in undertaking research using phenomenological psychology approaches, ethnomethodology approaches and other interpretivist approaches as distinct research approaches in their own right, rather than trying to combine some or all of them under some general umbrella term like 'qualitative research'.

The concept of 'perspectives'

It has already been pointed out that there is a tendency in the literature on interpretivism to use the terms 'understandings', 'meanings', 'beliefs', and 'perspectives' interchangeably and that, while this practice is not technically incorrect, since the terms largely mean the same thing, it is confusing. The position taken in this book is one which addresses the problem by using the term 'perspectives' consistently. Woods (1983: 7) gets to the heart of what perspectives are when he defines them as 'frameworks through which people make sense of the world'. Charon (2001: 4) arrives at a similar definition, but starts from a very basic position in stating that perspectives are made up of words. It is these words, he argues, that are used by the observer to make sense out of situations. He goes on to state that, as a result, 'the best definition of perspectives is a *conceptual framework*, which emphasises that perspectives are really interrelated sets of words used to order physical reality' and that the words we use cause us to make assumptions and value judgements about what we are and are not seeing. He also puts it another way (Charon 2001: 3) when he states that 'point of view' is 'the very best definition of what a perspective is'.

Becker et al. (1968: 34) adopt a similar position when they define perspectives as:

> A coordinated set of ideas and actions a person uses in dealing with some problematic situation, [they] refer to a person's ordinary way of thinking and feeling about and acting in such a situation. These thoughts and actions are coordinated in the sense that the actions flow reasonably, from the actor's perspective, from the ideas contained in the perspective. Similarly, the ideas can be seen by an observer to be one of the possible sets of ideas that might form the underlying rationale for the person's actions and are seen by the actor as providing a justification for acting as he does.

Charon (2001: 3) puts it yet another way again when he states:

> A perspective is an angle on reality, a place where the individual stands as he or she looks at it and tries to understand reality … a perspective is an absolute basic part of everyone's existence, and it acts as a filter through which everything around us is perceived and interpreted. There is no possible way that the

individual can encounter reality 'in the raw', directly, as it really is, for whatever is seen can only be part of the real situation.

This means that while human beings are limited by their perspectives in that they cannot see outside of them, these perspectives are also vital in that they make it possible for us to make sense of the world.

To make the latter point is not to argue that there is no truth at all, or that all opinions about reality are equally correct. The unfortunate situation is that, as Charon (2001) puts it, many people do believe that there is no truth at all. Reality, he argues, does in fact exist; 'there is something actually happening out there in the world – but we cannot know it completely or in any perfectly accurate way because we always see it through filters we are here calling perspectives' (p. 6). Crotty (1998: 44) makes the same point in a different way when he states that 'we do not create meaning. We construct meaning. We have something to work with. What we work with is the world and objects in the world'.

Another basic idea associated with perspectives is that they develop when people must choose between alternatives (Potts 1997: 19). Nevertheless, if certain sorts of situations occur repeatedly, the perspective may become a fixed part of an individual's way of coping with reality (Becker et al. 1968: 35). Also, there may be a need to distinguish between immediate and long-range perspectives. Furthermore, any given situation may not be interpreted in the same manner by everyone. At the same time, however, group perspectives, as has already been pointed out in the first part of this chapter, tend to develop. These are taken-for-granted ways of thinking and acting evolved by a group confronting similar problematic situations (Becker et al. 1968: 36). As Becker et al. (1968: 36) put it, they occur 'when people see themselves as being in the same boat and when they have the opportunity to interact with reference to their problems'. Such group perspectives apply to specific situations. They are ways of thinking and acting which have occurred as a result of certain institutional constraints, and serve as an answer to the problems these constraints cause (Potts 1997: 20).

It also needs to be recognised that not only can our perspectives change many times throughout our lives, but they can also change from situation to situation, and can do so many times during the same day. In other words, few of us have one perspective that we can apply to every situation we come across. In this regard, symbolic interactionists speak of perspectives as being 'situational'. Charon (2001: 7) elaborates on this as follows: 'In the classroom my perspective is that of teacher-sociologist; in my home it becomes father or husband; on a fishing trip it changes to "seasoned fisherman".' Each situation, he concludes, calls forth a different role, which means a different perspective.

Clarifying other key concepts

This final part of the chapter, as flagged in the introduction, clarifies three important distinctions which many tend to blur in developing eclectic approaches to interpretivist research: the distinction between 'behaviour' and 'action'; the distinction between 'perspectives' and 'perceptions', and the distinction between 'perspectives' and 'attitudes'.

Behaviour and action

One of the most basic ideas already mentioned regarding how the individual is viewed within the interpretivist paradigm is that all human action is meaningful and hence 'has to be interpreted and understood within the context of social practices' (Usher 1996: 18). In considering this, it is necessary to take on board immediately the importance of the term 'action'. Interpretivists speak of 'human action' rather than 'human behaviour' (Connole et al. 1993: 34). The significance of this is that while positivist scientists speak of events having 'causes' and 'human behaviour' is seen as the outcome of external influences, interpretivists speak of 'human actions' as having 'reasons'. In other words, actions are preceded by intentions which arise out of the perspectives which individuals hold; a position also consistent with the notion promoted at the end of the previous section of this chapter that one of the components of perspectives is that of 'reasons'. Furthermore, the position is that these perspectives create interaction between humans and are, in turn, created by this interaction.

Connole et al. (1993: 118–9) take up the distinction outlined above between 'behaviour' and 'action'. They point out that interpretivists deny that explanations of human activity can be elicited and measured by empiricist methods alone. On this, they draw attention to the view of Popkewitz (1984: 40–2) that we need to shift the focus of attention behind people's visible behaviour to the processes of negotiation of *appropriate* behaviours and, in so doing, investigate the social rules being used by those interacting. Connole et al. (1993: 119) elaborate on this view:

> Among several points he made was a reference to the classic distinction between two kinds of causation. The first is an event or action being brought about because of a prior event. The second is something done in order to cause a predicted consequence. In one the direction of cause-effect influence is forward in time as something occurs due to something happening before it. In the other the direction is backwards, with something being done at one time due to an intended future event. It is clear that all human behaviours cannot be adequately understood without bringing in the possibility of the second, conscious, intentional, in-order-to, cause-effect relationship.

This is the kind of thinking which has resulted in interpretivists favouring the use of the term 'action' over the term 'behaviour'.

Perspectives and perceptions

One regularly finds the concept of 'perceptions' utilised in interpretivist studies where there is no clear outline of the underpinnings in terms of epistemology, research paradigm, and theoretical approach. This is not very helpful because of the centrality of 'perspectives' in symbolic interactionism. Another complicating factor is that the concept of 'perception' is, in fact, a central concept itself within other theoretical approaches. Charon develops this point in a very helpful manner by, first of all, labelling symbolic interactionism as a distinct theoretical approach within one of two types of social psychology (Charon 2001: 21), namely, 'psychological social psychology' and 'sociological social psychology'. The notion of 'perception' is central to the former, which has its roots, to a large extent, in Gestalt psychology which developed in the late nineteenth and early twentieth centuries:

> Gestalt psychology emphasizes the central importance of 'perception' in human behaviour: The human being acts according to how the situation is perceived. Gestalt psychologists have attempted to isolate various principles of perception in order to better understand how the individual organizes the stimuli he or she confronts. Gestalt psychology as such is entirely psychological in its orientation, but because of the work of some Gestaltists a social dimension was added to the framework, which greatly influenced the direction of social psychology.
>
> (Charon 2001: 21)

Sociology, on the other hand, spawned sociological social psychology, which 'is distinct from much of psychology by de-emphasising the person as cause; it is distinct from much of sociology by de-emphasising the power of social patterns and society at large' (Charon 2001: 21). The main focus is on 'social interaction', which can be defined as the on-going, back-and-forth action that participants take towards one another. Also, while psychological social psychologists tend, by and large, to use surveys and laboratory experiments, sociological social psychologists focus on researching real-life events, such as interaction in a meeting or in the waiting room of a doctor's surgery.

A most important stream within sociological social psychology is symbolic interactionism. Here, as has been laboured repeatedly in this book so far, the concept of 'perspectives' is central. This is not to say that symbolic interactionists do not have a view on 'perceptions'. They do, but it has a much lesser status within this theoretical approach than does 'perspectives'. Charon (2001: 8) sums up this lesser status when he states that 'perspectives are not perceptions but are guides to our perceptions; they influence what we see and how we interpret what we see'. He takes up the same point in a different context when he states that language guides the individual through what his or her senses experience: 'It constitutes the individual's *perspectives*, and thus serves the function of alerting the individual to some parts of the environment and not to others' (Charon 2001: 65).

Perspectives and attitudes

In considering the symbolic interactionist's preference for the concept of 'perspectives' over that of 'attitudes' it is useful to consider once again the distinction made above between psychological social psychology and sociological social psychology. The basic question to be answered by those who espouse the former school is how other people around us influence our thoughts, feelings, and behaviours. By far the most important topic investigated by this branch of social psychology has been attitudes and attitude change. An attitude within this scholarly approach is usually defined as a person's set of beliefs and feelings towards an object, or class of objects, that predisposes the person to act in a certain manner when confronted by that object, or class of objects.

Symbolic interactionists, who are sociological rather than psychological social psychologists, conceptualise the individual very differently from those who are comfortable with the concept of 'attitude'. The latter, as already stated, is usually defined as being a fairly fixed and stable quality of an individual over time; and the image of the individual which is associated with it is that 'of a consistent, whole organism, responding to stimuli in situations according to this attitude brought to the situation' (Charon 2001: 38). In other words, an attitude is carried around from situation to situation. The external environment acts as a stimulus. The person first responds internally to an object, or to a class of objects. Then the person responds externally after having that internal response.

Symbolic interactionists reject this view as it promotes a notion of the individual as not being in control of his or her own action. As they see it, it is a view which is premised on a notion that the individual is passive and thus does not use the attitude; instead, the attitude directs the individual. By contrast, their concept of the individual is of an active being and they stress the importance of active definition of the situation. This is why they prefer the concept of perspectives. This concept captures the notion of a human being who interacts, defines situations, and acts according to what is going on in the present situation. Furthermore, because perspectives are conceptualised as dynamic and changing guides to interpretation and then to action, such action can never be totally predictable. The next chapter now seeks to outline a systematic way for engaging in research where one of the central concerns is trying to grasp participants' perspectives and how they act in the light of their perspectives.

Chapter 3

Posing the questions

A central position expounded throughout this book is that the interpretivist view of the individual, and particularly that based upon the symbolic interactionist theoretical position, is of one who is a manager of his or her environment. Elaborating on this position can lead to the development of different types of studies, as later chapters demonstrate in the form of research proposals. Nevertheless, it seems to me that before we can launch into pursuing any of these types of studies, we must first of all come to grips with more fundamental matters. In this regard, my contention is that there are two basic types of studies which can be developed from the symbolic interactionist view of the individual, particularly when it is considered in light of Blumer's three principles as outlined in the previous chapter. Furthermore, I contend that these form the foundational framework for engaging in all other kinds of related studies.

The two basic types of studies which can be developed from the symbolic interactionist view of the individual are as follows:

1 Studies aimed at generating theory on the perspectives which participants hold with regards to something;
2 Studies aimed at generating theory on how participants 'manage', 'deal with', 'or 'cope with' a phenomenon.

The second part of this chapter considers how to develop appropriate research questions for engaging in each of these two basic types of studies. Before moving to this, however, a number of points need to be clarified in order to get a clearer view of what each type involves.

The two basic types of studies

Studies of the first type can be viewed as 'frozen in time' studies. The concern is with generating theory about the perspectives which a group or groups have with regards to some particular phenomenon at a particular point in time. Thus, I have had students engage in studies on such areas as primary school principals' perspectives on what are 'good' schools, teacher educators' perspectives on what is a professional teacher educator, key stakeholders' perspectives within Fundamental Christian schools on their schools' programmes for the pastoral care of staff, high school principals' perspectives on the role of schooling in the promotion of the academic development of students, and NESB university academics' perspectives on the role which English-language proficiency played in their appointments to their positions. Such studies are valuable for reasons which will be discussed in some detail in the next chapter. At the same time, however, it is important to highlight here their lack of a longitudinal dimension. In other words, they tend not to be concerned with investigating the processes involved in the participants' construction of their perspectives, nor do they set out to track the perspectives from the initial point of investigation onwards to see how, if at all, they change.

Studies of the second type outlined at the commencement of this chapter, namely, those studies aimed at developing theory regarding how participants 'manage', 'deal with', 'or 'cope with' a phenomenon, do have a longitudinal dimension to them. One way of grasping what is involved here is to consider the notion that when we ask how participants 'manage', 'deal with', or 'cope with' situations, we are asking a particular type of question in 'shorthand' form. Phrasing the same question in its more extended form is really to ask a number of interrelated questions. To put it simply, as symbolic interactionists, what we are really doing when we pose the question: How do participants 'manage", 'deal with', 'or 'cope with' situations? is asking: What are the patterns that can be detected over a particular period of time from an investigation of:

i the perspectives which the participants have on a phenomenon at the outset;
ii how the participants act in the light of their perspectives;
iii the changes, if any, which take place in the participants' perspectives as a result of their actions;

and so on, as the cycle repeats itself time and again? In other words, there is a major focus on trying to generate theory about process.

It is necessary to elaborate a little on point iii above regarding a focus on 'changes, if any, which take place in participants' perspectives as a result of the responses to their actions'. What is being referred to here has already been taken up in some detail in the previous chapter in the exposition on the nature of 'perspectives' in noting that participants' perspectives may remain the same, may be reinforced, may be modified, or may change as a result of how they respond to how others respond to their actions. This, in turn, it will be recalled, may influence participants to act the same as they did initially, to modify their actions, to reinforce their actions or to change their actions. The challenge to the researcher is to try to detect patterns arising out of this constant interaction through in-depth studies carried out over definite periods of time.

It is also necessary to highlight the centrality of the term 'theory', or more specifically, that of 'generating theory', in each of the two types of central research questions which are the focus of attention in this chapter. Such a situation is different from that adopted by researchers who take a positivistic stance and are primarily interested in verifying or testing hypotheses about the nature of social life. To make this observation is not in any way to find fault with the work of positivist researchers. Rather, it is helpful in so far as it puts in context the publication of Glaser and Strauss' highly influential book, *The Discovery of Grounded Theory* (Glaser and Strauss 1967) – which will be considered in the next chapter within the context of its emergence historically – and the consequent great interest which it sparked in developing – or generating – social theory and concepts. A useful summary of how theory is defined in this and various other works of Glaser and Strauss is that it is an integrated framework of well-developed concepts and the relationships between them that can be used to explain or predict phenomena. It is for this reason also that it makes no sense to speak of 'findings' arising from interpretivist studies – the researcher does not find out anything. Rather, he or she generates theory, which can then be reported as one's 'results'.

In similar vein, it makes no sense to me to speak about 'triangulation' in such studies. Triangulation in the sense of using data from two or more sources in quantitative research in order to validate data through cross verification certainly makes sense in quantitative research. However, we are 'generating' theory, not using data to verify hypotheses. At the same time, however, we can, and should where possible, try to enrich the quality of data from which theory can be generated by gathering data in a qualitative research by using more than one qualitative research method.

Another point in need of elaboration regarding what is involved in each of the two types of studies which are the focus of this chapter centres on the practice of attributing the same meaning to the terms 'deal with', 'manage' and 'cope with' in symbolic interactionist studies and, indeed, sometimes even to the terms 'handle', 'respond to' and 'exercise control over'. I hold that while it is important for those commencing work in the field to recognise this practice, it is also important to recognise how two of these terms, namely, 'manage' and 'cope with', can be particularly confusing. Confusion centred on the use of 'manage' arises because readers unfamiliar with the interpretivist way of thinking are almost programmed to think of, and use the term only in terms of, scientific management. Thus, when one poses a question regarding how a group of participants manage some phenomenon or other, they automatically think that what is being asked is how they are managing in relation to how scientific management theorists state they *should* be managing. To take an example, imagine that a research project is being conducted in a factory setting. The data on one senior executive who reports that she suffers from stress indicates that she is regularly absent from work, comes in late in the mornings, and drinks alcohol to excess. The scientific managerialist would be likely to speak of this participant as not managing in the work place. The symbolic interactionist, on the other hand, in taking a non-judgemental approach, would be likely to speak in terms of the participant's regular absence from work, coming in late in the mornings, and drinking alcohol to excess as her way of managing his situation.

A similar confusion centres on an alternative way of using the term 'cope' to the way in which it is used by symbolic interactionists. What is being referred to here is the practice in a particular body of scholarship within psychology which has grown up around a psychological model of coping. Those working according to this model tend to evaluate responses according to either implicit or explicit criteria as to what *should* be involved in coping. In other words, they utilise pre-established standards to investigate the degree to which a person's responses can be judged to represent the level to which he or she is coping. Again, to use the example of the senior executive noted above, those working within the parameters of the psychologist's model of coping would view his actions as indicative of him not coping very well with his situation, while the symbolic interactionist would view them as the strategies he uses in order to cope.

To conclude on the latter point, then, the argument which has been made is that while symbolic interactionist studies of the second type noted at the beginning of this chapter are generally stated in terms of how participants 'deal with', 'manage', or 'cope with' particular phenomena, these terms mean the same thing within the interpretivist paradigm. Nevertheless, they can be confusing because the terms 'manage' and 'cope with' are also well-known terms associated with other paradigms and other theoretical positions, and in these situations they have a different meaning to what they have for interpretivists. Accordingly, the term used consistently throughout the remainder of this text is that of 'deal with'. This is because it is the most neutral of the various terms used by interpretivists and has the least potential to create misunderstanding.

Formulating studies in relation to questions on perspectives

Overall, the contention so far is that two main types of studies can be developed from a consideration of the central ideas of the symbolic interactionist theoretical approach located within the interpretivist paradigm. In order to progress from here in the development of a research plan, a number of steps need to be taken. Clearly, the first step that needs to be taken is to decide which of the two types of studies is appropriate for one's research area of interest. Once this has been settled upon, one needs to formulate one's focus of research into an appropriate statement of the aim of what is to be pursued. For example, if one decides on the first type of study, one would formulate an aim along the lines of the following adopted by various postgraduate students of mine over the past number of years:

- The aim of the study is to generate theory on teachers' perspectives on parental involvement in school decision-making.
- The aim of the study is to generate theory on the perspectives of Japanese teachers in Australia on what is effective teaching.
- The aim of the study is to generate theory on the perspectives of teachers in a state school system on the school development planning process in the schools.

- The aim of the study is to generate theory on the perspectives of key stakeholders on the quality assurance policy which is implemented in one private school sector.
- The aim of the study is to generate theory on the perspectives of teachers in Catholic schools on how to develop sustainable learning communities.
- The aim of the study is to generate theory on the perspectives of teachers in Fundamental Christian schools on the nature and purpose of schooling.

Similarly, if one decides on the second type of study, one would formulate an aim along the lines of the following studies also undertaken by various postgraduate students of mine over the past number of years:

- The aim of the study is to generate theory on how those university lecturers responsible for preparing distance education materials deal with the process.
- The aim of the study is to generate theory on how teachers in Fundamental Christian schools deal with the teaching of 'Human Origins'.
- The aim of the study is to generate theory on how parents deal with the home schooling of their children with disabilities.
- The aim of the study is to generate theory on how school administration teams deal with their work in a restructured education system.
- The aim of the study is to generate theory on how parents of children in the School of Isolated and Distance Education in Western Australia deal with their work as home tutors.
- The aim of the study is to generate theory on how parents of children diagnosed with Attention-Deficit/Hyperactivity Disorder deal with the schooling of their children with the disorder.

Each of the questions in these two groups is straightforward and unambiguous in light of the parameters established so far. Nevertheless, before the students settled upon these questions it was vital for them to establish that the issue of focus was a real issue for the participants and not just of academic interest to themselves as outsiders. If this had not been established, the likelihood is that the researcher would have designed a theoretically sound and neat research plan which could not have been implemented as she or he would have come up against a brick wall of non-responses. To put it another way, there is no point in designing a study about participants' perspectives on something, unless we are convinced before we commence the study that it is something about which they have fairly well formed views and that they feel sufficiently free to discuss these views.

Returning now to the matter of making progress in the development of a research plan, the second step which needs to be taken is that of taking one's stated aim and rephrasing it as a general question. In the case of the first example given above for studies of type one, this means that it would be restated as follows: What are teachers' perspectives on parental involvement in school decision-making? Similarly, the first example given above for studies of type two would be restated as follows: How do those who prepare distance education materials deal with the process?

At this point it is not so obvious how to proceed further. Certainly, our general research question, whether it relates to a type one or a type two study, is not very helpful on its own, particularly given the position expounded in the previous chapter that semi-structured interviews should constitute a central data-gathering method in both types of studies. What is being alluded to here is that it would be unlikely to be very productive to commence one's interviews by approaching participants and simply asking them to elaborate on their perspectives on the phenomenon under investigation. For one thing, they are likely to respond immediately, and quite understandably, with the question: What do you mean by perspectives? Second, semi-structured interviewing necessitates that we engage in conversations with participants through more down-to-earth questions.

The issue, then, is how to arrive at appropriate down-to-earth questions such that they will yield a quantity and quality of data which, when subjected to analysis, will allow us to generate theory regarding the participants' perspectives. Over the years of engaging in studies with aims along the lines of the two types of studies outlined at the commencement of this chapter, I have found it very helpful to focus my thinking along the following lines:

1 The general research question which is generated from the overall aim is always too broad to be answered directly.
2 What we need is a very specific set of data collection questions. A data collection question is, as Punch (2000: 27) puts it, 'a question which is asked in order to collect data in order to help answer the research question'. Punch elaborates on this by saying that sometimes many data collection questions will be involved in assembling the data necessary to answer one research question.
3 Some researchers term their list of data collection questions an '*aide memoire*', or a semi-structured interview guide. For symbolic interactionist studies of the types under consideration in this book, such a guide consists of those lists of questions deemed most appropriate at the beginning of the research in terms of having the potential to engage the participants in conversations across as wide a range of areas as possible. The objective is to yield data such that it is possible to grasp as fully as possible their perspectives on the phenomenon under investigation.
4 Notwithstanding the value of the position outlined in each of the preceding four points, we are still no wiser regarding how to develop a suitable list of data collection questions. One possible way of doing it which suggests itself would be to brainstorm colleagues and friends, have some informal conversations with individuals similarly located to those in mind for the study, and see what would come out of this activity. However, such an approach would not be very systematic and to pursue it would not involve following any particular chain of logic.

5 Much more productive is to take seriously the question stated above which participants would be likely to give us by way of reply were we to bluntly ask them what were their perspectives on something, namely: What do you mean by perspectives? The remaining part of this section of the chapter seeks to demonstrate that the exercise of unravelling into a number of component parts what we do in fact mean by the concept of perspectives gives us a very useful framework for logically arriving at a comprehensive list of data collection questions.

Much of the previous chapter focused on distinguishing the concept of perspectives from a variety of other concepts, particularly that of 'perceptions' and 'attitudes'. A number of useful definitions of perspectives was also offered, particularly that of Woods (1983: 7) 'frameworks through which people make sense of the world' and Charon's (2001: 4) 'conceptual frameworks'. These definitions have operated very well in this book so far by way of scaffolding the exposition and keeping considerations focused. Nevertheless, the astute reader must once again be having some uneasiness, this time in relation to the meaning of the term 'framework'. In particular, it is unlikely to have escaped many that the use of 'framework' in any definition implies a number of interrelated parts. In this case, what is being referred to are the interrelated parts of a perspective. This, then, begs the question: What are the parts that do in fact interrelate in any perspective?

Becker et al. (1968: 28–30) progressed towards answering the latter question when they contended that perspectives have several components, namely, a definition of the situation – a collection of ideas outlining the sort of situation in which action must be taken; an outline of the types of activities one may rightly be involved in; and finally, criteria of judgement. These components certainly correspond with the various aspects of the concept of perspectives as considered in the previous chapter. They pose problems, however, when considering how they might be used to develop guiding questions to facilitate the conducting of a research project with symbolic interactionist foundations.

Before developing this point further, it is important to clarify what is meant when referring to guiding questions. In particular, it is important to note that they are not logical subsets of the general research question such that if they were each dealt with, we would somehow have addressed the central research question. If we fail to take this point seriously we could find ourselves forgetting that, ultimately, our purpose is not even to answer a general research question, but rather to fulfil an aim, namely, to generate theory. Instead, what we are seeking in developing guiding questions is a set of questions which are deduced from our understanding of the central research question. Furthermore, this set of questions should be sufficiently comprehensive to facilitate the development at the commencement of our research project that which was already pointed out as being desirous: namely, an extensive list of data collection questions which at that point would seem to have the potential to engage the participants in conversations across a very wide range of areas in order to yield data regarding their perspectives.

It is certainly possible to pose guiding questions by utilizing the component parts of perspectives identified by Becker *et al.* and noted above. In other words, we can pose questions about 'one's definition of the situation', questions about 'the sort of situation in which action must be taken', questions about 'the types of activities one may rightly be involved in', and questions about 'criteria of judgment'. However, my experience is that it is very difficult to then translate these sorts of questions into data collection questions. Much more helpful in this regard is the position of Blackledge and Hunt (1985: 234); a position which is much clearer with regards to what is being referred to, while also being consistent with the position of Becker *et al.* In 2007, I laid out how these positions could be adapted to help in research design as they propose that the interrelated parts of the framework which goes to make up a 'perspective' consist of the participants' aims or intentions, their strategies, what they see as being significant for them, the reasons they give for their activity, and what they see as the expected outcomes of their activity (O'Donoghue 2007). This 'unpacking' exercise allows us to construct the following structure for the development of guiding questions in relation to the general research question regarding a study where the aim is to generate theory about participants' perspectives on a particular phenomenon:

1 What are the aims or intentions of the participants with regards to the phenomenon under investigation and what reasons do they give for their aims or intentions?
2 What strategies do the participants say they have for realising their aims and intentions and what reasons do they give for utilising those strategies?
3 What do the participants see as the significance of their aims or intentions, and their strategies and what reasons can they give for this?
4 What outcomes do the participants expect from pursuing their aims or intentions and what reasons can they give for this?

The following is an example of how one of my Doctor of Education students from Singapore, Ms. Jia Wen He, worked through each of the steps outlined in this chapter and used the above framework to arrive at a set of guiding questions for her study.

Project title

School-based career guidance programmes in junior colleges in Singapore: An interpretivist study.

Research aim

The aim of the study is to generate local theory about the perspectives of teachers of career guidance programmes in junior colleges in Singapore on their career guidance programme.

The issue

Guidance education has been an important aspect of public education in Singapore since its independence in 1965, and has undergone continual review and renewals. Studies on school-based guidance education in Singapore have addressed topics such as the evolving landscape of Singapore's guidance education, the professional training of counsellors, the perspectives of counsellors on school counselling, to the work values prized by Singaporean adolescents. However, there is little research that focuses on the perspectives of teachers of school-based career guidance programmes. Also, studies on career guidance in schools tend to focus on two main aspects: *career and identity development* of individuals (how career guidance reflects and develops the abilities, skills, and values of learners across different age groups) and *career counselling practices* (effects of counselling processes and counsellor characteristics, and what is appropriate for different profiles of students).

This study will complement existing research by examining *teachers' perspectives* on career guidance programmes in junior colleges in Singapore. The focus is on *programmes* because of they affect a greater number of students than do individual or small group counselling. Also, examining the perspectives of teachers in the context of their school is important; while the Ministry of Education (MOE) provides guidelines for guidance programs, schools have a degree of autonomy in designing and delivering their programmes, to fit the unique concerns of the school.

Central guiding question

What local theory can be generated about the perspectives of teachers of career guidance programmes in junior colleges in Singapore on their career guidance programme?

Sub-guiding questions

Four sub-guiding questions have been formulated in light of the component parts of perspectives as outlined above. These sub-guiding questions are not specific questions to be answered, but suggest themselves as guides to conversational questions that would generate data relevant to the study's central aim. They are as follows:

1 What are the teachers' aims with regards to conducting school-based career guidance programmes? What are their reasons for having the stated aims?
2 What are the strategies they say they use when conducting school-based career guidance programmes? What are their reasons for using these strategies?
3 What significance do they say they attach to their aims and strategies in conducting school-based career guidance programmes? What are their reasons for having the stated significance?

4 What outcomes do they expect with regards to conducting school-based career guidance programmes? What are their reasons for expecting the stated outcomes?

A series of conversational questions will be generated from these four sub-guiding questions. The nature of what will be developed needs to be such that I will have every reason to feel confident I can begin my research armed with a body of data collection questions with sufficient potential to engage the participants in conversations across as wide a range of areas as possible to yield data that will facilitate the generation of theory regarding their perspectives. At the same time, however, I will need to be open to the possibility that some of the data collection questions may be unproductive and will have to be dropped, while other more productive ones may suggest themselves during the interviews and will need to be pursued enthusiastically.

A second example taken from the proposal of Ms Carmen Cloria Zuniga Gonzales, who completed her Doctor of Education thesis under my supervision, is now provided.

Project title

The Curriculum for Secondary School History in Chile: A Study of the Perspectives of Key Stakeholders.

The issue to be examined in the project

The overall aim of the study is to generate theory about the perspectives of teachers of history in Chile regarding the secondary school history curriculum for the nation's schools. This is considered to be extremely important since it is teachers who implement the prescribed curriculum within classrooms. Thus, it is crucial to have an understanding of their perspectives on the curriculum that they currently have to implement to inform considerations for improvement and teacher professional development. A study of the situation throughout the whole country would be ideal. Time and other logistical constraints do not allow for this. On the other hand, it is held that an in-depth study of one major region, namely, in Valparaiso, could be highly instructive. While no claims will be made to generalise for the country more widely, a study undertaken in this one area should be of great value in helping to design further studies for examining the situation across Chile.

Background

Throughout the 1990s, 2000s, and into the present decade, the education system in Chile has experienced several changes. After 17 years of an authoritarian military regime, five successive democratic governments have identified education as a strategic tool to achieve economic development and a more just society. In this regard, curriculum reform has been promoted as an important feature in the search for quality. In line with this rationale, a new curriculum framework was introduced in 2010. Despite the extensive research and policy initiatives undertaken relating to curriculum reform, and associated research about the teaching of related school subjects such as sciences and mathematics in Chile, there has been little research undertaken on the teaching of history as a school subject.

General guiding question

What are the perspectives of teachers of secondary school history in Chile on the secondary school history curriculum for the nation's schools?

Sub-guiding questions

1 What are the teachers' aims with regards to the secondary school history curriculum in Chile? What are their reasons for having the stated aims?
2 What are the strategies they say they use when teaching the secondary school history curriculum in Chile? What are their reasons for using these strategies?
3 What significance do they say they attach to their aims and strategies in relation to the secondary school history curriculum in Chile? What are their reasons for having the stated significance?
4 What outcomes do they expect from teaching the secondary school history curriculum in Chile? What are their reasons for expecting the stated outcomes?

These questions will be broken down further into an *aide-memoire* of data-gathering questions (Punch 2000: 27), namely, questions suggesting themselves as the most productive line of inquiry at the commencement of the study. As the study unfolds, some of these data gathering questions may prove themselves to be redundant, while new and unexpected ones may arise.

A third example is taken from a proposal of a current PhD student of mine, Ms Tshe Wan Deema, from Bhutan.

Project title

Leadership at the Primary School Level in Bhutan: A Study of School Leaders in Remote Primary Schools in a Transitional Country.

The issue to be examined in the project

The proposed study seeks to generate theory regarding leadership at the primary school level in Bhutan, a developing country that has moved from being an absolute monarchy to being a constitutional monarchy. Not much is known about the nature of, and the contexts within which, school leaders work in remote schools in various settings. This includes remote schools in Bhutan. Here the education system, which was for long highly centralised, is now being decentralised. This adds an additional context to the school situation in the country.

The study being proposed will contribute to addressing the deficit in the existing literature on education leadership in relation to a variety of interrelated contexts. It will also, on a broader theoretical level, contribute to understandings on the importance of considering the neglected issue of context overall within educational leadership. Furthermore, it will contribute to understandings on the influence of context on leadership practices.

Background

Bhutan is a tiny landlocked country in Southeast Asia, with an area of approximately 38,394 square kilometres. It is located between China and India. It has a total population of 768,577. The country has been ruled under a monarchy since 1907, when the First King was enthroned. In 2008, the Fourth King of Bhutan introduced democracy to the country and changed the form of government from that of an absolute monarchy to that of a constitutional monarchy. Since then, the country has had two general elections.

Ever since the establishment of the monarchy, the development of education has been emphasised, along with other development activities. The introduction of a Western system of education in Bhutan started as recently as 1961. Since then, English has been used as a medium of instruction in the schools and the curriculum has been borrowed from India. The main subjects taught were English, mathematics, Hindi and Buddhist scriptures (Wangmo and Choden 2011).

In the early 1960s, the country started its planned national development activities, with the implementation of the First Five Year Plan. This was designed to run from 1961 to 1966. Basic infrastructure facilities, including roads, power, communication systems, transport, agriculture and animal husbandry, were established. Considerable progress was also made in the field of education. By 1966, there were 108 schools, with an enrolment of 15,000 students.

In 2008, the system of government changed from being an absolute monarchy to being a constitutional monarchy. A new constitution was adopted and the country had its first general election. This has had implications for 'modernizing' education because since then the minister for education has been appointed by the government rather than by the king. Also, government education policy is now discussed in Parliament. The general education structure consists of 11 years of free basic education from pre-primary to grade ten. Since early 2010, the national education system has been aligned with the principles of Gross National Happiness, which is the country's national philosophy. This philosophy places more importance on people's well-being than on the country's economic development.

Not much, however, is understood about the background to the ways in which school leaders are implementing education in schools in Bhutan. This raises a further issue currently gaining a lot of attention from educationists, namely, the importance of considering context when studying leadership. In Bhutan, five main contexts can be identified: 'urban', 'semi-urban', 'rural', 'remote', and 'difficult' (MoE/RS 2012). There is a particular need to concentrate on the perspectives of school leaders on their work in all of these contexts, including the 'remote' districts. The latter are facing very challenging circumstances in terms of climate, isolation, transport, and the communication systems. Thus, they constitute a potentially valuable site for contributing to our current knowledge base on issues confronted by leaders at the school level in challenging circumstances associated with remoteness.

General guiding question

What are the perspectives of school leaders in remote primary schools in Bhutan on their work?

Sub-guiding questions

1 What are the aims of school leaders in remote primary schools in Bhutan in relation to their work? What are their reasons for having the stated aims?
2 What are the strategies that school leaders in remote primary schools in Bhutan say they adopt to achieve their aims in relation to their work? What are their reasons for using these strategies?
3 What significance do they say they attach to their aims and strategies in relation to their work? What are their reasons for having the stated significance?
4 What outcomes do they expect from their work? What are their reasons for expecting the stated outcomes?

Significance of the research

1 It will provide a broad historical background to primary school leadership in Bhutan.
2 It will develop an understanding of the nature of the context within which school leaders work in Bhutan and the strategies they use for dealing with the complexities of their work.
3 It will help to inform processes of school leadership preparation, development and support in Bhutan.

4 It will provide a valuable framework for researchers wishing to engage in related studies on other levels within the education system of Bhutan and elsewhere, and suggest developments for the future.

The same kind of careful planning needs to be undertaken regarding the second type of studies, namely, those aimed at generating theory regarding how participants deal with a particular phenomenon. Such studies, it will be recalled, necessitate trying to discover patterns over a period of time from an investigation of:

i the perspectives which participants have regarding a phenomenon at the outset;
ii how the participants act in the light of their perspectives;
iii the changes, if any, which take place in the participants' perspectives as a result of their actions.

The approach to initial data gathering regarding participants' perspectives is exactly the same as for the first type of studies. Subsequent data-gathering sessions aimed at uncovering changes, if any, in perspectives over time, however, while likely to be guided at the beginning by the same schemes as those developed for use in the initial session, may take new and unexpected turns as participants relate their positions. Researchers have to be prepared to pursue any new line of thought on the part of the participants, even if they have been unanticipated. This is because, as has already been argued, it is that which is important to the participant which is paramount, not what might be important to the researcher. At the same time, however, researchers should still be guided when developing their data collection questions – even those which suggest themselves 'on the spot' – by a desire to canvass across the five areas of participants' aims or intentions, their strategies, what they see as being significant for them, the reasons they give for their activity, and what they see as the expected outcomes of their activity.

It is also important when engaged in studies of the second type to investigate how participants act in the light of their perspectives. Ideally, this should be done by adopting the approach of Wolcott (1973) when he shadowed a school principal for an extensive period of time, after which he went on to write *The Man in the Principal's Office* and more recently (Rigg (2017) produced the equally valuable *The Woman in the Principal's Office*, albeit using a different qualitative research approach). Over this period, he was not only in a position to make copious notes regarding the principal's actions, but also to regularly seek clarification in order to make sure that what he thought he was observing was in fact what was happening. The importance of engaging in such clarification is what some interpretivists are referring to when they caution us to make sure that 'a blink is not a wink'.

Most researchers, and particularly new researchers, do have neither the time nor the resources required for adopting the approach of Wolcott. Consequently, they have to do the best they can. Normally, this involves planning a set of interview questions regarding participants' actions to be asked as recall questions during the same session when one is interviewing them about their current perspectives on the phenomenon in question. It is also possible, however, to develop a picture of participants' actions by communicating with them at regular times between interviews through phone and email contact, as well as by encouraging them to keep a diary. Some of the details of what is involved are outlined in Chapter 6.

Given the extent to which there has been mention so far in this chapter of interviewing, observations and document study, it would be reasonable to expect that one should now be offered a detailed exposition on such data-gathering and data-analysis approaches. I hold, however, that such an exposition makes more sense when outlined within exemplars of research proposals and of actual studies undertaken and also if one, first of all, has a fairly clear idea as to what the outcome of such data gathering and analysis would be. So far, all that has been indicated regarding the latter is that it should result in the development of theory. But what might that mean? And, equally important, what might be the value in such theory? The following chapter now turns to these matters.

Chapter 4

What is theory and what is its value?

The last chapter was concerned with the two basic types of interpretivist studies which can be pursued based on symbolic interactionist foundations. The aim of such studies, it will be recalled, is to generate theory regarding the perspectives which participants hold with regard to a particular phenomenon, and regarding how participants 'deal with' that phenomenon. This chapter now considers what is meant by theory within these types of studies. It then goes on to consider the sorts of populations with which it is normal to work when generating such theory. Finally, it provides an overview on the range of arguments which are used as justifications for the value of engaging in studies aimed at theory generation.

What is theory?

Lewins (1992: vii) provides us with a very good starting point in considering what is theory. He characterises social science research as being mainly theory testing or theory generation. He clarifies the distinction as follows:

> Compare, for instance, two common statements from medical practitioners: 'I think the patient has hepatitis but I will need to do some tests to confirm it'; and 'I think we will need to do some tests to see if we can establish why the patient is ill'.

In the first example, the starting point is a theory about why the patient is ill. This guides the choice of evidence needed to confirm it. The approach is different in the second example. Here the doctor hopes to arrive at 'a theory or a diagnosis' (Lewins 1992: vii) after the evidence has been gathered. Lewins goes on to illustrate his point further by asking us to compare the following examples from a statement in a courtroom:

Example 1: The prosecution argues that the accused committed the crime and we will produce evidence to support the claim.
Example 2: At an earlier stage in the case the police asked 'Who committed this crime?'

Again, theory testing is implied in the statement by the prosecution and theory generation is implied in the question by the police.

Put briefly, the steps in theory testing are as follows. First, hypotheses are developed. These are propositions which accord with 'the simple propositional logic; that is, if this theory is true, then I should be able to observe the following (if A then B)' (Lewins 1992: 47). This is followed by 'operationalisation'. What is involved here is the making of decisions as to what will count as evidence for the sub-concepts in the hypotheses. We then test the hypotheses by carrying out the research and analysing the results.

Theory generation research, by contrast, involves ending with a theory rather than starting with it. Here it is useful to recall the definition of theory presented in the previous chapter, namely, that it is an integrated framework of well-developed concepts and the relationships between them that can be used to explain or predict phenomena. This is a definition which gets one away from any notion that theory has to be so involved that it is really too complex to concern the great majority of us. Rather, it emphasises that theories are statements about how things are connected. To put it another way, theory consists of two parts, namely, the things to be connected and the connection itself. LeCompte and Preissle (1993: 120) elaborate on this by stating that the things to be connected are the concepts, and the connections or relationships 'show how concepts, categories, or constructs can be linked together once they have been identified'.

Another value in the definition offered above is that it makes clear that while theory can function as a predictor of phenomena, it does not necessarily have to do so. LeCompte and Preissle (1993: 119) approach this matter in a slightly different way. They speak of certain theories centring 'on understanding and interpretation of the meaning of constructs rather than explanation of phenomena'. On this, they elaborate as follows:

> Theories which explain general phenomena may be predictive ('every actions causes an equal and opposite reaction'). They also may be retrodirective or descriptive. Retrodirective and descriptive theories are similar in that both are explanations of phenomena tied to particular situations, but they differ in their time referent. Retrodirective theories address things which happened in the more or less distant past, such as historical explanations of the causes of specific revolutions; descriptive theories are more oriented to things close in time, such as an explanation of how a given university faculty responded to the policies of a dean.
>
> (LeCompte and Preissle 1993: 118)

Again, this distinction is very helpful for present considerations. To speak in LeCompte and Preissle's terms, this book is not concerned with theories which are predictive. Rather, the concern is primarily with theories which are descriptive, although some consideration is also given in the chapters in Part II to the generation of retrodirective theories. Such theories are worthy of generation, even if their qualities do not include prediction. While the final part of this chapter, as already indicated, will consider in detail what these qualities are, it is useful to start thinking about the matter at this point. In this regard, one could not do much better than to ponder the point made by LeCompte and Preissle (1993: 119) who point out that while theories which explain individual cases cannot be used to predict the cause of a different kind of case, 'they can be used in a comparative fashion to alert researchers to themes or events which might be common to similar phenomena under different conditions'.

Another way of looking at this is to highlight the distinction which is often made between 'nomothetic theories' and 'ideographic theories'. The former is developed as general laws of human behaviour which have predictive qualities, while the latter is designed to explain particular events or human actions within specific cultural contexts. Again, this book is concerned with the development of ideographic theory rather than nomothetic theory. Ideographic theory corresponds somewhat with the well-known notion of substantive theory, while nomothetic theory has a correspondence with formal theory. Strauss and Corbin (1990: 174) make the distinction between substantive and formal theory as follows: any substantive theory evolves from the study of a phenomenon situated within one particular context. A formal theory, on the other hand, emerges from a study of a phenomenon examined under many different types of situation. By way of example, they state that if one is interested in 'status' one could study the status of executives within an organisation. Because the theory which would be generated would be the product of a study of the phenomenon within one particular situational context, it would be substantive theory. On the other hand, one might, as they put it:

> study status in several types of situations, say: the status of politicians at the national level, the status of persons within families, the status of socialites within a given city, and the status of various professional ranks within academic institutions.
>
> (Strauss and Corbin 1990: 174)

This level of study is what is required in order to generate formal theory. They summarise by saying that it is not the level of conditions that makes the difference between substantive and formal theories, but the variety of situations studied.

To recap then, the focus in this book is on the generation of ideographic or substantive theory, with the orientation being more on things close in time than on how things happened in the more or less distant past. In considering what might be involved in this regard it is now useful to progress to considering that ideographic or substantive theory is not some homogenous entity; rather, different varieties of theory can be developed through analysis of data produced in studies of the types considered in the previous chapter. The remainder of this section of the chapter is concerned with outlining the most common of these varieties.

The first variety of theory which can be considered is 'description'. On this, Taylor and Bogdan (1998: 135) state:

> any good qualitative study, no matter how theoretical, contains rich descriptive data; people's own written or spoken words, their artefacts, and their observable activities .... researchers try to convey a sense of being there and experiencing settings firsthand ... researchers attempt to give readers a feeling of 'walking in the informants' shoes' – and seeing things from their point of view. Thus, qualitative research should provide 'thick description' of social life.

Lewins (1992: 26) also makes the point that description in research reports is never just 'mere' description. He states that when we describe anything, whether it is for everyday purposes or for scientific research, 'we describe it with the categories and concepts of our major preoccupation in mind'.

A second variety of theory which can be considered is that of concepts which can be generated from the data gathered in the research. Strauss and Corbin (1990: 61) define concepts as 'labels placed on discrete happenings, events and other instances of phenomena'. They go on as follows:

> Science could not exist without *concepts*. Why are they so essential? Because by the very act of naming, we fix continuing attention on them. Once our attention is fixed, we can begin to examine and ask questions about these phenomena (now, of course, labelled as concepts).
>
> (Strauss and Corbin 1990: 62)

To put it another way, concepts are vital because they give us a language by which we can speak about a phenomenon. This is particularly important when investigating an unexplored topic. Once a set of concepts has been developed, whole new areas can be identified for research because we now have a language for articulating the issues involved.

Bogdan and Biklen (1982: 156) provide a list of what they call 'families of codes' which can be used to analyse data and lead to the generation of a variety of concepts, including the following:

1. Concepts that describe the setting under investigation.
2. Concepts that refer to 'sequences of events, changes over time, passages from one type or kind of status to another' (Bogdan and Biklen 1982: 156). They are generated by collecting data on a person, group, organization, or activity over time and perceiving 'change occurring in a sequence of at least two parts' (Bogdan and Biklen 1982: 156).
3. Concepts that refer to regularly occurring kinds of behaviour.
4. Concepts that refer to 'particular happenings that occur infrequently, or only once' (Bogdan and Biklen 1982: 156).

5 Concepts that refer to 'the tactics, methods, ways, techniques, plays and other conscious ways people accomplish various things' (Bogdan and Biklen 1982: 156).
6 Concepts that refer to 'regular patterns of action among people not officially defined by the organizational chart' (Bogdan and Biklen 1982: 156).

These by no means constitute the total sum of concepts which can be developed. Nevertheless, it is possible to classify the total variety of concepts into two types, namely, those derived from an 'emic' – from phonemic – perspective and those derived from an 'etic' – from phonetic – perspective; emic represents an insider's perspective and etic represents the outsider's. In other words, concepts can be organised in terms of (a) those which represent participants' 'definitions of the situation', participants' perspectives, and participants' ways of thinking about people and objects; and (b) those generated by the researcher where it is considered that several pieces of data seem to have certain structural properties in common, yet are not identified as such by the participants.

A third variety of theory which can be considered is that of categorising. Strauss and Corbin (1990: 61) define a category as a classification of concepts. This classification, they state, is discovered 'when concepts are compared against one another and appear to pertain to a similar phenomenon'. The concept then which is developed is a higher order, more abstract concept, called a category. A category can, in turn, be developed into its 'properties' and its 'dimensions'. The properties of a category are its characteristics or attributes. Strauss and Corbin (1990: 71) offer the example of 'watching' as a category. Among its properties are 'frequency', 'extent', 'intensity', and 'duration'. Each of these properties can be 'dimensionalised' or broken down into its dimensions. Thus, the dimensions of 'frequency' extend from 'often' to 'never', the dimensions of 'extent' extend from 'more' to 'less', the dimensions of 'intensity' extend from 'high' to 'low', and the dimensions of 'duration' extend from 'long' to 'short'. Again, with such categories at one's disposal one is armed with a framework by which one can speak about phenomena in ways hitherto not possible and one can locate specific instances of a phenomenon somewhere within the framework. On this also, Woods offers some useful advice relating to tests of adequacy which can be brought to bear in the generation of categories, along with indicators as to when initial attempts may need to be revised (Woods 2006: 26).

A fourth variety of theory which can be considered is that of propositions. A proposition is defined by Taylor and Bogdan (1998: 134) as 'a general statement of fact grounded in the data'. They go on to offer the following example of a proposition: 'Attendants use evasion strategies to avoid getting caught violating institutional rules'. They explain that, like concepts, propositions are generated by poring over the data. 'By studying themes … and relating different pieces of data to each other' they say, 'the researcher gradually comes up with generalizations' (Taylor and Bogdan 1998: 134). Woods views the process in similar light. As he sees it, 'categories can be put together in separate groups around a common theme'. The researcher might then try to 'conceptualise the material and raise it to a higher level of understanding, so that it might inform our general understanding of such issues' (Woods 2006: 32). It is through this process that propositions can be arrived at.

A fifth variety of theory is that of models. Lewins (1992: 21) describes a model as a simplified representation of something existing in the world. Its function is to provide a fairly clear picture of something which in reality is somewhat more complicated. Lewins (1992: 21) gives, as an example, a street directory, stating:

> It is obvious that particular streets and places do not exist as parallel lines and dots, but such a scale representation of the real world is explanatory to the extent that it becomes possible to answer questions such as 'where am I?' when one is lost.

In summary, a model is constructed in order to try to denote in a relatively simple manner the crucial parts of a very intricate situation.

The sixth variety of theory which can be considered is that of typologies. These, to put it simply, are classification schemes. Again, they can be both classification schemes used by the participants and those generated by the researcher. Furthermore, they point to relationships and interconnections, thus providing a foundation for comparison. A particular form of typology is Weber's (Aran 1967) 'ideal type'. It provides a basic method for comparative study because it is founded on the 'earned distinctions' of individuals. As such, it is seen as providing a 'rationalizing reconstruction of a particular kind of behaviour' (Aran 1967: 204). Shils and Finch (1949: 90) have explained that 'An "ideal type" is formed by the synthesis of a great many diffuse, discrete, more or less present and occasionally absent concrete individual phenomena which are arranged ... into a unified analytical construct'.

It should not be inferred, however, that being classified as belonging to a 'type' indicates that a predetermined or inflexible set of actions will always be enacted by particular individuals when they are faced with a specific set of conditions. Rather, an 'ideal type' is a device which allows us to establish similarities as well as variation in a concrete phenomenon. Therefore, the basis of a typology which is comprised of 'ideal types' is that under specific conditions, individuals who are considered to belong to a particular 'type' will tend to engage in actions and interactions which are similar to others of this 'type'. When, on occasions, individuals engage in actions which are atypical of the 'type' to which they have been assigned in relation to the way they deal with a particular phenomenon, it should not be adjudged that the overall typology has failed, or that it has some inadequacies. The efficacy of a 'grounded typology' lies not only in its capacity to describe regular and predictable patterns of actions and interactions, but also in its capacity to focus attention on 'intervening conditions' (Strauss and Corbin 1990) which can lead to atypical actions.

While the six varieties of theory mentioned above are by no means the only way in which one can characterise what is possible through analysis, it is important also to note that theory development of the type considered in this book does not include the development of 'laws' or of 'causal theories'. These levels of theory relate to nomothetic rather than ideographic studies. Laws 'posit the recurring nature of particular relationships' (Lewins 1992: 21) and causal theories posit 'the conditions under which the event being explained happens'. Silverman (2005: 349) summarises the point being made here in very simple terms when he states that 'why' questions are usually best answered by quantitative methods.

Selecting participants

In order to obtain data for the generation of theory of the sort considered in the previous section of this chapter one usually, though not always, needs to select participants for interview and observation. Stating this immediately poses for many the following question: How many participants do we need to have? From considerations so far, it is clear that, since the studies in which we are interested are ideographic, one is by definition restricted to understanding particular events or human actions within specific cultural contexts. This immediately places a limit on the number of participants required. Equally, one is not obliged to work with a large number of participants located within such limits, since the aim is to generate theory rather than test hypotheses. To put it simply, a much smaller number of participants is required to generate heuristic devices or 'tools' by which we can speak intelligently about the phenomenon under investigation than is required if we are trying to discover 'findings' which are generalizable from the results of a study of a sample of a population to the total population.

Knowing, however, that one is not expected to work with a large number of participants still does not indicate how many is enough. The challenge in this regard is a methodological one, where methodology, as will be recalled from Chapter 1, is viewed as a strategy, plan of action, process, or design to link our paradigm-guided questions with particular methods. At this point it is necessary to backtrack a little and call to mind that the methodology, which it was indicated in Chapter 1 would be explicated in this book because of its relationship to the interpretivist paradigm and the symbolic interactionist position within it, is that of 'grounded theory'.

Punch and Wildy (1995: 2) state that grounded theory is best defined as a research strategy whose purpose is to generate theory from data. This strategy, as Charmaz (2002: 675) puts it, consists of guidelines that aid the researcher in the following ways: '(a) to study social and social psychological processes; (b) to direct data collection, (c) to manage data analysis, and (d) to develop and abstract theoretical frameworks that explain the studied process'.

Charmaz goes on to explain that grounded theory researchers collect data and analyze it simultaneously from the initial phases of research. Furthermore, as they proceed they take the view that some of the data collection questions developed in the initial stages of a study could become redundant as a study progresses, while other unanticipated ones could emerge.

The latter point highlights one of the major reasons why at no stage in this book do I encourage researchers to use computer-assisted qualitative data analysis software (CAQDAS). Some people wrongly assume that all of one's data can be collected initially and then analysed using a computer package. Also, such packages cannot conduct qualitative data analysis on their own. Rather, when they are used, the researcher has to create the categories in the first instance. Furthermore, the software cannot interpret the significance of what one has collected. It merely collates data and records the work of the analyst. Ezzy (2002, 132) has made this argument forcibly:

> The software limits the richness of the data that can be analysed. The primary way in which 'richness' is lost is through the decontextualisation of data by CAQDAS software. Code-and-retrieve methods of data analysis, both manual and computerised, break up data into chunks, and these chunks are sorted into groups according to categories to which they relate. ... the code-and-retrieve methodology encourages short segments of data to be viewed out of context, and not clearly linked to the more general interpretative frames utilised by participants.

He concluded by stating that 'rich' data include references that 'explain the relationship of the events under description to a more general cultural and interpretative framework'.

Here it is also instructive by way of further background to recall Punch and Wildy's (1995: 2) observation that the history of grounded theory is, in fact, quite short. A useful overview of this history is provided by Creswell (2005: 396–7). Here, as in most other accounts, the origins of grounded theory are traced back to the 1960s when Glaser and Strauss published two major works in medical sociology concerned with dying in hospitals (Glaser and Strauss 1965, 1968). In 1967, they also published a companion 'how we did it' book entitled *The Discovery of Grounded Theory* (Glaser and Strauss 1967). According to Strauss and Corbin (1994: 275), this work had three purposes: to offer a rationale for theory that was grounded, to suggest the logic for and specifics of grounded theories, and to legitimate qualitative research undertaken in a rigorous manner.

Over its short history grounded theory has split into two different, yet largely related, positions. Charmaz (2002) refers to these as objectivist and constructivist. The objectivist position, she states, emphasises the viewing of data 'as real in and of themselves' (Charmaz 2002: 677). This position, she goes on, 'assumes that data represent objective facts about a knowable world. The data already exist in the world, and the researcher finds them' (Charmaz 2002: 677). Thus, it is a position very much in harmony with the positivist paradigm. Strauss and Corbin (1990), on the other hand, with Chicago school of sociology influences, brought grounded theory in the direction of the interpretivist paradigm by developing an approach which 'places priority on the phenomena of study and sees both data and analysis as created from the shared experiences of researcher and participants and the researcher's relationships with participants' (Charmaz 2002: 677).

The identification of grounded theory with the interpretivist paradigm resulted in quite a degree of controversy between Glaser and his followers in the one camp and Strauss and Corbin and their followers in the other. The most open controversy centred on Glaser's rejection of what he saw as over-codification of explicit procedures for qualitative data analysis by Strauss and Corbin (1992). Anyone interested in the nature of the controversy would do well to read the account of it presented by Atkinson et al. (2003: 148–52). This, however, is not the place to enter into a discussion of the pros and cons of either position. Rather, the stance adopted here is that the fundamental approach common to both positions is most appropriate when a study is designed within the interpretivist paradigm, and particularly where the theoretical foundation is that of symbolic interactionism; a position upheld by Chenitz and Swanson (1986: 3–15).

Fundamental to grounded theory is that it is an inductive approach to data gathering and analysis. It is oriented, as Taylor and Bogdan (1998: 7–8) put it, to developing 'concepts, insights, and understandings from patterns in the data rather than collecting data to assess preconceived models, hypotheses, or theories'. 'A theory,' they hold, 'may be said to be grounded to the extent that it is derived from and based on the data themselves'. On this, they refer to Lofland (1971), who described this kind of theorizing as 'emergent analysis' and who pointed out that the process is one which is creative and intuitive as opposed to being mechanical. At the same time, Taylor and Bogdan (1998: 8) are not naive enough to claim that pure induction is possible. As they put it, 'We can never escape all of our assumptions about the world. Even an interest in social meaning directs our attention to some aspects of how people think and act in a setting and not to others'. The goal, they conclude, 'is to make sure the theory fits the data and not vice versa'.

With whom, then, do we commence our largely inductivist-oriented research? The standard approach is to, first of all, imagine the ideal research setting. This, in the words of Taylor and Bogdan (1989: 19), 'is one in which the observer obtains easy access, establishes immediate rapport with informants, and gathers data directly relating to the research interests'. Being 'ideal', of course, means that the situation to which we would like to gain access never fully exists, but one should do one's best to approximate it as much as possible. Having done so, one then commences one's research usually by interviewing one participant. (It is hardly possible to be more inductivist than this!) Once the first interview has been completed, analysis can commence.

At this juncture it is helpful to consider Crabtree and Miller's (1992) observation that four major analysis styles tend to be used by the wide range of qualitative researchers. These are termed the 'quasi-statistical style', the 'template analysis style', the 'immersion/crystallization style', and the 'editing analysis style'. The following summary of each is based on extracts from the very useful overview provided by Polit et al. (2001: 382):

> *Quasi-statistical analysis style:* The researcher reviews the content of the narrative data, searching for particular words or themes that have been specified in advance. The result of the information is information that can be analysed statistically. For example, the analyst can count the frequency of occurrence of specific themes, or can cross-tabulate the occurrence of certain words.
>
> *Template analysis style:* The researcher develops a template or analysis guide to which the narrative data are applied. The units for the template are typically behaviours, events, or linguistic expressions (e.g. words). A template is more adaptable than a codebook in the quasi-statistical style. Although the researcher may begin with a rudimentary template before collecting any data, it undergoes constant revision as more data are gathered. The analysis of the resulting data, once sorted according to the template, is interpretive and not statistical.
>
> *Immersion/crystallization:* This style involves the analyst's total immersion in and reflection on the text materials, resulting in an intuitive crystallization of the data.
>
> *Editing analysis style:* The researcher acts as an interpreter who reads through the data in search of meaningful segments. Once segments are identified and reviewed, the interpreter develops a categorization scheme and corresponding codes that can be used to sort and organise data. The researcher then searches for the patterns and structure that connect the thematic categories. The grounded theory approach typically incorporates this style.

While there may be occasions when students engaging in research of the type – which is the focus of this book – may draw upon the first three styles outlined above, our concern is almost totally with the fourth style. Here, as concepts are generated they are compared and clustered – 'the constant comparative method' – until categories are formed (Charmaz, 2014). This process is assisted by asking oneself constant questions of the data, particularly the question: What is this an example of? – 'the method of constant questioning'.

The processes of constant comparison and constant questioning are referred to by Polit et al. (2001: 385) as follows:

> The researcher asks questions about discrete events, incidents, or thoughts that are indicated in an observation or statement, such as the following:
>
> What is this?
> What is going on?
> What does it stand for?
> What else is like this?
> What is this distinct from?

Important concepts that emerge from close examination of the data are then given a label that forms the basis for a categorization scheme. These category names are necessarily abstractions, but the labels are generally sufficiently graphic that the nature of the material to which it refers is clear.

Operating in this manner, one moves on to the next participant and the next one, in each instance building analysis upon analysis. In other words, the researcher is regularly involved in generating hypotheses about categories and about their relationships and interrelationships, and then testing these hypotheses with data. In this way, the process is also deductive. Equally, it means that data collection and data analysis occurs in parallel and repeatedly, rather than consecutively as a one-off set of activities.

The next question then is: On what basis is each subsequent participant chosen? The grounded theory response to this is captured in the notion of 'theoretical sampling'. Taylor and Bogdan (1989: 83) summarise this notion as follows:

> In theoretical sampling the actual number of 'cases' studied is relatively unimportant. What is important is the potential of each 'case' to aid the researcher in developing theoretical insights into the area of social life being studied. After completing interviews with several informants, you would consciously vary the type of people interviewed until you had uncovered the full range of perspectives held by the people in whom you are interested. You would have an idea that you had reached this point when interviews with additional people yielded no genuinely new insights.

Adopting a theoretical sampling approach facilitates the generation of the full range and variation in a category. Also, as a category is being developed in this manner it is constantly tested against new data as it is collected. A particular strategy utilised in this regard is that of seeking out negative cases in order to disprove hypotheses and thus further refine emerging theory.

The idea in grounded theory, then, is that data collection and analysis continues until categories become saturated. Saturation refers to the inability to develop categories further in terms of their properties and dimensions no matter how much new data are collected. Experienced researchers adopting this approach appreciate that they may stop at any level of analysis where saturation has been reached in relation to just some categories, and then report their results. They are also comfortable with the notion of Burgess (1982) that researchers may formulate and reformulate their research, developing it out where they judge that it is yielding a poor return for effort and contracting it where it appears to be too broad in scope.

A beginner, however, quite understandably, often seeks from the outset to work within a clearer set of parameters, not least so that a reasonable prediction can be made regarding the length of time which will need to be spent on the study. There appears to me to be at least two main ways in which such parameters can be established. The first is to harness Stainback and Stainback's (1984: 299) notion of 'modified analytic induction'. They elaborate on this notion as follows:

> a modified analytic induction strategy has been developed for practical purposes. In the modified approach, the researcher may tightly define a population, thus limiting the applicability of the description of theory to a specifically defined group. Or, a researcher may determine the number of cases he/she has the resources to handle in an investigation and simply base the theory and testing of the theory on those cases, making no claim that the theory is inclusive beyond the defined set.
>
> (Stainback and Stainback 1984: 299)

This is somewhat akin to the notion of Adelman et al. (1976: 141) of a case as a bounded system 'within which issues are indicated, discovered or studied so that a tolerably full understanding of the case is possible'. Within the bounded system chosen, of course, one still has to theoretically sample. An example of one case study undertaken along such lines is presented in the next chapter.

Another slightly different way to narrow the focus of study is to define the area of interest so tightly from the beginning that the full population which could be studied is so small that all can be participants in the research. An example of a study undertaken along such lines is presented in Chapter 6. Before proceeding to these chapters, however, a short exposition on the value of generating theory of the type which they report is now offered.

What is the value of this kind of theory?

The next obvious major question to be posed from considerations so far is: What is the value in theory developed through studies of the types being proposed here which are idiographic and are based on data collected from relatively small populations? For some, this sort of question is irritating and they are inclined to retort with the question: What is the value in historical studies or philosophical studies? What they imply through such a response is that within the academic world there are great bodies of work which are considered of value for reasons other than that of having practical relevance. In particular, the contention is that such work can be academically and intellectually relevant in its own right. While the same contention can be made in regards to studies of the type which are the focus of interest in this book, it is instructive to consider that an extensive set of arguments regarding their practical value have also been articulated for many years. What this final part of the chapter now outlines is an overview on these practical arguments. It does so under three main headings: (i) arguments for the value of the theory developed in terms of its importance for bringing about change in the situation studied; (ii) arguments for the value of the theory developed in terms of its potential for contributing to professional development programmes; (iii) arguments for the value of the theory developed in terms of its generalizability to situations other than the ones studied. There is, however, quite a degree of overlap in the three groups of arguments.

The value of the theory generated for bringing about change in the situation studied

The necessity of understanding people's contextual realities before introducing changes in the hope of improving the quality of education in any context is well summarised by Fullan (1982: 149) as 'in order to effect improvement, that is, to effect an introduced change which has the promise of increasing success and decreasing failure, the world of the people most closely involved must be understood'.

This position has also been taken up by others, including Dove (1986: 212). What they emphasise is that the first step in the process of improving the quality of education should be to aim at understanding the contextual reality. Hargreaves (1993) has considered this matter in some detail and what he had to say can be summarised in the following short account.

Hargreaves (1993: 149) spoke of the 'immunological capacity' of interpretivist studies, and especially symbolic interactionist studies. He contended that many social policies fail and nowhere is this more evident than in education where, he held, innovations frequently fail quite disastrously. The one common reason for this, he argued, is as follows:

> in grafting new ideas onto schools, we do it with so little knowledge about the nature of the everyday world of teachers, pupils and schools that our attempted grafts (and various forms of major and minor surgery) merely arouse the 'anti-bodies' of the host which undermine our attempts to play doctor to an educational patient.
>
> (Hargreaves 1993: 149–150)

He went on to argue that symbolic interactionist studies can help provide us with the necessary understandings, 'for only when we understand the precise nature of the host body can we design our innovatory grafts with any confidence that they will prove to be acceptable' (Hargreaves 1993: 150). Fullan (1982) made a similar argument in his contention that central-level bureaucrats who are trying to promote change could benefit from reflecting on interpretivist studies. This, he argued, is because to effect improvement, that is, to introduce change that promises more success and less failure, the world of the people most closely involved in implementation must be understood.

There is also another aspect to this argument. Theory in the form of detailed description can function to familiarise policy-makers with how those who are expected to implement change understand their world. Hargreaves (1993: 149), however, has reminded us of the importance of also generating concepts, categories, propositions, models, and typologies to this end. At its most basic, this involves *naming* features 'of the complex commonsense knowledge of members of society'. Through this process, he argued, we are provided with 'a language for speaking about that which is not normally spoken about: the ineffable is rendered articulate' (Hargreaves 1993: 149). He concluded with an example from the world of education as follows:

> Recent interactionist work in the field of education shows the extent to which teacher skills rest upon tacit knowledge. Teachers have no explicit conceptual apparatus in which to express and communicate these skills – and they reject the traditional language of the educational sciences to that end. By its designatory function, symbolic interactionism can provide such a language.
>
> (Hargreaves 1993: 149)

Finally, he argued that the 'language' produced through analysis can also be put before the research participants, acting as a mirror which 'reflects man [*sic*] back to himself'. This can provide the participants with 'an opportunity to judge and appraise the reflection' they see and, perhaps as a result, seek to change themselves and their professional world.

The relevance of the theory generated in one setting for professional development programmes in other settings

Theories of the sort being considered in this book are usually developed in just one setting. However, they can also have relevance for professional development programmes, not only for those in this setting, but also for those working in other settings. Indeed, they can be instructive to an international audience. As Sultana (1991) puts it, they can expose stakeholders involved in similar circumstances in various other parts of the world to material which could help them in clarifying and sharpening their own perspectives. Another way of putting this argument is that the insights provided by a theory can provide a framework for developing enlightenment and guiding activity since it can 'speak' to others in similar and related contexts who share some of the same concerns.

This position also serves to highlight another point, namely, that many uninformed readers can have unrealistic expectations of what a good theory can offer, in particular in terms of expecting clear directives for practice from theory. Such expectations, as Entwistle pointed out over 30 years ago, often betray a misunderstanding of the very nature of theory. He developed this point as follows:

> Demands are made of theories for guidance which, in their nature, it is impossible for them to supply. There never can be a one-to-one relationship between theory and practice if by this we mean theory which predicts every contingency in a practical situation. A theory gains its relevance to every conceivable situation by being an exact account of none of them .... The fault for the theory-practice gap may lie not in the theory but in the unrealistic expectation of practitioners.
>
> (Entwistle (1971: 98)

The same point regarding the limitations of theory was made by William James (1958: 15) back in 1892, when he commented as follows regarding the function of the study of psychology for educationists:

> You make a great mistake if you think that psychology, being a science of the mind's law, is something from which you can deduce definite programmes and schemes and methods of instruction for immediate classroom use. Psychology is a science, and teaching is an art. An intermediary inventive mind must make the application, by using its originality. The science of logic never made a man reason rightly, the science of ethics never made a man behave rightly. The most such sciences can do is to help us catch ourselves up, check ourselves, if we start to reason or behave wrongly; and to criticise ourselves more articulately if we make mistakes. A science only lays down lines within which the rules of the art must fall, laws which the follower of the art must not transgress; but what particular thing he shall positively do within those lines is left exclusively to his own genius. And so while everywhere the teaching must agree with the psychology, it may not necessarily be the only kind of teaching that would so agree; for many diverse methods of teaching may equally well agree with the psychological laws.

For many decades this position was overlooked as research in the professions, including education, became preoccupied with attempts aimed at the invention and discovery of sure-fired prescriptive models which would lead to easily generalisable solutions in each area (Hopkins 1993). Eisner (1983), for one, however, became instrumental in providing compelling arguments which enabled scholars and practitioners in the field of education to question such preoccupation. He made the case that due to the changing uniqueness of the practical situations that make up the domain of education, only a portion of professional practice can be usefully treated in the manner of a prescriptive science. The gap between general prescriptive frameworks and successful practice is, he held, dependent more on the reflective intuition, the craft, and the art of the professional practitioner than on any particular prescriptive theory, method, or model.

To apply this position to considerations of professional development programmes for participants other than those who take part in studies leading to the generation of ideographic theory is to argue that such theory can, in the language of Stenhouse (1975), aid in the development of the capacity of educationists to understand relationships and make judgements by constituting frameworks for others within which they can think. In similar vein, symbolic interactionist studies of the sort being discussed in this book may constitute one source to assist us in breaking away from a notion of continuing professional development as being concerned only with instrumental ends achievable through 'the recipes of tried and true practices legitimated by unexamined experiences or uncritically accepted research findings' and towards one of 'developing reflective practitioners who are able to understand, challenge and transform' (Sachs and Logan 1990: 479).

Generalisability of theory developed in one situation to other situations

No claim can be made for the 'generalisability' of interpretivist theories, including those developed in symbolic interactionist studies, in the sense in which researchers working within the positivist paradigm can claim generalisability for their theories. This position is very much the same one that underpins the recent work of Uhrmacher et al. (2017) where he promotes an approach to qualitative which is in parallel to that running throughout this book and which is termed 'educational criticism and connoiseurship'.

At the same time, this is not to argue that there can be no generalisability. Stake (1978), for example, has argued that interpretive studies undertaken with small populations may be in harmony with the reader's experience and thus a natural basis for generalisation. In other words, readers can relate to the study and perhaps gain an understanding of their own and others' situations. This is what is referred to when it is stated that a theory can have 'reader or user generalisability'. As Kennedy (1979), in the same vein, put it, generalisability is ultimately related to what the reader is trying to learn from such studies.

Lancy (1993: 165) has provided a yet different angle on this, stating that such an approach 'is comparable to the law where the applicability of a particular precedent case must be argued in each subsequent case'; the reader must decide whether the results apply or not. This is similar to the argument of Strauss and Corbin (1994: 279) when they state:

> Grounded theories … call for exploration of each new situation to see if they fit, how they might fit, and how they might not fit. They demand an openness of the researcher, based on the 'forever' provisional character of every teacher. For all that, grounded theories are not just another set of phrases; rather, they are systematic statements of plausible relationships.

A related argument is that insofar as theory developed through this methodology is able to specify consequences and their related conditions, the theorist can claim predictability for it, in the limited sense that if elsewhere approximately similar conditions obtain, then approximately similar consequences should occur (Strauss and Corbin 1994: 278).

On the latter matter, Lincoln and Guba's (1985) notion of 'transferability' is instructive. They have contended that, unlike researchers operating in the positivist tradition who strive for high levels of 'external validity', those who operate in the interpretivist, or what they call the 'naturalistic paradigm', cannot specify the external validity of an inquiry; rather 'he or she can provide only the thick description necessary to enable someone interested in making a transfer to reach a conclusion about whether transfer can be contemplated as a possibility' (Lincoln and Guba 1985: 316).

Consequently, emphasis is placed on the concept of 'transferability' and the associated responsibility for providing an accurate and comprehensive 'data base' that would make transferability judgements possible on the part of potential 'appliers' (Lincoln and Guba 1985). For this reason, the presentation of any theory developed should, as much as possible, be both conceptually 'dense' and interlaced with relevant extracts from the data.

Interpretivist studies can also be seen as having generalisability in the sense outlined by Uhrmacher (1993: 89–90). Building his ideas on those of Eisner (1985), he has argued for the production of cases which describe school life, interpret that life by exploring the meanings and consequences of education events, and assess the significance for education of events described and interpreted. This 'thematics' approach, Uhrmacher (1993) states, is related to generalising in social science research. He goes on to argue that, rather than make formal generalisations, one can provide the reader with an understanding of the major themes that run through the cases under study. In turn, these themes can provide the reader with theories or guides for anticipating what may be found in other situations; 'these theories provide guidance, not prediction' (Uhrmacher, 1993: 90). Thomas (1997) offers a similar view in his identification of four broad uses of theory in inquiry in the field of education and the social sciences.

Finally, Hargreaves (1993) makes the point that micro-theories of the sort produced in symbolic interactionist studies are 'a potential source of correction to macro theories, which frequently oversimplify, underestimate or ignore the complexity of the detailed operation of relevant factors in actual social settings'. To put it differently, there is much scope for using symbolic interactionist studies 'as a basis for a critical reading of a macro theory, and then actively to seek out the micro implications' with a view to undertaking the necessary empirical work to 'provide an empirical testing ground' (Hargreaves 1993: 150).

Chapter 5

An example of a 'perspectives' study

Introduction

So far this book has emphasised that two main types of studies can be conducted where the central underlying principles are those of the symbolic interactionist theoretical approach within the interpretivist paradigm. The first of these types consists of studies where the central research question is formulated in terms of participants' perspectives on 'things'. This chapter now presents an exemplar of one way of presenting theory generated within a study of this type.

The study

This chapter outlines the first set of three sets of results of a study conducted for the degree of Doctor of Education by Dr. Sarah Ekin, under my supervision in the Graduate School of Education at The University of Western Australia. The central aim of the study was to generate theory on the perspectives of language teachers of German in Western Australia on what is an effective teacher of German. In line with this, the central research question which guided theory generation was as follows: What are the perspectives of secondary school teachers of German in Western Australia on what is an effective teacher of German? The question was pursued in the case of teachers located within the Perth metropolitan area in the State of Western Australia (WA).

The central proposition of the theory that was generated is that teachers of German within WA adopt a very pragmatic stance in their considerations on what is an effective teacher of the language within the mainline school system. They identify three competencies in regard to this. The first competency, they say, relates to an ability to motivate students. The second competency, they say, relates to the adaptability of teachers of German. The third competency, they say, relates to dealing with the constraints presented by having to teach and learn German in a secondary school classroom.

In relation to each competency, teachers emphasise the importance of having a clear notion of the outcome they expect and the importance of planning to realise this outcome. They also emphasise the importance of using appropriate pedagogical strategies to help students achieve the competency. Also, the secondary school teachers of German articulate reasons for each of these emphases.

The remainder of this chapter now presents a detailed introduction to the first competency, namely, the ability to motivate students. It opens with an elaboration on the nature of this competency. The emphasis placed on the importance of having a clear notion of the outcomes one should expect as a result of the existence of this competency is then considered. This is followed by an outline of the planning approach that secondary school teachers of German consider they should adopt. Pedagogical strategies considered appropriate in relation to the outcome and the planning are then outlined. Throughout the exposition on each of these matters the reasons offered by secondary school teachers of German for their perspectives are detailed.

The nature of the first competency: The ability to motivate students

Secondary school teachers of German hold that for students to learn German, they need to have a willingness to learn the language. Further, they hold, for students to demonstrate this willingness, teachers need to be able to show that learning German and learning about the cultures of German-speaking countries is useful. Also, to motivate students to learn German, teachers of German need to awaken a sense of curiosity about the language and its related cultures and they need to challenge students to want to learn the language. Equally, motivating students to learn German often requires building a rapport with them. This relates back to the first of the three competencies considered in this chapter that teachers of German feel they have to deal with in order to be an effective teacher of the language.

The first competency being referred to is the ability to motivate students. Three themes were generated on this. The first theme relates to promoting a desire amongst students to learn German and the perceived influence of this on the expected outcomes, the required planning approach, and the associated pedagogical strategies considered important by the teachers of German. The second theme relates to promoting students' extrinsic motivation to learn German. The third theme relates to promoting students' intrinsic motivation to learn German. Finally, these three themes are not hierarchical.

Promoting a desire amongst students to learn German

The first theme relates to teachers promoting a desire amongst students to learn German. Teachers of German recognise that for students to gain a level of written and oral competence in German so that they are capable of communicating in the language, they need to want to learn German and they also need to choose to learn the language and learn about German-speaking countries. Thus, the desire to learn German is comprised of two aspects. The first relates to a willingness to learn the language and the second relates to building an interest in language and culture in students. The former is related to students' attitudes towards learning a second language and to students' level of desire to invest the time and energy required to learn a second language, while the latter, namely, building an interest in language and culture in students, relates to how an effective teacher of German is able to positively influence a student's willingness to learn a language and to learn about another culture. Each of these is now considered.

Having a willingness to learn the language

Teachers of German perceive that for students to begin to learn German and then to choose to learn German beyond the compulsory years of language education, they need to have a willingness to learn a language in general, and a specific willingness to learn German. However, students' desire to learn a language cannot be presupposed. On this, teachers of German observe that among WA students and parents there is an Anglo-centric mindset. This mindset reveals itself in negative attitudes towards people who speak another language and in the expectation that people who come to Australia should speak English.

The result, it is felt, is a lack of interest in, and a lack of impetus regarding, learning another language. Effective teachers of German, therefore, it is held, seek to awaken and instill in students a willingness to learn German beyond the compulsory years of language education in schools. As one participant put it: "One can do so many fantastic things to get the students motivated. You 'get' the young ones (primary school students) with film stars, costumes and food". Another participant agreed, while stating that "my predecessor wouldn't teach in the junior school. It's mickey-mouse German. But that's where you win. You've got to get them down there".

Building an interest in language and culture in students

Along with encouraging a willingness in students to learn a second language, effective teachers of German consciously, it is held, generate students' interest in the language, in culture generally, and in the culture of German-speaking countries. They do this through creating a balance between teaching language and teaching about culture in their lessons. One teacher described the process thus:

> We do talk about what happens in Germany and in Europe. How society is built up, how it has evolved over time. Especially in Year 12, it is about how families have developed: the roles between men and women. Emancipation – which kids don't know about: 'what is emancipation?' How women got jobs over time. How it changed from being a mum and working at home and (then to) getting an education.

By adopting such an approach, it is held, students will seek to expand their language repertoire to express themselves and may seek to find out more outside the classroom about culture.

Promoting extrinsic motivation to learn German

The second theme related to the nature of the competency of secondary school teachers of German to motivate students to learn the language is concerned with the extrinsic motivation to learn it. Effective secondary school teachers of German, it is held, recognise that they can influence this extrinsic motivation by demonstrating the usefulness of what the students learn, especially to beyond the classroom. Teachers explain that for students to recognise the usefulness of German, he or she needs to establish a balance in lessons between emphasising language and emphasising culture. This means that classes have to have language content that the students find useful to use. Second, the teacher needs to provide cultural content from German-speaking countries that contributes to the students' sense that learning about German-speaking countries, or people, traditions, lifestyles and culture, is useful and valuable to them.

It is also held that students need to be able to recognise usefulness when, of their own volition, they choose, for example, to watch a film in German or to listen to songs in German. Related to this, teachers of German believe that students should be able to choose to use German in their free-time activities because they are confident in their German language competence. Also, an awareness of increasing competence in the German language becomes evident to the students, it is held, when they see their language learning progress in the increasingly complex language activities undertaken in the classroom, as well as in the interactions in German that they have with other students and with their teachers both in the classroom and outside. In relation to this, an effective teacher of German, it is held, should be able to provide students with strategies such that when they are faced with the situation of trying to understand a new text with unfamiliar words, they should, as one teacher put it, have the following perspective:

> This is not exotic. You're just solving a problem. You're taking what you know and it's helping you to work out what you don't know. It's exactly what you do in maths, you do in science. You do it when you go out into the world.

Teachers also argued that for students to be able to do this, "you have to make links! You've got to make links to the real world too. They're what's called your enduring understandings".

Teachers of German also consider that an effective teacher is one who is able to get students to see that German has relevance beyond the classroom. On this, they contend that an effective teacher of German tries to provide content which results in students gaining a sense of curiosity about the language and culture of German-speaking countries. The culmination of this curiosity, combined with further learning of the language and cultures of German-speaking countries, is students independently seeking out opportunities to use their language and cultural knowledge beyond the classroom. This may seed in their minds the idea of taking a holiday in a German-speaking country, using the language with German speakers while on holiday, or gaining access to German-language resources on the internet.

Promoting intrinsic motivation to learn German

The third theme relating to the nature of the demand to motivate students to learn the language is that teachers should attempt to promote their intrinsic motivation to learn German. They observe that when students show an interest in an aspect of German, or German-speaking cultures, such as the language's structure, or German cars, or modern German history, they can become intrinsically motivated to learn the language. This can be considered in terms of an effective teacher of the language being able to motivate students to have a sense of curiosity about German and German-speaking cultures, and also to being able to challenge students to develop a desire to learn the language. These are now considered in turn.

Awakening a sense of curiosity about German and German-speaking cultures

Teachers of German argue that they are able to bring students to appreciate German-speaking cultures. The result, they hold, is that those who are interested in learning about these cultures are open to having their sense of curiosity about them further awakened. However, they also hold that in the case of students who have little prior knowledge of, or interest in, German and German-speaking countries, different teaching and learning strategies need to be used to awaken a sense of curiosity. Thus, it is held, the immediate aim of an effective teacher of German should be to motivate students to learn German in the classroom.

Another aim, it is held, should be to awaken students' curiosity about German and German-speaking countries so that they might choose to use their language competence beyond the classroom. This might take the form of searching German language websites at home for information relating to their areas of interest, or conducting a conversation with a German tourist they meet in the street. A further aim might be for students to continue learning German at tertiary education level or to go to Germany to study at a university.

Challenging students to have a desire to learn German

Along with awakening a sense of curiosity about German and German-speaking cultures, teachers of German argue that in order to be an effective teacher an important facet of motivating students is challenging them to desire to learn the language. They offer three reasons for this. First, teachers hold that challenging students to desire to learn German by holding high expectations of their ability to learn it results in students who desire to invest the effort required to gain competence in the language. Second, students who rise to the challenge and achieve well in class tests, or who can hold a conversation with the teacher in German, gain a sense of achievement. Third, teachers of German hold that by providing activities that are both aligned to students' abilities and yet are still challenging ensures that students do not become bored.

Expected outcomes because of the first competency

Another aspect of the perspectives of secondary school teachers of German on what are effective teachers of German is that they expect certain outcomes in relation to the first competency, namely, the ability to motivate students. This section discusses the matter in relation to perceived enriching outcomes that can stem from learning German. They are now discussed in turn.

Enriching outcomes from learning German

This theme relates to two features of student motivation to learn German identified by teachers of German as being important to recognise in order to be an effective teacher of the language. The features encompass moving students beyond being monolingual individuals and diluting their Anglo-centric worldview. Each is now considered in turn.

Moving students beyond being monolingual individuals

There are two ways, it is held, that teachers of German can assess whether or not their students have moved beyond being monolingual individuals. The first way is when students demonstrate their competence in using German in formal classroom exchanges. On this, effective teachers of German, it is argued, pay attention to the accuracy and content of the students' written and spoken output and compare it to the teaching and learning in previous classes. Development in the students' German language skills is then seen as indicating improved competence. This, in turn, is seen as evidence of a desire to move away from monolingualism. The second way, it is held, that a teacher has been effective in realising a move away from monolingualism is when students engage in conversations in German outside of the classroom. This can involve student initiation of the exchange, the content and the amount volunteered, or the teacher being able to elicit this by furthering the conversation.

Diluting students' Anglo-centric worldview

The second enriching outcome of the demand on effective teachers to motivate students to learn German, it is held, is teachers having succeeded in diluting students' Anglo-centric worldview. As one teacher put it, "taking them out of the very Anglo-centric mindset of Australia, where the expectation is that everybody who comes here speaks English, and speaking a foreign language – by some people anyway – is still considered to be quite rude".

Teachers of German believe that an Anglo-centric worldview acts against students perceiving a need for, or expressing an interest in, learning another language. So, an effective teacher, it is held, should "make the link that languages make the link with other countries and cultures. (It is) trying to open the kids eyes as well a little bit. (because) … it's not only just Australia or other English-speaking countries in the world". "After all," it is regularly said, "there are more countries in the world that don't speak English than actually do."

The planning approach teachers consider that they should adopt

Organisation plays a significant role in teachers' private and public lives. Full-time teachers in WA usually have 40 contact hours a week with students. Some schools, especially independent schools, also expect a regular commitment from teachers to conduct extra-curricular activities. Organisation for teachers also includes lesson preparation, assessment, (including marking and attending moderation meetings), and participating in professional learning. Against such a scenario, teachers of German believe that lesson preparation is the key planning approach for effective teachers aiming to motivate students to learn German. They identify three categories in such preparation. These are the planning approach to lesson content, the student focus when planning lessons, and the planning approach to being well-prepared. These categories are now looked at in turn.

The planning approach to lesson content

The first planning approach teachers of German say assists effective teachers in keeping students motivated to learn German is to focus on lesson content. They indicate that both individual lessons and blocks of lessons need to achieve a balance between a focus on language and a focus on culture (including development of students' knowledge about Germany, Austria, Switzerland, and Liechtenstein). One reason offered for the importance of maintaining a balance between these content elements is to reduce the likelihood of students growing bored with a class that is too focused on any one aspect of the subject. Another reason offered is that it is important to try to encompass the interests of all students who are learning German. A further reason is to ensure that students can leave every class with the sense that they have learned something. A fourth reason offered is that it will lead to students wanting to continue learning German later on in their education.

Student focus when planning lessons

The second planning approach teachers of German identify as being a characteristic of an effective teacher of the subject is that there should be a student focus when planning lessons. They identify three aspects of this. First, effective teachers of German should focus on students when designing the content of their teaching and learning programme for a given class. Here, they should take into account their individual students' interests and abilities. On this, one teacher claimed:

> they've all got an interest for something. They've all got a pastime – a thing they are passionate about. Everybody has got some sort of interest, or passion. You can engage with everybody on some level. We've just got to find that level, that common ground.

Second, effective teachers of German should adopt a student focus when preparing activities focused on grammar, syntax, and vocabulary. These, it is held, should be selected based on individual students' strengths and weaknesses. Third, effective teachers of German, should, when planning lessons, focus on the preparation and provision of feedback. An effective teacher of German who operates in this way will, it is held, ensure that students are interested, engaged in, and enthusiastic about learning German. In addition, they will reduce student boredom and behaviour problems in class.

The planning approach to be well-prepared

Effective teachers of German who are well-prepared, it is held, are also those teachers who organise their out-of-school time in such a way as to have adequate time to engage in research for lessons and to collect, collate, create, and adapt teaching materials. In order to be well-prepared also, it is argued, they need to manage their outside-class teaching time. In the associated preparation time, they should write formative assessments, prepare individualised feedback on completed work, and develop differentiated teaching and learning programmes for their students.

One reason cited by the teachers of German as to why it is important to be well-prepared is to ensure that a lesson runs smoothly. Another reason offered is that students will be able to better demonstrate some learning of German, or learning about German-speaking countries. A third reason is that it will ensure that there is less time and opportunity available for poor discipline. This, it is argued, is because students will be interested in, engaged in, and be challenged by, the teaching and learning activities. The fourth reason offered for the importance of being well-prepared is that students will recognise and acknowledge the work and effort that the teacher of German has invested in preparing the lesson, and this will lead to an increase in their motivation to learn German.

The pedagogical strategies considered appropriate in relation to the outcome and the planning

Teachers of German detail three categories of strategies that are used by effective teachers of the subject to motivate students when learning it. These relate to personal time management skills. They also relate to pedagogical knowledge, subject knowledge, and subject-pedagogical knowledge of German. Further they relate to student focus. Each of these categories is now discussed in turn.

Personal time management skills

Explicit skills for the management of time may be part of teachers' pre-service teacher preparation. They usually relate to planning teaching and learning programmes and individual lessons to align with the prescribed curriculum and programmes of assessment. While acknowledging the importance of these skills, teachers of German also describe other skills related to personal time management that are perceived to be crucial to motivating students to learn German. These relate to managing personal time outside of the classroom and the requirement that one make a personal commitment to the teaching and learning of German.

MANAGING PERSONAL TIME OUTSIDE THE CLASSROOM

Effective teachers of German, it is held, need to consciously manage their personal time outside of the classroom. The reason offered for this is that it is necessary to find a balance between the time they spend working on classroom-related activities, attending professional learning events, and maintaining a personal life. Effective teachers of German, it is held, can use various strategies for this. For example, some might focus on managing their free-time on weekends and holidays, where they might devote 50 per cent of their free-time to school related work, and the other 50 per cent to their personal life.

MAKING A PERSONAL COMMITMENT TO THE TEACHING AND LEARNING OF GERMAN

An effective teacher of German, it is held, also has a personal commitment to the teaching and learning of the subject. It is argued that this is evident inside the classroom in the rapport that teachers build with their students, in the personalised attention they give to students' learning, and in the layout of the classroom, including the types of posters, realia, and learning materials used. Also, commitment to teaching and learning German by engaging in teaching-related activities outside of the classroom is deemed to be significant. Examples offered of such commitment are making videos for the classroom, collecting reading materials and current music while on holidays in German-speaking countries, taking students on school trips to German-speaking countries or to cultural events in the local area, organising cultural days or a cultural week at school, making links with primary schools and universities through mutual visits, organising interschool speaking competitions for students, setting up e-pal opportunities, trialling new teaching ideas and materials with friends and colleagues, and attending State and national conferences for teachers of German. Also, this level of commitment to the teaching of languages, it is held, should continue throughout one's career in order to be an effective teacher.

Pedagogical knowledge, subject knowledge and subject-pedagogical knowledge of German

Teachers of German identify pedagogical knowledge, subject knowledge and subject-pedagogical knowledge as three categories of knowledge that assist effective teachers of the subject to motivate students to learn German. These should be drawn upon, it is argued, in relation to innovation in teaching and learning German, to formal and informal professional learning, and to the necessity of continually updating teaching and learning materials. Each of these is now discussed in turn.

INNOVATION IN TEACHING AND LEARNING GERMAN

An effective teacher of the language, it is held, should be involved in innovation in teaching and learning the language. Thus, the position is held that an effective teacher of the subject should combine the use of textbooks, realia, reality-based resources, and new technologies in individual lessons. The reason offered for this combining of resources is to avoid giving students a wrong, and often out-dated, impression of German and German-speaking countries that is, it is argued, often present in textbooks.

PROFESSIONAL LEARNING FOR A TEACHER OF GERMAN

Teachers of German hold that the goal of undertaking professional learning is to motivate students to learn. On this, they consider that effective teachers should participate in two forms of professional learning throughout their professional life. The first, it is held, is formalised professional learning, and the second, informal professional learning.

Teachers in WA are required to undertake six days of professional learning per year. Teachers of German often elect to participate in professional learning that is focused on the teaching and learning of the German language, and on the cultures of German-speaking countries. One reason offered for this practice is that they sense that they feel somewhat isolated in school. This is because one is often the only teacher of German in a school. So, teachers of German consider that an effective teacher of the language will seek camaraderie by availing themselves of professional learning opportunities with fellow teachers of the language to improve pedagogical knowledge, subject knowledge, and subject-pedagogical knowledge.

Teachers of German consider that an effective teacher is also one who considers it important to improve one's ICT skills, and one's knowledge of the official syllabi and assessment guidelines. It is also held that it is important to learn about new classroom management strategies and pastoral care practices.

Teachers of German also consider that to be an effective teacher of the language it is important to recognise that professional learning might be informal. Some, for example, say that they can learn new pedagogical skills in discussions with colleagues who teach other subjects, including how to better implement ICT in their teaching and learning programmes. For others, it is held, informal professional learning might be pastoral in nature and focus on individual students and their abilities. Yet others offer collaboration with languages teaching and non-languages teaching colleagues in preparation for, and in the running of, a 'languages week'.

CONTINUOUS UPDATING OF TEACHING AND LEARNING RESOURCES

Teachers of German perceive that their continuous updating of teaching and learning resources is important if they are to be effective teachers of the language. It is also held that the nature of students changes over time, as do their interests, and that this requires that they regularly think about the teaching resources they use. Official changes to the curriculum and assessment requirements for German also force teachers to update their resources. Another driver for updating resources in order to be an effective teacher of the language is attendance at professional learning opportunities and in-country visits, during which one is likely to be introduced to new resources related to the latest trends in German-speaking countries.

Student focus

The third strategy, it is held, that should be used by effective teachers of German to motivate students to learn the language is to focus on the students. This relates to lesson preparation, to teaching and learning, and to activity outside the classroom. Strategies offered by teachers of German to maintain such a student focus are now considered.

STUDENT FOCUS IN LESSON PREPARATION

As a strategy, an effective teacher of German, it is held, should concentrate on students' interests and abilities when selecting teaching and learning material for lessons. Further, it is held that because materials and resources often go out of date quickly and students' interests vary from class to class, and from year to year, one should be constantly on the look out for new, interesting, and stimulating resources. Examples offered include finding and selecting a new film, article, or music that appeals to the interests of the class, or to an individual student's interests.

STUDENT FOCUS IN THE TEACHING AND LEARNING OF GERMAN

Teachers of German contend that the lack of prescription in the curriculum and syllabus documents for German in WA enables one to focus on students in designing one's teaching and learning programmes. Also, it is perceived that an effective teacher is one who considers it important to pique students' interests and to challenge them through the choices one makes in one's teaching and learning programmes. These choices can relate to directing the lesson content towards students' interests and abilities and towards adaptive classroom management.

Lesson content directed at students' interests and abilities

Teachers of German hold that effective teachers of the language direct two aspects of the lesson content towards students' interests and abilities in order to keep them motivated to learn German. These relate to the vocabulary content and to the content of the materials. These, it is argued, should, in turn, be selected by employing three identifiable strategies. The strategies offered relate to building rapport with students, to broadening a set topic to encompass students' interests, and to focusing vocabulary and grammatical structures at the ability level of individual students.

The first strategy that effective teachers of German use, it is held, is building rapport with students. It is further held that to do this, teachers have to get to know their students, including what their students like and what they dislike. Teachers of German who have this knowledge about their students, it is argued, are able to develop a differentiated curriculum to the best of their capacity. As one teacher put it:

> teachers tend to teach in their own preferred learning style. I could see that in myself … I'd say, relative clauses, "yeah they're hard. Five steps: tick them off as you go. When it gets to the end, it's got to be right". Because that's the way I think, sequentially. What I wasn't reaching properly was, number one, the frustration of the boy who wants to know: what's your task, what do I have to do and I'll do it for you. … or, the one that has to see the big picture, the helicopter view. That was a real eye opener for me.
>
> (AU)

The challenge to effective teachers, then, is not to use the same teaching and learning style with all students, not to lecture to students, and not to focus lessons on their own interests.

Effective teachers of German who can build rapport with students, it is argued, are also those able to achieve the twin goals of students gaining competence in the language and understanding aspects of German-speaking cultures. They are also those able, it is held, to encourage students to be enthusiastic about learning German. Further, building rapport with students, it is offered, ensures that effective teachers of German can observe changes in their students' interests from school year to school year.

The second strategy that effective teachers of German should use in relation to directing lesson content at students' interests and abilities is to broaden out the topics prescribed on the syllabus. This can be achieved by adapting such language content as vocabulary, language chunks and grammar to include language related to the current students' interests and abilities. Further, effective teachers augment the prescribed visual, aural and written stimuli with realia, and visual and audio stimuli, directed at students' interests and abilities.

A third strategy that effective teachers of German use, it is held, is pitching vocabulary and language chunks at the level of language competence of the individual students. This can be achieved by adapting the teaching and learning activities related to new vocabulary, syntax and grammatical structures to students' abilities, and by teaching complex structures to high-achieving students. The first reason teachers of German offer for using this strategy is that classes for German in WA often have students of mixed ability which results in diversity in the pace of learning in class. The second reason teachers of German offer for using the strategy is that by pitching language content at each student's level of language competence, one should be able to recognise what one has previously learned, where one's weaknesses in German lies, and what one can further achieve. The third reason teachers of German offer for using the strategy is that directing language content at individual students' abilities introduces an element of positive competition to the class. The fourth reason teachers of German offer for using the strategy is that students who are learning interesting and challenging language content are not likely to grow bored and become distracted.

Adaptive classroom management

The ability to be adaptive in classroom management practices is viewed as important in order to be an effective teacher of German. Teachers identify various strategies that an effective colleague should employ in relation to this. One of these is to draw up classroom rules collaboratively at the beginning of the year. Further, teachers of German hold that to be an effective teacher of the language, it is important to be consistent in following the class rules.

Teachers of German also hold that effective teachers of the language conduct conversations in German with students outside of the classroom. These can be informal conversations in the school grounds as well as formal discussions when the teacher of German is in the role of pastoral care provider. The following quote demonstrates a common strategy teachers of German employ in this regard:

> I make sure that I know them. Get their name right, that's a good start! You've got to know what sport they play. Who won on the weekend, because we play sport, every Saturday. One, two, three of them, ... four of them, are younger brothers of boys I've taught before .... It's a case of, you know the older brother, "so, what's Antony doing?" and we have a little bit of chitchat before class, just about their family. Knowing them is really, really important. (AU)

One reason offered for this practice is to demonstrate to students that German is more than a subject taught and learnt in a classroom. The aim is that adopting it should lead to students viewing German as a language of normal conversation.

Conclusion

The central research question which guided theory generation in this study, it will be recalled, was: What are the perspectives of secondary school teachers of German in Western Australia on what an effective teacher of German is? The central proposition of the theory generated from data gathered within this context is that teachers of German within WA consider that an effective teacher of the language within the mainline school system is one who has developed and honed specific competencies in order to teach and learn the language. This chapter has detailed the first of the competencies, namely, the ability to motivate students.

Chapter 6

An example of a study on how participants 'deal with' a particular phenomenon

This chapter presents an exemplar of the write-up of the second main type of study which can be conducted where the central underlying principles are those of the symbolic interactionist theoretical approach within the interpretivist paradigm, namely, studies where the research question is formulated in terms of how participants 'deal with' 'things'. The background to the study is the trend over the past 35 years towards the 'inclusion' of students with intellectual disabilities into the mainstream of education rather than having them educated in the separate environment of the special class or special school. This development has posed challenges for teachers and has also resulted in the generation of a research agenda.

The particular focus of the study reported here – which was undertaken with Dr Ron Chalmers – was on the 'inclusion' of children with severe or profound intellectual disabilities into the 'regular' classroom setting in the state of Western Australia (WA). The aim was to generate theory on how teachers in rural and remote schools in WA who had no specific training for the education of children with disabilities 'dealt with' their classroom work when they were placed in the position of including a student with a severe or profound intellectual disability in their class. A certain amount of 'thick' description is used in the presentation, with a liberal use of quotes so that 'voice' can be given to the views of the participants and to give the reader a sense of what it would be like to be in a similar situation. Attention is also given to presenting the wide range of concepts developed and to the relationships between them. Furthermore, it is demonstrated how the theory generated was such that propositions emerged and a typology was constructed.

Following engagement in open and axial coding, the process of selective coding was commenced by developing a 'general descriptive overview of the story' (Strauss and Corbin 1990) which represented the emerging theory. The main story seemed to be about:

> *how regular teachers in rural and remote schools who have had no specific training for the education of children with disabilities deal with their classroom work when they are placed in the position of having a student with a severe or profound intellectual disability included in their class. In general, the 'inclusion' of such students impacts widely on the teacher both in terms of their in-school life*

> *and their out-of-school life. For all teachers, 'inclusion' has a significant impact on their classroom work.*
>
> *There are three types of teachers in terms of the 'areas of life' in which the phenomenon of 'inclusion' is significant: the 'technician', the 'strategist' and the 'improviser'. 'Technicians' (type A) deal with their classroom work by focusing on classroom organisation issues. They 'selectively adapt' aspects of their teaching classroom organisation practices in response to the impact of 'inclusion'. For the 'technician', 'inclusion' has an impact primarily on their in-school life. 'Strategists' (type B) deal with their classroom work by focusing on classroom organisation and teaching methodology issues. They 'selectively adapt' aspects of their teaching methods and teaching techniques in response to the impact of 'inclusion'. For the 'technician', 'inclusion' has an impact on their 'in-school life' and their 'professional' life at home. 'Improvisers' (type C) deal with their classroom work by focusing on classroom organisation, teaching methodology and curriculum content issues. They 'selectively adapt' the content of the curriculum in response to the impact of 'inclusion'. For the 'improviser', 'inclusion' has an impact on their 'in-school life', their 'professional' life at home, and their general life.*
>
> *While all teachers initially focus on and selectively adapt aspects of their classroom organisation and management, type B teachers widen their focus and begin to adapt their teaching methods. Type C teachers take the additional step of selectively adapting the curriculum.*

Selective adaptation is a complex theory which is constructed of five distinctive categories: (1) receiving, (2) accepting, (3) committing, (4) adapting, and (5) appraising. Each of these categories, in turn, are comprised of processes and sub-processes. This 'story' was used as the basis for generating the fully integrated theory about how teachers 'deal with' their classroom work in an 'inclusive' classroom.

How teachers 'deal with' their work in inclusive classrooms

The theory of selective adaptation

The theory of 'selective adaptation' which emerged from the data represents the basic social-psychological process by which regular classroom teachers deal with their classroom work when one member of their class has a severe or profound intellectual disability. The theory is now presented in two parts. The first part is an outline of what is meant by selective adaptation. This provides a background to the second part, namely, a 'grounded typology' of teachers with regards to how they deal with their classroom work in an 'inclusive classroom'.

The meaning of 'selective adaptation'

Teachers tend not to make radical changes or transformations to their classroom organisation, teaching methods, or curriculum content when responding to the challenges of managing their classroom work in an 'inclusive' classroom. Rather, where changes are made, they tend to be carefully considered modifications of existing teaching practices. In other words, teachers 'deal with' their classroom work in an 'inclusive' classroom by 'selectively adapting' aspects of their 'normal' practices. Each of these categories will now be considered in turn.

CATEGORY 1: 'RECEIVING'

Once teachers become aware that they will have a student with a severe or profound intellectual disability as a member of their class they begin to gather information about 'inclusion'. The processes that teachers use in this regard are categorised within the theory of 'selective adaptation' as 'receiving'. Kelly gave general expression to this notion of 'receiving' as follows:

> I spent a lot of time with the deputy discussing the whole thing. I wanted to find out everything I could about the whole deal, about what I was entitled to and what was expected of me. This was a whole new ball game for me and I just wanted to know the rules.

Teachers engage in the processes associated with 'receiving' with greatest intensity at the start of the school year. However, they also utilise the processes at subsequent times to deal with situations which arise in relation to specific aspects of managing their classroom work.

Within 'receiving' there are three distinct but interrelated processes: *clarifying*, *analysing*, and *checking*. *Clarifying* is the term that has been given to the process by which regular classroom teachers find out about 'inclusion' and its myriad elements. A comment made by Lily captures what is involved:

> I wanted to know my rights in this area. I wanted to know if I had to take a child with such problems. I even thought about contacting the union to get some advice about inclusion. I knew that more and more of these children were moving into regular classes, but I didn't know very much about it at all.

Teachers used a wide range of strategies when 'clarifying'. The more 'formal' of these strategies were discussions with representatives of the Education Department and union officials. Other 'formal' strategies included participation in training programmes and professional development programmes designed to increase teachers' skills in the education of students with disabilities. 'Informal' strategies included discussions with colleagues and school administrators, and casual conversations with friends and family members.

While the combination of strategies used to gain information varied among teachers, the overall outcome was that, during the course of the year, each of the teachers received a substantial amount of information about all aspects of 'inclusion'. Teachers used this information as the basis for making decisions about how they would respond to the new conditions that they would encounter in their 'inclusive classroom'. In particular, the information was used to guide their decision-making in relation to what they saw as the main facets of classroom work: classroom organisation, teaching strategies, and curriculum content.

Scrutinising is the process through which teachers examine closely the information they receive about all aspects of 'inclusion'. In particular, it is the process through which they analyse individual pieces of information and then reconcile them with their current overall understanding of 'inclusion'. As Joan put it:

> I was given conflicting advice about where Nola [disabled student] should be seated in the class. On the one hand, I was told that she must be in with the other kids and then I was told that for practical and safety reasons she should be at the desk on her own. It was up to me to balance the principles of inclusion with the practical task of running the class.

This process can be likened to the construction of a jig-saw puzzle whereby each piece of information has significance for the whole picture of 'inclusion' and the emerging picture has significance for each of the pieces.

As a direct result of engaging in 'scrutinising', teachers' overall understanding about 'inclusion' can change significantly over a school year. The process of closely examining information about a wide range of specific issues associated with 'inclusion' tends to have a cumulative effect on their overall understanding of the phenomenon. In the words of one teacher in the present study, 'the big picture about inclusion kept changing as the year wore on because I was forced to think about all aspects of it very thoroughly'.

Checking is the process used by teachers to compare and contrast the information they receive about 'inclusion'. Amie explained as follows how she engaged in this process:

> Already I've got a few ideas about how to 'take advantage' of having Sophie in the room. It will be a good opportunity to teach the others about acceptance and tolerance, and being thankful for what you've got. But I am not sure how far you can take it. I am not sure if I should be drawing attention to Sophie [disabled student] or not. I'll have to check this out with the visiting teacher.

'Checking' stems from a reluctance on the part of teachers to accept any information, advice, or suggestions about the broad range of issues associated with 'inclusion' without corroboration. It can relate to a single issue or situation, or it can be a lengthy process involving complex issues and multiple sources of information. In this regard, the teachers in the present study frequently sought the views of the principal, other teachers and teacher-aides about very specific matters related to the student with the disability. Also, each of the responses was considered and compared with the teachers' prevailing views about 'inclusion'. As with 'clarifying' and 'scrutinizing', the intensity with which teachers in the present study engaged in the process of 'checking' was greatest at the commencement of the school year. However, they also continued to engage in 'checking' well into the second half of the school year.

Teachers in the study recognised early in the school year that there was no specific source of information from which they could obtain answers to many of their questions about inclusion. Schools were particularly lacking in this regard. As a result, they tended to seek out and compare the views and opinions of school administrators, 'experts', colleagues, and friends about matters related to 'inclusion'. The advice and opinions of 'experts' such as specialist teachers, therapists, and psychologists constituted a particularly important element of the 'checking' process.

The regular visits to schools by professional staff enabled the teachers in the study to compare and contrast information from an external source with the school-based information about 'inclusion'. 'Checking' of this type between external and internal sources was done for a variety of purposes. On most occasions, the advice of visiting professional staff was sought by teachers to support their own understandings about 'inclusion' or to endorse their current classroom practices. The advice of 'experts', however, was used by some of the teachers to question or challenge the advice or instructions given by the principal or other school administrator. There were also occasions when the views of one visiting 'expert' were used to challenge the advice of others. For example, therapists, psychologists, and members of the visiting teacher service reported that they felt the information and advice they provided was often manipulated or used in ways that would suit the specific purposes of teachers or school administrators. To avoid becoming the 'pawns' in the 'checking' processes which were occurring in particular schools, they became somewhat guarded in the release of information and sensitive to the processes they would use to offer advice in school.

CATEGORY 2: 'ACCEPTING'

Once teachers have satisfied themselves that they have developed an understanding of the broad conceptual underpinnings of 'inclusion' and that they have received useful information about specific aspects to this approach to the education of students with disabilities, they begin to consider the implications of this new educational phenomenon for themselves and for others. They do this through *assessing impact*, *values clarifying*, and *reconciling*.

Assessing impact is the process through which teachers make initial judgements about the overall impact that 'inclusion' will have on their classes. Jodie voiced her thought patterns in this regard in the following manner: "There's no doubt that I'm going to be spending a lot of extra time developing individual educational plans and thinking up new ways of teaching." Teachers 'assess impact' by creating a mental image of what the year ahead will look like and by visualizing the changes that they believe they will have to make to their existing classroom work-practices.

A significant feature of 'assessing impact' is that it tends to be based on information 'received' by teachers rather than on the outcome of their direct experience of 'inclusion'. In other words, the initial judgements that teachers make about 'inclusion' are strongly influenced by what they find out about this educational phenomenon from outside the classroom. As a result, the outcome of 'assessing impact' is largely dependent upon the accuracy and reliability of information that has been 'clarified', 'scrutinised', and 'checked' by the teachers; major processes which, it will be recalled, constitute the first major category within the theory of 'selective adaptation', namely, 'receiving'.

Values clarifying is the process through which teachers examine 'inclusion' within the values framework they hold in relation to the education of students with intellectual disabilities. Mary was engaging in this process when she stated:

> I have no doubt that inclusion is the right thing to do. The days of segregating children with disabilities are behind us. But teachers are going to need a lot of support and advice to make sure that all kids in the class get a fair deal.

In 'values clarifying' teachers ask themselves two types of questions. The first type is along the following lines: Does 'inclusion' fit with my own values in relation to human rights, equity, ethics, and social justice? The second type of question they ask is along the following lines: Does the practice of 'inclusion' fit with my own values about education?

The outcome of the process of 'values clarifying' influences significantly the extent to which teachers 'selectively adapt' their classroom practices in an 'inclusive classroom'. It was found that teachers who were generally supportive of the practice of including students with intellectual disabilities in mainstream schooling tended to be more prepared to adapt their classroom practices than were teachers who either did not support 'inclusion' or who were uncertain about 'inclusion'.

Reconciling is the process through which teachers examine 'inclusion', or specific aspects of it, in relation to their existing personal and professional frameworks. June used the term when reflecting on her experiences at the commencement of the school year:

> I found it difficult to reconcile 'inclusion' with my life at this time. Up until the start of this year I had my teaching career on track and I knew where I was heading. This was a big change for me in many respects. I had to think carefully about it [inclusion] to see how it would influence my life.

She went on to give a detailed account of those aspects of her life she considered may have been influenced by having a student with a severe intellectual disability as a member of her class. In analysing this account, a series of recurring questions which she asked herself became clear: How will this 'inclusion' affect my career? Will the experience increase or decrease my opportunity for transferring to another school? Will it enhance my opportunity for promotion within the education system? How will 'inclusion' affect my relationship with colleagues? What impact will it have on my personal life? Consideration of these and other questions led this teacher to make an overall assessment of the likely impact of 'inclusion' on her professional and personal life.

Significantly, the outcome of the process of 'reconciling' also influences the extent to which teachers 'selectively adapt' their classroom practices in an 'inclusive' classroom. In those cases where teachers form the view that 'inclusion' will have a positive overall impact on their personal and professional lives, the extent to which they are willing to adapt their existing classroom practices is greater than it is for teachers who form negative views about the impact of 'inclusion'. As in the case of 'assessing impact', however, the outcome of the process of 'reconciling' is influenced significantly by teachers' experiences of 'inclusion'. Initial judgements made by them about the likely impact that 'inclusion' will have on their personal and professional lives will tend to be amended after they have had experience with managing an 'inclusive' classroom.

CATEGORY 3: 'COMMITTING'

The third major theoretical category of 'selective adaptation' is 'committing'. 'Committing' is a category comprised of three processes: ***deciding***, ***rationalising***, and *explaining*. Through these processes teachers develop a consistent 'point-of-view' about 'inclusion'. This then leads them to engage in a range of actions and interactions aimed at justifying the particular point-of-view they have taken about 'inclusion', both to themselves and to others. In this regard, John made the following comment:

> I gave a lot of thought to my teaching during first term. Towards the end of term I realised that I would have to make some decisions. Was I going to make 'inclusion' work or was I going to fight against it. I felt I had to become more definite in my approach. So I decided to give it my best shot. But I could easily have gone the other way. I can see how some teachers become negative and say it can't work. I didn't. I decided to make it work.

Through the process of ***deciding*** which is exemplified in this extract, teachers adopt a particular stance in relation to 'inclusion' which, in turn, influences the nature and extent of the adaptations they make to their classroom work practices.

The stance taken by teachers in relation to 'inclusion' after engaging in the process of 'deciding' can vary significantly from one teacher to the next. While some teachers develop a strong commitment to 'inclusion' based either on axiological or educational grounds, others reject this approach to the education of children with disabilities and, as a result, spend the remainder of the school year implementing a policy to which they have little or no commitment. Perspectives which range between these two 'points-of-view' can also develop as the outcome of the process of 'deciding'.

The time it takes to reach the point of 'deciding' upon a particular 'point-of-view' in relation to 'inclusion' also varies significantly between teachers. In some instances teachers engage in the process of 'deciding' during the first few days in which they have responsibility for an 'inclusive' classroom. Other teachers, however, will not develop a firm position on 'inclusion' until midway through the school year.

Rationalising is a process in which teachers justify to themselves the particular stance they have adopted about 'inclusion'. Liz was engaging in this process when she stated:

> I was quite open with the deputy principal. I told him that I was setting up the classroom and establishing routines that would take care of Jane's needs, but that I would be relying heavily on the teacher aide to work with her. I am happy to put time into preparing her programme, but I can't take time away from all the other kids during class time.

Through engaging in such 'rationalising', teachers use information, advice from others, and personal experiences which support their stance. Also, they tend to downgrade, trivialise, or reject information or advice which conflicts with the stance they have taken.

While teachers talk with their friends and colleagues, particularly in the early part of the school year, to 'clarify' and 'check' information about 'inclusion', they also use these discussions to *explain* the stance they have taken. A typical 'explanation' was along the lines of that offered by Joan:

> I think there will be more gains than losses for me in this. I've already learnt a lot of new things about my teaching so far this year. By making changes to the way I teach I am going to get more satisfaction and the class is going to work more effectively.

As with 'rationalising', teachers tend to use the process of 'explaining' to criticise or reject viewpoints about inclusion which conflict with their own. Also, as they gain experience with 'inclusion' they tend to speak with increased conviction about their own views, interlacing their contributions to conversations with examples drawn from their own experiences in managing an 'inclusive' classroom.

CATEGORY 4: 'ADJUSTING'

'Adjusting' is the 'core category' of 'selective adaptation'. Thus, it represents the central phenomenon around which all the other categories are integrated. It consists of three major processes: *selecting*, *reacting*, and *initiating*.

Selecting involves teachers identifying aspects of their classroom work practices they are going to change in response to 'inclusion'. As Lily put it: "I knew that I would have to give my teacher assistant a lot more responsibility, far more than I would normally allow. I made a conscious decision to give her a more direct and responsible role."

For all teachers, the 'selecting' process tends initially to be focused on classroom organisational practices. Some teachers then move beyond this somewhat narrow focus and 'select' elements of their teaching strategies for change. Yet another group of teachers takes the additional step of 'selecting' particular aspects of the content of the curriculum for change.

Reacting is the process whereby teachers make changes to their classroom practices in response to a particular experience or set of experiences they have had when teaching in an 'inclusive' classroom. In this regard, John explained how he was preparing himself for what was to come: "There is no doubt that this will be a big learning year for me. It will be a real opportunity to learn more about teaching kids with disabilities. I am already booked in for two training programmes in Perth."

Through 'reacting', teachers attempt to change particular classroom practices with which they are dissatisfied and make adjustments which they believe will improve the way the classroom is operating. The overall aim of the process is to make a positive change in current practices which, in turn, will enhance the capacity of the teachers to deal with their classroom work.

The time taken for teachers to 'react' to particular classroom situations can vary significantly from one teacher to the next. While some teachers are prepared to make significant changes across a broad range of their existing teaching practices in a short period of time, others take a more measured approach and attempt to consolidate one change before moving on to the next. Also, while factors such as professional and life experiences, and the capacity and willingness to implement change, have a significant influence on the time taken for teachers to 'react' to classroom situations with which they are dissatisfied, the 'point-of-view' that teachers adopt towards 'inclusion' through engaging in the processes of 'deciding', 'rationalising', and 'explaining' will also have an influence on the pace of change. This notion of 'point-of-view', it will be recalled, was considered under 'deciding', the first major process of the third category of the theory of 'selective adaptation'.

Initiating involves teachers making preemptive changes which are based on the information they have received about 'inclusion' through the processes of 'clarifying', 'scrutinising', and 'checking', or on the 'point-of-view' they have adopted in relation to the education of students with intellectual disabilities in regular classrooms. The following comment from Becky indicates what is involved in this process:

> It took a lot to implement the friendship roster for Kelly [disabled student]. My lunch breaks and recess times were taken up with this. I gave it my best shot because I had been told that it would have positive results.

Through engaging in this process, teachers make changes on the basis of the conditions they anticipate they will experience in the 'inclusive' classroom.

Motivation for teachers to engage in 'initiating' can stem from a range of sources. There were many examples in the present study where teachers made changes to their regular practices, especially in relation to classroom organisation, as precautionary measures to increase safety for the student with the disability, for other students, or for adults in the classroom. Other changes were motivated by the concern of the teachers to ensure that they were implementing classroom practices consistent with current practices in relation to 'inclusion'. In most cases, however, 'initiating' was motivated by the desire to establish an effective classroom environment which would result in productive outcomes for all students in the class.

CATEGORY 5: 'APPRAISING'

The fifth and final category of the theory of 'selective adaptation' is 'appraising'. It consists of two major processes, namely, 'assessing' and 'judging'.

Assessing is the process used by teachers to estimate the magnitude or quality of the outcomes of the adjustments they have made to their regular classroom practices in response to 'inclusion'. Heather gave the following example of such an adjustment:

> The change we made to the arrangement of desks and equipment has been very successful. I've been able to set up a reading corner and the kids can move about without falling over things. It also feels as though we have more space. The room seems bigger.

'Assessing' can be a simple process in which teachers examine the direct effects of specific changes they have made to the classroom. This is rarely the case, however. The complex and dynamic environment of classrooms is such that most changes made by teachers have a number of interrelated consequences. Therefore, it is often the case that the process of 'assessing' involves an examination of the impact of changes on and between the disabled student, the other students, the teacher aide, and the teacher. Teachers use a variety of strategies to 'assess' the outcomes of the adjustments they make to their normal classroom practices. These range from 'objective', statistically-based techniques such as counting the number of times the student with the disability will engage in a particular type of behaviour, through to 'subjective', intuitive methods of assessment.

The study also indicated that teachers tend to use their own observations of what is happening in the classroom as the basis for 'assessing' the outcomes of adjustments they have made. However, the observations of colleagues, school administrators, and in some cases students, can also have an impact on their 'assessments'. Most teachers in the present study were eager to engage their colleagues in discussions about the changes they had made in their classroom practices and sought their views about the impact of the changes.

Judging is the process through which teachers draw conclusions about the value of the outcomes of the adjustments they have made to their current classroom practices. The following was June's 'judgement':

> When I look back to the start of the year and think about how the classroom was operating, I know that the new approach was worth the pain in making the changes. I was very uncertain about my capacity to teach all the students in the class and to keep things under control if I chose to spend a lot of time with Michelle each day. I know that the experts might be saying that I am relying too heavily on the teacher aide, but I really don't think there is any better way of going about it.

When they engage in this process they are asking: Have the adjustments I have made in my normal classroom practices increased my capacity to deal with my classroom work? The judgements they make in this regard lead them to consider whether to persist with the changes, revert to their previous classroom practices, or implement alternative adjustments. The findings from this study clearly show that in situations where teachers 'judge' that the changes they have made have not resulted in an increased capacity for them to deal with their classroom work, they either make new changes or revert to previous practices. Where changes have been 'judged' by the teacher to be effective they are retained or, in some cases, modified in an attempt to gain further improvement in classroom operations.

A 'grounded typology' of teachers regarding how they 'deal with' their classroom work in an 'inclusive classroom'

A major outcome of the study being reported here was the generation of a 'grounded typology' of teachers with respect to how they deal with their classroom work in an inclusive classroom. The typology is based on three propositions which build upon the meaning of 'selective adaptation' outlined in the previous section. The first proposition is that teachers can be classified into three 'types' in relation to the extent to which they 'selectively adapt' aspects of their classroom work in an 'inclusive classroom'. The second proposition is that the 'inclusion' of a child with a severe or profound intellectual disability into regular classrooms can have a significant impact on the professional and personal lives of teachers. The third proposition is that there is a correspondence between the degree to which teachers 'selectively adapt' aspects of their classroom work and the extent to which their lives are affected by 'inclusion'. Each of these propositions will now be considered in turn.

Proposition One

The extent of 'selective adaptation' varies amongst teachers. For some teachers, labelled 'the technicians', the adaptation is limited to the area of classroom organisational matters. This includes, for example, making changes to the regular layout of the classroom or implementing new routines or procedures. Other teachers, labelled 'the strategists', move beyond this somewhat narrow focus and 'selectively adapt' their teaching strategies and methods. For a third category of teacher, the 'improvisers', 'selective adaptation' also extends to the content of the curriculum.

All teachers tend to focus initially on and 'selectively adapt' aspects of their classroom organisational practices in response to 'inclusion'. There are many examples in the data which indicate that teachers are eager to attend to the technical aspects of 'managing' the 'inclusive' classroom before turning their attention to other areas to 'adapt'. As Amie remarked: "it's like anything in teaching, you've got to attend to the basics before you can move on to the fancy stuff".

The time taken for 'strategists' and 'improvisers' to shift their focus to 'selectively adapting' beyond classroom organisational matters varies from one teacher to the next. Some of them move beyond this narrow focus within a few days of the school year commencing, while others make the transition many weeks or even months into the year. Similarly, the time taken by the 'improvisers' to commence 'adapting' the content of the curriculum also varies amongst the teachers in this category. The situation with regards to the present study can be illustrated as shown in Table 6.1 below.

Table 6.1 Teachers classified by type and the approximate timing of their transition through the stages of 'selective adaptation' in the 41-week school year

Teacher	*Teacher type*	*Selective adaptation of classroom organization*	*Selective adaptation of teaching methods*	*Selective adaptation of curriculum content*
Joan	technician	Week 3		
John	technician	Week 2		
Jean	technician	Week 2		
Becky	technician	Week 3		
Mary	strategist	Week 1	Week 2	
June	strategist	Week 5	Week 5	
Lily	strategist	Week 2	Week 3	
Heather	strategist	Week 5	Week 7	
Liz	improviser	Week 1	Week 2	Week 8
Amie	improviser	Week 1	Week 2	Week 18
Kelly	improviser	Week 2	Week 2	Week 12

Proposition Two

For some teachers, the 'inclusion' of a student with a severe or profound intellectual disability in their class has a significant impact on their 'in-school' life. For other teachers, 'inclusion' has an impact both on their 'in-school' life and their 'professional work at home'. For a third category of teachers, 'inclusion' has an impact on their 'in-school' life, their 'professional work at home', and their 'general life'.

(a) The impact of 'inclusion' on teachers' 'in-school' life

For each of the teachers in the present study the 'inclusion' of a student with a severe or profound intellectual disability in their class had an impact on their 'in-school' life. At various times during the working year issues associated with 'inclusion' dominated their working lives. Conversations with colleagues were frequently interlaced with discussions about disability issues, principals frequently sought information about the students with disabilities, parents frequently asked questions about the implementation of 'inclusion', and non-teaching staff often offered opinions about the 'new approach' to educating students with disabilities. While for some the impact was minor, for others their exposure to 'inclusion' resulted in a significant change in the regular pattern of their lives at school. They spoke often about the increased demands on their time which resulted from managing an 'inclusive classroom' and the restrictions this placed on their ability to participate in the regular activities of the school.

Throughout the course of the year most of the teachers in the study reported that the task of managing an 'inclusive classroom' had affected in some way their relationships with their colleagues. For example, mid-way through the school Becky made the following comment:

> I've really noticed a change in my relationship with the others. There seems to be a bit more distance between me and them and I'm still trying to work out why. It may just be my imagination, but I think they may be giving me more consideration because of the extra work involved in looking after Angela [disabled student]. Even the boss seems to be treating me with kid gloves. It's very subtle but it's also a bit spooky.

Other teachers attributed their changed relationships with colleagues to the increased workloads associated with managing an 'inclusive classroom'. As Joan put it:

> I don't have the same amount of time to mix with the staff during breaks. I used to spend a lot of time in the staffroom during recess and lunch but I can't do that any more. I am not moaning about it. It's just a fact of life. But it's got to have an effect on my role with the staff. That's OK.

The teachers also spoke about how the increased demands on their time which resulted from managing an 'inclusive classroom' placed restrictions on their ability to participate in regular activities at school.

There were also, however, a number of positive features in the relationships between the teachers and their colleagues as a consequence of 'inclusion'. Diane was particularly pleased that her status in the school had been enhanced because of the increased responsibility which was associated with teaching a student with very high support needs. This highlights another general area in which 'inclusion' has an impact on the 'in-school' lives of regular teachers. Indeed, most of those in the study provided examples to illustrate the increase in the overall level of responsibility and accountability which is associated with 'inclusion'.

A final area in which 'inclusion' has an impact on teachers 'in-school' life is related to the attention focused on the 'inclusive classroom'. Joan spoke of 'operating in a goldfish bowl' when referring to the many visits she received from therapists, psychologists, and visiting teachers. Similarly, Mary was concerned about the ongoing attention her class received during discussions at staff meetings as a result of 'inclusion'. Yet again, John spoke of the inordinate amount of time spent during 'Parent and Citizens' meetings discussing the operation of his classroom and in particular matters pertaining to 'inclusion'.

(b) The impact of 'inclusion' on teachers' 'in-school' life and their 'professional work at home'

While the impact of 'inclusion' is felt in a myriad of ways by all teachers in relation to their 'in-school' life, others also feel the impact on their 'professional work' which is done at home. The following examples from the data illustrate the impact that 'inclusion' has on teachers in this regard:

> I'm thinking a lot more about why I am planning to do things. It takes a lot more time but I think it's making things easier at school.
>
> (Mary)

> I learnt early on that you cannot skip a week of planning and preparation and run on automatic. You can't wing it and you can't just rely on last year's programmes. You have to think about things carefully, especially at home in the evenings.
>
> (June)

> I'm a lot more disciplined in my preparation at weekends. This inclusion has got me into a good routine.
>
> (Heather)

> My husband and the kids said a few things at the start of the year. They noticed how much more time I was spending on preparation at home at night and at the weekends.
>
> (Lily)

One of the most common changes to a teacher's professional work at home is an increase in the overall amount of time spent planning and preparing. A general view held by the teachers in the present study is that this additional planning and preparing is required to ensure they can deal with their classroom work effectively. At the same time, however, while some of them were concerned initially about this increased time commitment, as the year progressed they were generally pleased with their own abilities to reduce the amount of additional planning and preparation time required. Also, despite the additional time spent, it was possible for some teachers to stop 'inclusion' impacting beyond this realm of their lives.

(c) The impact of 'inclusion' on teachers' 'in-school' life and their 'professional work at home' and 'their general life'

For a third group of teachers within the present study, the impact of 'inclusion' was felt in their 'general lives', including interactions with their families and friends, leisure pursuits, hobbies, holidays, and entertainment activities. The following examples from the data illustrate this:

> Inclusion dominated my home life for a while. It is one of those things that we as a family tended to talk about over meals, on week-ends, any time.
>
> (Liz)

> It is a routine topic of conversation with my friends. They are really interested because of Sophie's [disabled student] degree of disability. Sometimes I raise the topic and sometimes someone else will. I guess it is because I have started to think a lot about social justice issues. My mind goes to it all of the time.
>
> (Kelly)

> During the first few weeks I was worried about the safety issues. I kept on thinking about my responsibilities and what would happen if anything went wrong. I used to wake up at night worrying.
>
> (Amie)

While these and other extracts from the data illustrate the impact that 'inclusion' can have on the 'general lives' of teachers, the study also found that the extent of this impact declined during the latter half of the school year. The following comment made towards the end of the school year by Liz was typical of the explanations given to account for this decline in the impact of 'inclusion': "It's like anything in teaching, after a while you just get used to it."

Proposition Three

Considerations so far have focused on the classification of teachers according to the extent to which they 'selectively adapt' their classroom work and on the classification of teachers according to the extent to which their lives are affected by 'inclusion'. What now follows is an exposition on the correspondence which was found to exist between these two series of classifications.

For 'technicians' – teachers who tend to restrict the 'adjustments' they make in their regular classroom practices to the area of classroom management – the impact of 'inclusion' tends to be confined to their 'in-school' lives and does not impinge to any significant extent upon either their 'professional work at home' or their 'general life'. There are very few examples in the data which indicate that teachers classified as 'technicians' are particularly concerned about, or give special consideration to, issues associated with 'inclusion' either during their planning and preparation time at home or during the general course of their lives. An exception in this regard was voiced by Becky as follows:

> This inclusion stuff nearly destroyed a dinner party we gave last term. I was really surprised by the passion it stirred up amongst a couple of my friends. They took opposing views on the practice of having really disabled kids in our schools and I had to become the umpire. Everyone joined in, everyone had an opinion. I was really surprised.

Becky was surprised by the incident because, as she commented, "it was the first time that inclusion ever became an issue for me outside school".

For 'strategists' – the teachers who 'selectively adapt' both their regular classroom organizational practices and their teaching strategies – the impact of 'inclusion' extends beyond their lives at school to also affect their 'professional work at home'. Teachers in this category regularly spend periods of time at home on matters related directly to 'inclusion'. However, like the 'technicians', the 'general lives' of the 'strategists' tend not to be affected by 'inclusion'. For 'improvisers' – the teachers who 'selectively adapt' their regular classroom practices, their teaching strategies and the content of the curriculum – the impact of 'inclusion' is felt across three areas of their lives, namely, 'in-school life', 'professional work at home', and 'general life'. As the following comment made towards the end of the school year by Amie, an experienced teacher, illustrates, the lives of teachers in this category can be affected significantly by 'inclusion':

> Even my mother noticed a change in me during the first few months. She said she was concerned about me. Maybe it was because I was talking a lot more about my work than I did in previous years. But she knew that I had been

> very keen to make this [inclusion] a success and she also knew that it was taking a lot of my time and energy.

Amie's deputy principal also noticed the impact that 'inclusion' was having on her:

> It's become a big part of her life this year. She's certainly given 100 per cent to make sure that Marnie gets the best chance in school.

These and other examples from the data support the finding that teachers who tend to make the widest range of adjustments to their classroom work practices are also the teachers most widely affected by 'inclusion'.

Conclusion

The emergence of 'inclusion' as a central concept underpinning much of the policy direction regarding the education of students with severe or profound intellectual disabilities has generated considerable attention in recent years. The associated research agenda incorporates an extensive range of topics and issues, and there have been calls for the undertaking of a variety of empirical studies from both the quantitative and qualitative research perspectives. In particular, there have been calls for studies which will increase our understanding of the phenomenon of 'inclusion' from the perspectives of the people involved, including teachers, parents, school administrators, and students. In the field of 'inclusion' for people with severe disabilities, there is a need for studies which detail what is naturally occurring. The study reported in this chapter was conducted as one contribution to this call.

Part II

Extending the range of interpretivist studies

So far the focus of this book has been on the two main types of studies that arise directly out of the central principles of the symbolic interactionist theoretical approach within the interpretivist paradigm, namely, studies where the aim is formulated in terms of participants' perspectives on 'things' and studies where the aim is formulated in terms of how participants 'deal with' 'things'. To pursue such questions is to engage in research which was defined in Chapter 1 as 'big theory' research. In Chapter 1 also, it was pointed out that other types of 'big theory' research can be undertaken within the interpretivist paradigm by adopting other theoretical approaches, including phenomenology and ethnomethodology. Furthermore, it was argued that the position adopted throughout this book is one which does not favour an approach based on the argument that symbolic interactionism, phenomenology, and other theoretical positions within the interpretivist paradigm can be combined loosely to underpin an eclectic research approach. Neither does the development of such a research approach by combining theoretical approaches from various paradigms find favour. This is not to argue against eclectic research approaches in principle; rather, it is to maintain that in order for any such research approach to be put forward as defensible, rigorous logical arguments need to be mounted to make crystal clear what is involved. The latter, of course, would necessitate a separate book.

At the same time, it is not being argued that the only types of interpretivist studies which can be undertaken using symbolic interactionism as the underpinning theoretical approach are the two main types outlined at the commencement of this chapter. In recent years, I have engaged in research projects on my own, with colleagues, and with students, which were conceptualised within the parameters of four related types. These are the focus of the proposals outlined in the next seven chapters.

Chapters 7 is a proposal for a 'frozen in time' study and Chapter 8 is a proposal for a 'deal with' study. The next five proposals indicate various related types of studies that can be based on these two fundamental types. The first three of these relate to 'policy studies', 'life history studies', and 'interactionist historical studies', respectively, while Chapters 12 and 13 relate to the 'problem-focused' variety.

A point not to lose sight of, however, is that while studies with terms such as 'policy', 'life history', and 'problem-focused' in their titles can be underpinned by a variety of foundations other than those of interpretivism and symbolic interactionism, the concern in Part II is with studies where interpretivism and symbolic interactionism are chosen as the central foundations. Each chapter makes this very clear, illustrating what is involved through an outline of a series of research proposals. Also, it is recognised that the substantive areas which are the focus of the proposals in the chapters could also have led to proposals to engage in research conceptualised within other paradigms. For example, it is not too difficult to imagine policy studies being undertaken within the critical theory paradigm, or life history studies being conceptualised within the poststructuralist paradigm.

Within each proposal a research topic is identified and is located both contextually and within a body of research literature. The emphasis then shifts to detailing a research plan demonstrating how the research topic can be conceptualised within the interpretivist paradigm. Overall, such a plan is useful as it allows one to see how each of the component parts could possibly be developed so that they could become the early chapters of a thesis. At the same time, it is recognised that as a study unfolds there could be good reasons for structuring a thesis differently.

While the general pattern noted above holds for all seven proposals, there are also certain ways in which the proposals deviate from each other. Some of these differences will now be highlighted to emphasise a belief that not only is there room for flexibility in proposal development, but also that such flexibility may be necessary and is to be encouraged. First, there is the idiosyncratic matter of some researchers favouring certain terms over others, even though what is meant is invariably the same. Thus, we find 'the background' being used as a heading in Chapter 7, but what is being indicated is no different than what is outlined under 'the research context' in Chapter 8.

The proposals also vary in the length of the expositions given on such matters as selection of participants, approaches to be adopted in data gathering, and the modes of data analysis to be utilised. Again, I would argue that there is no hard-and-fast rule about this. Sometimes the decision is made in the light of required word-lengths by student research committees in universities, or by grant-awarding bodies. Other times, a judgement is made by the researcher as to the extent to which he or she thinks those assessing the proposals may need to be educated on issues of method, particularly if there is a suspicion that judgements may be made by using criteria other than those used by interpretivists. Finally, before moving on to those chapters on the proposals in question, it is necessary to make one other point, namely, that there would appear to be further 'types' of studies which could be added to the five considered. To date, however, I have not explored them in any detail and so will not dwell on them here.

Chapter 7

A proposal for a perspectives study

This chapter outlines a proposal to conduct a research project conceptualised as a 'perspectives'-focused project, one of two dominant foci emphasised in this book so far. I developed the proposal with Mr. Niall McCalum in 2009 when he was studying for a Doctor of Education degree in the Graduate School of Education, The University of Western Australia. His particular interest centred on school leadership teams in Western Australian high schools with culturally diverse student populations.

Title

School leadership teams in Western Australian high schools and culturally diverse student populations

The aim of the study

The aim of the proposed study is to generate theory about the perspectives of leadership teams in four Western Australian government high schools on the education of students from culturally diverse populations in their schools.

As a result of immigration to Australia over the past 60 years, the nation has become very culturally diverse. Successive governments since the Second World War encouraged migration to increase the population, including that of skilled workers. In recent years there has been a significant increase in diversity among the countries of origin of migrants, including refugees (Australian Bureau of Statistics 2008). This has come about in part due to globalisation, conflicts, and natural disasters in many countries and often means that students attending schools have different languages, religions, and customs that create challenges for them and the staff in schools. Also, some migrant groups can face discrimination and racism. Young refugee students are particularly at risk due to the combined effects of traumas associated with exile, migration, and resettlement (Olliff and Couch 2005). Research on such issues shows that the result for some migrant pupils can sometimes be academic underachievement, and high dropout rates and behaviour problems in schools (Shields 2004). The challenge for leadership teams and teachers is to provide an effective and relevant curriculum and a learning environment which caters for the academic, social, and emotional needs of culturally diverse students. This, in turn, calls for a variety of studies to inform practice. The study proposed here is one response to the specific Western Australian context for the need which exists.

The emerging importance and focus on leadership teams has been driven by a desire to develop 'collaborative modes of work performance' (Gronn 1998: 3), often resulting from notions of devolution of responsibility from the 'top' of organisations to enhance productivity and staff engagement (Cranston and Ehrich 2005). With the implementation of education changes and an increased complexity of school management through devolution, principals have embraced the opportunity to share new tasks and decision-making with teams (Cardno 2002; Gronn 2003). Studies have previously focused on the perspectives of the students and their teachers. However, very few studies have focused on the perspectives of the leadership teams.

Definition of terms

For the purposes of this study, the following definitions will be used:

- 'Migrants' and 'immigrants' will be used interchangeably to refer to people who have moved from their country of birth to reside in another country.
- 'Refugees' are defined as people who has left their country of origin and cannot return to it 'owing to a well founded fear of being persecuted for reasons of race, religion, nationality, membership of a particular social group or political opinion' (UNHCR 1992: 5).
- 'Perspectives' are defined as frameworks through which people make sense of the world (Woods 1992).
- 'Theory' is defined as 'a set of well-developed concepts related through statements of relationship' (Strauss and Corbin 1990: 15).

The background

International migration means crossing the frontiers which separate one of the world's 200 states from another (Castells 2000). Since the end of the Second World War international migration policies have undergone major changes due to global economic, social, and political changes on a vast scale. Tight controls by governments have been eroded by the ease of travel by potential migrants, by family reunions, by regional treaties between countries, and by an increasing flow of undocumented migrants, including refugees (Appleyard 2001). As a result of these changes, international migration has become an issue of major concern in many countries.

Until the 1960s, the Federal Government in Australia adopted a policy of assimilation, known as the 'White Australia policy', which required migrants to shed their cultures and languages and to become indistinguishable from the Anglo-Australian population. In the mid-1960s, the Government moved to a policy of integration, which did not expect minority cultures to give way totally to the dominant culture. Neither, however, did it encourage ongoing cultural diversity. Further changes followed the 1978 Galbally report (Galbally 1978) on migrant services, with the Government adopting a policy of multiculturalism, which recognised the right of migrants to maintain their cultural identities, encouraged and assisted migrants to do so, and promoted equal opportunity and access to services (Roth 2007).

Concurrently, patterns of immigration have changed over the past 25 years, with an increased diversity among the countries of origin of migrants resulting in a great diversity of small and emerging ethnic communities in Australia (Khoo 2003). This is particularly evident in the case of refugees and asylum seekers who have come from countries such as Sudan, Iraq, Afghanistan, Burma, Liberia, Sierra Leone, Eritrea and Congo (ABS 2008a). The main shift in associated Australian Government policy in the last decade has been the increase in temporary worker migration, including temporary skilled workers (Khoo 2003).

Over the last 25 years, Australia's immigration programme has been divided into two categories:

- Migration for skilled and family migrants. This category made up 71.7 per cent of the overall migration program in 2005–2006 (ABS 2008b). Unlike many previous migrants, the skilled migrants, who arrived after 1996 had an immediate higher socioeconomic status later reflected in the educational performance of their children (Hill and Allen 2001; Khoo 2003). The major regions of birth of these migrants were Asia (51%), Europe (29%) and Africa and the Middle East (8%) (ABS 2008b).
- Humanitarian migration for refugees and others with humanitarian needs. Of the 12,100 humanitarian settlers in 2006, North Africa and the Middle East (52%) accounted for the origin of the greatest proportion, followed by sub-Saharan Africa (27%) and central Asia (13%) (ABS 2008b).

One clear need of migrants in Australia over the years has been for English-language support. Prior to the 1970s, there was limited English as a Second Language (ESL) provision for migrants in mainstream education. In the late 1970s, however, the federal and state governments started to train ESL teachers and establish 'Intensive English Centres' (IECs) for migrant students. The time students spent at the IECs varied from state to state. In Western Australia (WA), students could stay at the centres for up to 12 months before moving to a mainstream school. Currently, gaining access to the IECs and ESL support in mainstream classes depends on the visa class of one's parents.

In most cases, the children of migrants on temporary visas are ineligible to enrol in an IEC.

Focusing on WA in particular, there has been a large increase in the number of migrants in the state since the 1970s. Many of these have come from Malaysia, South Africa, Singapore, India, Hong Kong, Vietnam, and China, thus reflecting the Indian Ocean Pacific Rim focus (Burnley 2001). By 2006, 12 per cent of the overseas-born population in Australia lived in WA, and 87.2 per cent of these were living in Perth (ABS 2008a). Burnley (2001: 321) describes Perth as 'a non-segregated and diverse multicultural landscape'. In 2007, there were 4,500 students in WA identified as needing ESL support either in mainstream schools or at an IEC. Most of these students come from the Sudan, with significant numbers also coming from Burma, Afghanistan, Kenya, the Congo, and China (DET 2008).

Over the last decade, migration patterns have changed in ways that bring new challenges to the school system. These challenges have taken on a new complexity due to political and economic circumstances around the world, and through both forced and voluntary migration (Walker 2005).

In WA schools, teachers and leadership teams face new challenges as they endeavour to cater for the schooling, emotional, social, and family needs of their culturally diverse student population. This proposed study will investigate the perspectives of the leadership teams in four WA high schools concerning the culturally diverse student populations in their schools. The next section in the proposal is an overview of the literature on the education of culturally diverse students.

Substantial and original contribution to knowledge

This proposed study aims to make several substantial and original contributions to knowledge:

i It will provide substantive theory in an area where no such theory currently exists.
ii The theory will prompt other studies into an under-researched area.
iii The theory will have relevance for school leaders and to Department of Education and Training (DET) policy-makers in WA who are responsible for catering for the needs of students from culturally diverse backgrounds as well as for such personnel more widely.

Overview of the related literature

The main areas which are dealt with in the research literature on the education of culturally diverse students can be categorised into four interrelated areas, namely, schooling issues, emotional issues, social issues, and family issues. Each of these will now be considered in turn.

Schooling issues

Studies overseas have shown that many students who are migrants, or who come from a language background other than English, perform at a level below that of other students (Marks 2005; Walker 2005). In England, for example, research findings indicate a widespread underachievement of some minority ethnic groups (Blair 2002; Walker 2005). Shields (2004: 111) adds that among minoritised children in the USA, 'there are high failure and dropout rates, an over-identification of behaviour problems, and placement in low-level academic programs'. The amount of formal schooling the students received in their country of origin was also cited as a major factor in the academic success of migrant students in the USA (Anisef et al. 2008) and in Australia (Christie and Sidhu 2002; Earnest et al. 2007). However, Hill and Allen (2001) warn that it is dangerous to overgeneralise about the educational performance of immigrant children because the pattern varies among ethnic groups. Studies in Australia have also found that some migrant students experienced difficulties in being in a classroom environment and accepting the rules and social conventions (Olliff and Couch 2005).

The increased diversity of origins of Australia's population is also reflected in the diversity of languages spoken at home and at school. Being proficient in English for culturally diverse students is crucial for their education and future employment (Olliff and Couch 2005; Earnest et al. 2007). In addition, the education level attained by immigrants is one of the most significant indicators for successful resettlement (DIMIA 2005). On this, Olliff and Couch (2005: 42) state that 'English represents the key to a possible future containing education, employments and a reasonable standard of living'.

The level of English proficiency of migrants in Australia has a major impact on their transition into mainstream education and employment (Cassity and Gow 2005; Olliff and Couch 2005). Language is a major barrier to learning until children become competent in speaking, reading, and writing in English (Driver and Beltran 1998; McBrien 2005; Olliff and Couch 2005). Allen (2002) suggests that migrant children may be competent at spoken, colloquial English, but considerably behind in academic English.

The transition from IECs to mainstream schools was found to be a problem for many migrant students in Australia (Cassity and Gow, 2005; Miller et al. 2005). Researchers have argued that 12 months in an IEC is not long enough for many students to become proficient at English (Hakuta et al. 2000; Olliff and Couch 2005). Also, over a decade ago, Iredale and Fox (1997) pointed out that many high school students in New South Wales in need of specialised ESL instruction do not receive any such assistance.

Many teachers feel ill-equipped to respond to the challenges of teaching culturally diverse students and find the existing curriculum and resources inadequate to their needs (Miller et al. 2005). In response, researchers have called for training programmes for teachers to provide them with the knowledge and expertise to teach culturally diverse students (Allard and Santoro 2008; Hill and Allen 2004).

Emotional issues

Researchers in the United States have indicated that education is crucial in facilitating the socialisation and acculturation of some migrant children (Eisenbruch 1988; Hones and Cha 1999; Sinclair 2000). Acculturation is the change in an individual that results from contact with a different culture (McBrien 2005). During acculturation, changes can occur in a person's sense of identity, values, and beliefs and many people experience acculturative stress as they try to adapt to a new culture. On this, Anisef et al. (2008) reported that stresses associated with resettlement by first and second generation migrant students in the USA include loneliness, isolation, and a lack of friends. In the particular case of refugee children, education can provide them with important psychological supports by re-establishing routines, a sense of normalcy and hope for the future, as well as interaction with peers, with trusting adults, and with opportunities for expression and exploration of feelings, ideas, hopes, and concerns (Nicolai and Triplehorn 2003).

Research in Australia also suggests that one of the major challenges for recently-arrived young people is to identify with a community to which they can safely belong (Cassity and Gow 2005). For many young people, schools provide a primary place of belonging. Post-migration difficulties include concerns about their family not living in Australia, difficulties with employment, and difficulties adjusting to cultural life in Australia (Schweitzer et al. 2006).

Many refugees who come to Australia may suffer from trauma from civil conflicts, such as torture, rape, family separation and loss, and community breakdown. Some may also have faced displacement from their country and had extended stays in refugee camps (Earnest et al. 2007; Francis 2007). These traumatic experiences make a difference to students' interest in, and capacity for, learning (Christie and Sidhu 2006). Unless these refugee children are fully engaged in what they are learning, they can become disruptive and lack. Children in particular are most vulnerable in these circumstances because they also have to cope with the many developmental challenges encountered by any young person (Adjukovic and Adjukovic 1993).

Social issues

Studies overseas have shown that culturally diverse students have been confronted with social ostracism and bullying as a result of stereotypes held by native-born students (Anisef et al. 2008; McBrien 2005). Hamilton and Moore (2004) also found from their review of the literature that there is a high likelihood of students who are refugees in Western countries being the target of bullying and racism. Rutter (2003) found that in many United Kingdom (UK) schools, newly-migrated refugee children, particularly those who spoke little English, were the target of bullying from UK-born students. Racism is a serious concern for educational leaders as it can be most evident is at the school level.

In a study conducted in Melbourne, White and Perrone (2001) investigated 117 young people in so-called ethnic youth gangs. Young people they interviewed spoke of 'street fights' which were seen as violent, occasionally involving weapons, and often linked to racism. They also referred to group conflict which was also evident in the form of 'school fights' which included verbal and physical assaults, and again were often associated with racism. The researchers found that there was a strong link between ethnicity and group behaviour involving street and school-based conflicts. A lack of understanding and appreciation of other young people's backgrounds, histories, and cultures is seen to contribute to some of the tensions between diverse groups. For many young people interviewed, being part of a gang or ethnic group was a rational way to protect themselves and was a major source of social connection (White and Perrone 2001).

Mansouri and Kamp (2007) studied Arab-Australian youth in Melbourne and found that 'racism and social exclusion were factors of concern readily and repeatedly identified by students' (Mansouri and Kamp 2007: 100). The authors concluded that the effects of racism had a significant influence on the students' social experiences and educational attainment. Studies undertaken in Australia by Allen (2002) have also demonstrated that in the specific case of refugee students many are ridiculed or alienated because of their insufficient English skills, or strong accents.

In a WA study of African refugee students, Haig and Oliver (2007) found that racism and bullying exists in schools and that African refugees particularly encounter high levels of racism and bullying. Students reported being ostracised by mainstream students and were often excluded from groups and activities. The study also found that there was tension between African refugees and Aboriginal students. Haig and Oliver (2007: 55) state that 'these groups of students both identified as "black" Australians and this is creating difficulties'.

Family issues

Schmid (2001) found from his research in the USA that the socioeconomic status of the parents has a strong effect on the achievement of culturally diverse students. 'A more cohesive, stable and resourceful home environment leads to higher educational attainment' (Schmid 2001: 73). Children who come from immigrant families in which both parents are present perform better and have lower drop-out rates than children raised in single-parent families.

McBrien's (2005) study in the USA found that many young refugees and their parents had unrealistic educational expectations which was also found in similar studies in Australia (Cassity and Gow 2005; Olliff and Couch 2005). Earnest et al. (2007) found that most of the adolescents interviewed in their study of refugee students in WA felt that their parents/guardians had a difficult time adjusting to Australia, experiencing difficulties with language barriers, an inability to find work, and isolation. Parents were not able to provide the emotional support or help with homework due to their poor levels of English and schooling. The young people also identified the disruption of family structures, loss of friendship, peer support, isolation from culturally similar communities, and lack of involvement in the community outside of school as affecting their social engagement (Earnest et al. 2007).

Although there are a number of studies into the education of culturally diverse students in Australian schools, very little research has been undertaken to understand the phenomenon from the perspective of leadership teams in schools. This proposed research will thus be significant in examining this area. In particular, the theory which will be developed should prove instructive for policy-makers in helping to cater for the specific needs of these students.

Research plan

Theoretical framework

The aim of the study proposed here is to generate substantive theory about the perspectives of leadership teams in four WA government high schools on the education of students from culturally diverse populations. This requires a method of investigation that allows for the interpretation of social phenomena. Therefore, the study will be conducted within the interpretivist theoretical framework of symbolic interactionism, which places primary importance on the social meanings people attach to the world around them and how they respond to them (Taylor and Bogdan 1998). One of most basic ideas of interpretivism is that all human action is meaningful and hence 'has to be interpreted and understood within the context of social practice' (Usher 1996:18). Interpretivists examine the meanings that phenomena have for people in their everyday settings (O'Donoghue 2007).

Blumer (1969) has argued that social research should be based on three principles: human beings act towards things on the basis of the meanings they have for them; the meanings of such things are derived from or arise out of the social interaction that one has with others; and meanings are handled in and modified through an interpretive process used by the person in dealing with the things encountered. Adopting these principles as a foundation for the present study requires that the perspectives of the leadership teams in each high school are explored on the education of 'culturally diverse students'.

It is important at this point to further explain the concept of 'perspectives'. Woods (1992) defined perspectives as, 'frameworks through which people make sense of the world'. Blackledge and Hunt (1985: 234) identified the following key components that further define perspectives:

- The aims and intentions (so it can be asked what an individual aims to do in a particular situation).
- Strategies that they use to achieve their aims.
- The significance that an individual attaches to the situation.

- The reasons that individuals give for the aims, strategies and significance they have to a particular situation.

These components provide a framework for this study as it seeks to determine the perspectives of leadership teams regarding their culturally diverse student populations.

The research aim

The aim of this study, it will be recalled, is to generate theory about the perspectives of leadership teams in four WA government high schools on the education of the students from culturally diverse populations.

The central guiding question

What is the best theory I can generate regarding the perspectives of leadership teams in WA high schools on the education of the students from culturally diverse populations?

Guiding questions

The following guiding questions have been formulated in the light of the above-mentioned framework and will form the basis of the first round of interview questions:

i What are the aims or intentions of the leadership teams in regards to their culturally diverse student populations? What reasons do they give for these intentions?
ii What strategies do the leadership teams say they have for realising their aims and intentions and what reasons do they give for utilising those strategies?
iii What do the leadership teams see as the significance of their aims or intentions, and their strategies and what reasons can they give for this?
iv What outcomes do the leadership teams expect from pursuing their aims or intentions and what reasons can they give for this?

Research methods

Grounded theory methods will be used for generating theory which is grounded in data systematically gathered and analysed from the empirical world in question (Strauss and Corbin 1994). Fundamental to grounded theory is that it is an inductive approach to data gathering and analysis. It is most appropriate when a study is designed within the interpretivist paradigm and particularly where the theoretical foundation is that of symbolic interactionism (O'Donoghue 2007). In addition, O'Donoghue (2007: 32) states that studies 'that are aimed at generating theory on the perspectives which participants hold with regard to something' are consistent with the symbolic interactionist view.

Grounded theory methods consist of simultaneous data collection and analysis, with each informing and focusing the other throughout the research process (Charmaz 2005). This set of practices offer a logic for composing conceptual elements that hinges on their articulation through close reading, comparison, and attendant conceptualisation of data (Locke 2001). Glaser (1992: 13) also states that grounded theory is useful to 'researchers and practitioners in fields that concern themselves with issues relating to human behaviour in organisations and groups'.

Adopting what has come to be known as a 'theoretical sampling' approach in grounded theory facilitates the generation of the full range and variation in a category (O'Donoghue 2007). The data collection and analysis continues until theoretical saturation is achieved; that is, until no new data are showing new theoretical elements, but are confirming what has already been found (Punch 2005). A particular strategy utilised in this regard is that of seeking out negative cases in order to disprove hypotheses and thus further refine emerging theory (O'Donoghue 2007).

Selection of schools

This study aims to generate theory rather than test hypotheses. Therefore, one is not obliged to work with a large number of participants (O'Donoghue 2007). By limiting the number of cases to four schools, it will enable the researcher to develop theoretical insights into the perspectives of the leadership teams in their natural setting. Adelman et al. (1976: 141) describe a case as a bounded system 'within which issues are indicated, discovered or studied so that a tolerably full understanding of the case is possible'. Each school will be treated as a separate case.

Purposive participant selection, or selection in a deliberate way, with some purpose of focus in mind (Punch 2005) will be used to select the schools based on the high proportion of students – at least 40 per cent of the total student population –from culturally diverse backgrounds in each school. The number of culturally diverse students will be determined from data available from the Department of Education and Training in Western Australia. Two of the four high schools will be from high socio-economic areas and one will have an IEC attached. The other two schools will be from low socio-economic areas and one will have an IEC attached to the school. Government secondary schools have been selected as they have high proportions of culturally diverse student populations and the author has greater access to these schools.

Selection of the participants

In this proposed study, the leadership teams in four Western Australian high schools will comprise the participants. The leadership teams in each government secondary school will include the principal, two or three deputy principals, the heads of 'learning areas', and the programme coordinators. Generally, the leadership team will consist of 11 members.

Data collection

For this study, qualitative research methods of data collection will be employed because of their concern for the empirical social world and their suitability for fieldwork. Data collection and data analysis are closely woven in grounded theory research and are part of an iterative process rather than independent activities. Two methods commonly used in qualitative studies, namely, interviews and document analysis, will be used in this study (Taylor and Bogdan 1998).

Interviews

Qualitative interviewing, according to Kvale (1996) and Rubin and Rubin (1995), is a kind of guided conversation in which the researcher carefully listens 'so to hear the meaning' of what is being conveyed (Rubin and Rubin 1995: 7). The goal of a qualitative interview is to see the research topic from the perspective of the interviewee, and to understand how and why they come to have this particular perspective (King 2004). It is one of the most powerful ways to understand others. In-depth qualitative interviewing fits grounded theory methods particularly well (Charmaz 2003; Goulding 2002; Minichiello et al. 1995). It provides 'an open-ended, in-depth exploration of an aspect of life about which the interviewee has substantial experience, often combined with considerable insight' (Charmaz 2003: 676).

Semi-structured interviews (Minichiello et al. 1995; Taylor and Bogdan 1998) will be the primary means of data collection for this study. Semi-structured interviews are generally organised around a set of predetermined open-ended questions, with other questions emerging from the dialogue between the interviewer and interviewee.

The interviews will take place in a setting where the participants feel comfortable talking about important issues (Taylor and Bogdan 1998). Each interview will take between one and two hours and each participant will be given a copy of the *aide-memoire* or interview schedule prior to the interview to allow them to reflect on the questions (McHugh 1994). It also provides guidance in conducting the interview while still permitting flexibility to ask probing questions. For this proposed study, the four guiding questions will form the basis for generating the interview or conversation questions.

Participants will be given verbatim interview transcripts to modify as required as this provides the best data base for analysis (Merriam 1988). The participants will be given the freedom to elaborate, refine, modify, or alter their transcript until they are satisfied that the views presented in the transcript are an accurate reflection of their perspectives. Follow up interviews will be held with selected participants to further clarify categories and concepts raised in the initial interviews.

In keeping with grounded theory methods, where data gathering and analysis are conducted concurrently, these interviews will also be used to gather supplementary data about the concepts which emerged from the analysis of the initial interviews. Participants will also be asked to confirm, validate, and verify the emerging concepts and propositions based on the analysis of the data collected. Punch (2005) states that this strategy, called 'member checking', is useful in seeking to ensure the internal consistency and coherence of the study. The transcribed interviews also allow for the use of quotations in the descriptive and analytical section of the dissertation. The interviews will be tape-recorded with the consent of the participants.

Documents as a source of data

The second major source of data will be documents, both historical and contemporary. They are a rich source of data for social research and provide the conceptual density required for authentic research (Punch 2005; Strauss 1987). They can also be important where an intersecting set of different methods and data types are used in a single project (Denzin 1989a; Hodder 1994). The range of documents which will be perused includes various types of DET policies, reports, and other relevant documents, together with state and federal documents relating to immigration and federal policies for ESL and culturally diverse students will be analysed.

Data analysis

Grounded theory methods of analysis are directly aimed at generating abstract theory to explain what is central in the data (Punch 2005). Grounded theory is consistent with the symbolic interactionist view of human behaviour and it tends to make its greatest contribution in areas where little research has previously been undertaken (Strauss and Corbin 1990). Although grounded theory is a highly inductive approach, it also takes on a deductive aspect as the researcher moves back and forth in their thinking to examine the generalisations and give them specific meaning throughout the analytic process (Punch 2005; Strauss 1987).

At each stage of the data analysis, Strauss and Corbin (1990) and Glaser (1978) state that the researcher needs to develop theoretical sensitivity, which refers to a personal quality of the researcher to be aware of the subtleties of the meaning of data. Theoretical sensitivity assists in the development of categories, as well as their relationships to each other. The analysis of data in this study will involve two major types of coding, namely, open coding and axial coding (Glaser 1992; Strauss and Corbin 1990). While each if these is a distinct analytic procedure, it is often the case that the researcher will alternate between the two modes of analysis, a practice which followed in the present study. The coding procedures will be applied flexibly and in accordance with the changing circumstances throughout the data gathering, analysis, and theory formulation. The two types of coding and how they will be used in the study will now be described.

Open coding

Open coding is defined as 'the process of breaking down, examining, comparing, conceptualising, and categorising data' (Strauss and Corbin 1990: 61). Open coding is the part of the analysis where the phenomena are named and categorised through a close examination of the data. During this stage of analysis, the raw data from interviews and documents are broken down into sentences, phrases, or words and each incident, idea, or event is given a name. Once phenomena have been identified in the data, concepts can then be grouped around them (Strauss and Corbin 1990). The process of open coding stimulates the discovery not only of categories but also of their properties and dimension. Glaser and Strauss (1967) describe the use of writing code notes and theoretical memos to capture an idea that has been sparked by an incident or phrase during the data collection phase. Memo writing connects the barebones analytic framework that coding provides with the polished ideas developed in the finished draft (Charmaz 1994).

Axial coding

In this second stage of analysis, the categories that have been developed are interconnected with each other using a process called axial coding (Punch 2005). Axial coding is a set of procedures whereby data are put back together in new ways after open coding, by making connections between categories (Strauss and Corbin 1990). The researcher moves between inductive and deductive thinking, as properties suggested by the data are verified against other incidents in a 'constant interplay between proposing and checking' (Strauss and Corbin 1990: 111). In axial coding the focus is on specifying a category (phenomenon) in terms of the conditions that give rise to it, its context, the action/interaction strategies by which it is handled, and the consequences of those strategies. These specifying features of a category give it precision, and they are referred to as theoretical codes (Glaser 1978) or coding paradigms (Strauss and Corbin 1990).

In this stage of analytic activity, the aim is to provide organisation for the conceptual categories developed. Diagrams are often helpful in displaying the relationships between categories. Strauss and Corbin (1990) state that diagrams are the graphic representations of the relationships between concepts. Diagrams, like memos, grow conceptually in complexity, density, clarity, and accuracy as the research and analysis progress.

Ensuring the quality of the data

For this proposed study, the combination of 'thick description', semi-structured interviews, and close analysis of relevant documents, is likely to result in a holistic understanding of the phenomenon. Punch (2005) states that the description of the phenomenon must specify everything a reader needs to know in order to understand the findings. Second, the research report needs to provide sufficient information about the context of the research so that a reader can judge the transferability or generalisability of its findings (Lincoln and Guba 1985).

Another practice which will promote the internal validity of this study is 'member checking' (O'Donoghue 2007). Punch (2005) states that this process involves taking the interview transcript back to the interviewee before the analysis to check that the record is accurate. Second, it also means 'taking the developing products of the research – its concepts, its propositions, the emerging cognitive map – back to the people being studied, for confirmation, validation and verification' (Punch 2005: 255).

In qualitative studies, O'Donoghue (2007: 197) argues that external validity relates to the proposition that the reader or user is able to 'generalise' the findings of the study. In other words, it relates to the extent to which the study's findings relate to the reader's own situation. In order to enhance the possibility of this kind of 'generalisability', it is imperative that the study provides a rich, 'thick description' of the phenomenon in question. Readers' judgements about the appropriateness of the transferability of findings to other contexts can thereby be based on sufficient information (O'Donoghue 2007).

For the proposed study, the notion of 'dependability' (Lincoln and Guba 1985: 316) has been adopted. This means that the reader should concur with the research findings, taking into consideration the data collected. The main technique to be used to enable the dependability of results is the 'audit trail'. This will allow the researchers to take the reader through the work from beginning to end so that the process by which conclusions have been drawn can be made apparent (O'Donoghue 2007: 197). People will thereby be able to judge the dependability or trustworthiness of the outcomes. Therefore, in keeping with audit requirements, the following information will be collected and stored: interview tapes, transcripts, documents, data analysis, memos, diagrams, and field notes.

Chapter 8

A proposal for a study of how people 'deal with' a phenomenon

This chapter outlines a proposal to conduct a research project conceptualised as a 'deal with' project, the second of the two dominant foci emphasised in this book so far. I developed the proposal with Dr. Helene Metcalf when she was studying for a Doctor of Education degree in the Graduate School of Education, The University of Western Australia. Her particular interest at the time was on how nurse educators were dealing with a locally developed 'problem-based learning' (PBL) curriculum in undergraduate nurse education.

Project title

Towards a theory of how nurse educators deal with a locally developed problem-based learning (PBL) curriculum in undergraduate nurse education

The research aim

The aim of this study is to generate substantive theory about how nurse educators who have not previously taught a PBL curriculum 'deal with' such a curriculum in undergraduate nurse education in their first year of involvement in a BSc (Nursing) degree. Stating the central research aim in these terms implies that a qualitative research approach within the interpretive paradigm will be adopted. The specific methodology will be grounded theory, which essentially advocates the utilisation of empirical data in order to generate a theory. Thus, the theory produced will be a product rather than a preconception (Borgatti 2002). Qualitative modes of analysis consistent with the grounded theory approach, particularly 'open', 'axial' and 'selective coding', will also be utilised.

Definition of terms

Theory can be defined as an abstract explanation describing how different factors or phenomena relate (Macnee and McCabe 2008).

The term 'deal with' refers to 'the patterns that can be detected over a particular period of time from an investigation of the interactions between participants perspectives and their actions' (O'Donoghue 2007: 33).

BSc (N) or Bachelor of Science (Nursing) is a three-year undergraduate degree, completion of which entitles the graduate to register with the appropriate statutory body. In the case of Western Australia this would be with the Nurses Board of Western Australia (NBWA).

Problem-based learning (PBL) students progressively acquire knowledge and skills through dealing with a succession of contextual problems (Boud and Feletti 2003: 14).

The context

Undergraduate nurse education has been under global review for the past 30 years, with a particular focus on where and how nursing programmes are designed and delivered. It is now five years since a position paper from the National League for Nursing (1990) in the United States of America (USA) threw down a challenge to nurse educators worldwide calling for a re-examination of curricular processes, and in particular how nursing education programmes were designed. This challenge was clearly to provoke nurse educators to revisit what they were striving to accomplish and how student teaching and learning facilitated practice. Following on from this trend, the Australian National Review of Nurse Education in the Higher Education Sector (Reid 1994) recommended that in the design and delivery of courses, university schools of nursing need to take into account the health care needs of the community, the goals and targets of health services, the requirements of the employers of nurses, and the need for responsive and flexible graduates.

The latter position is consistent with the view of Creedy and Alvi (2003) who suggest that changes in nurse education are inseparable from the changes in nursing practice. The same point is echoed by Heath (2002:11) who suggests that the rapid changes in healthcare prompts the need for changes in nursing education. Heath also calls for solutions that set standards and build a capacity to address and plan for change. What is required, she argues, are not prescriptive models of education and training that will become outdated before they are implemented. Rather, faculty, students, consumers, and nursing service personnel must work in partnership to design innovative educational systems that meet the needs of the health care delivery system now and into the future.

While many schools of nursing have risen to this challenge and have sought to integrate innovative strategies within their curriculum, a closer look reveals that much of this innovation has focused on adding to or rearranging content within the curriculum, rather than being a significant paradigm shift. In addition to this ineffective reshuffling of content, the National League for Nursing (USA) identified that many nurse educators are unaware of contemporary teaching practices in nursing practice, with many nurse educators continuing to teach as they were taught (Diekelmann 2002) and for a health care system that no longer exists (Porter-O'Grady 2003). The challenge therefore for those involved in the preparation of nurse education is to adopt a more relevant pedagogical approach to deliver an innovative, evidence-based curriculum that is flexible and responsive to student needs, incorporating contemporary teaching and learning processes. Many have responded by promoting curricular changes favouring the use of PBL in nurse education (Creedy and Alvi 2003). This is consistent with a notion that the intention and purpose of the nursing curriculum should be educationally valuable and creditable. Also, it responds to those who claim that the curriculum should prepare nurses on an occupational and professional basis.

The university at which the present researcher is working has embraced such notions and will be introducing a locally developed curriculum centred on PBL within the first six months of 2008. This will be introduced into a newly-created Bachelor of Science (Nursing) three-year programme. The challenges this programme will generate during its introduction and in particular within the first year are acknowledged. The researcher firmly believes in this innovation on the grounds that nurses in health care settings need to be effective critical-thinkers and problem-solvers in what is becoming a constantly changing environment. Nevertheless, she will make a sustained effort to take a 'distanced' and 'non-judgemental' stance when engaged in the empirical part of the proposed study.

The decision to engage in the study was influenced largely by Clancy's (2005) suggestion that PBL may be considered one of the most significant educational innovations of the past 30 years. While the literature discusses the advantages and disadvantages of this approach, it appears that the role of the facilitator is an area that warrants further exploration. In particular, there is a need to generate theory on how teachers 'deal with' the changes required of them in their teaching. Thus, the present author believes the proposed study, in responding to this need, will prove a valuable contribution to the field.

Literature overview

Burns and Grove (2004) suggest that the primary purpose for reviewing relevant literature is to gain a broad background or understanding of the information that is available related to the research problem of interest, in addition to gaining some background information. It is also suggested that, in reviewing literature for grounded theory, the purpose is to combine the information in the literature with the theory generated in the study. The first step in the literature review process is to seek out available studies pertinent to the author's proposed research area. To this end, the current author initially carried out an electronic search by utilising CINAHL (Cumulative Index for Nursing and Allied Health Literature), a widely available database specifically for nursing research. This was then further expanded to include a search through Google Scholar, a widely available database. The latter search was undertaken using three key headings: The curriculum in nurse education, PBL in the tertiary sector, and the introduction of PBL into the nursing curriculum. The following review is structured around these three headings. Within each section discussion is centred around identifying and exploring key concepts. An analysis in terms of relevance informed by currently available literature is also provided.

The curriculum in nurse education

There appears to be growing discontent in various quarters with the university curriculum, since the move from vocational training in nurse education, to that of a university degree. Within the literature, there appear to be a variety of definitions of the term 'curriculum'. Stenhouse (1975) suggests that the curriculum is an attempt to communicate the essential principles and features of an educational proposal in such a form that is open to scrutiny and is capable of effective translation into practice. In a similar vein, Skilbeck (1975) suggests that the curriculum refers to the learning experience of students in so far as they are expressed or anticipated in educational goals and objectives, plans and designs in school environments. Similar again is the position of Bevis and Murray (1990: 8). They define 'curriculum' as 'an accumulation of composite learning activities that have been carefully designed in order to enable the achievement of specific educational goals'.

A variety of curriculum models (where curriculum is understood in the sense indicated above) within nurse education have been under scrutiny in Australia. The Australian Universities Teaching Committee (AUTC) commissioned a study entitled 'Learning outcomes and curricular developments in major disciplines: Nursing' (Clare et al. 2002) which explored current curricula and clinical education models in nursing education. This report highlighted a lack of empirical evidence for the effectiveness of existing curriculum models. Focus groups identified such nursing curricula issues of concern as excessive content and assessment, inconsistency between university staff, and a difficulty in understanding the Australian Nursing and Midwifery Council (ANMC) competencies.

Quite clearly then the need to change nursing curriculum in Australia was an issue in the early years of this century. This reflected developments in the USA where the National League of Nursing (1990) called for exploration of new pedagogies and new ways of thinking about the curriculum. It was suggested that it is no longer sufficient to change the curriculum by randomly inserting new topics into a course or rearranging the sequence of topics. Rather, there needs to be a radical reform of the nursing curriculum. Taking up the same point, Clancy (2005) argues as follows:

> If nursing has changed so dramatically and it appears that it will continue to change, as nurses' move into more and more diverse and challenging areas. Have educators and curriculum designers made the necessary changes to produce a nurse capable of dealing with excessive changes or has the teaching and learning styles of the educators and the curriculum remained the same as

> it has done for the past thirty years. All that seems to have happened within this new knowledge explosion is that curriculum content has got larger and larger and students are expected to sit more and more assessments. It might be suggested that the time is ripe for nurse educators to look at re-evaluating their current styles of teaching.
>
> (p. 2)

She concludes by saying that the time is ripe for a renewal of the nursing curriculum, which includes keeping up to date with knowledge and developments. But it is also time to introduce innovation into teaching, which suggests a more fundamental change in terms of values and beliefs.

Problem-based learning

The application of PBL in education is not new. Evenson and Hmelo (2000) suggest that Dewey, one of the key educational theorists in the early part of the twentieth century, was one of the first to conceive the notion of a 'problem situation'. He recommended that students should be presented with real-life problems and then helped to discover the information required to solve them. It took time before this approach influenced the world of medical education. Indeed, it was not until the late 1960s that the McMaster medical school in Ontario, Canada, pioneered the first completely problem-based medical curriculum, with Maastricht University in the Netherlands following suit in 1974 (Maudsley 1999).

When exploring the literature there does not appear to be a single definition of PBL accepted by all. This is not surprising as it is considered an approach rather than a single method or technique. Nevertheless, Barrows and Tamblyn (1980), two of the major contributors to the field, provided a useful definition when they stated that PBL is 'the learning which results from the process of working towards the understanding of, or resolution of a problem' (p. 1). Similarly, Gibbon (2005) stated that on PBL 'we take a collection of information, pertinent to the problem, we learn a little about each and synthesis it to solve the problem like a jigsaw'. Boud and Feletti (2003: 1) took a slightly different view when they suggested that 'the principle idea behind problem based learning is … that the starting point for learning should be a problem, a query or a puzzle that the learner wishes to solve'. In addition, they acknowledged PBL as one of the most powerful teaching methodologies designed to encourage students to take responsibility for their own learning. They suggest that the PBL approach provides students with the motivation to actively pursue the concepts and principles which they need to lead a fulsome life.

Regarding students, Engel (1997) suggests that when PBL has been adopted as the mainstay for a variety of curriculum its application is expected to fulfil two distinct purposes. One is to use PBL as a method that will assist students towards a specific set of objectives which will be useful to them throughout their professional life, irrespective of their profession. Here he is referring to 'generalizable competencies'. These include the following:

- adapting to and participating in change;
- dealing with problems, making reasoned decisions in unfamiliar situations;
- reasoning critically and creatively;
- adopting a universal or holistic approach;
- practising empathy;
- appreciating the other persons point of view;
- collaborating productively in groups or teams;
- identifying own strengths and weaknesses and undertaking appropriate remediation.

The advantages for students in using PBL was evaluated in a study carried out by Deretchin and Contant (1999). Using a self-reporting instrument given to 540 medical students, they also concluded that there was a positive trend towards students embracing PBL as a method for lifelong learning.

However, these authors also highlighted some concerns over faculty involvement, with students acknowledging dissatisfaction over the level of faculty support. The issue of faculty engagement was also explored by Walker and Lofton (2003) who add a word of caution and suggest that in order for PBL to be successful academics need to consider strategies to support students' induction into the process of PBL. When exploring the issue of supporting students and facilitation by academics, Drinan (1991) suggests that there are not enough quality facilitators and that perhaps this is because our traditional education systems are unlikely to encourage the facilitation skills required of a PBL teacher.

The introduction of PBL into the nursing curriculum

Biley and Smith (1999) acknowledge that the increase in nursing degree programmes and other recent changes in nurse education, practice, and policy have prompted the need for education programmes capable of producing graduates who can explore options, who are articulate, and who have the capacity to develop decision-making skills. As a result, many nursing schools worldwide are appreciating the potential of PBL as an appropriate technique to develop the desired type of nurses (Creedy and Alvi 2003). On this, and as already highlighted, there appears to be increasing interest in the implementation of PBL within the nursing curriculum. Again, while the definitions of PBL within this domain may vary slightly according to institution and discipline, Cheek et al. (2007) suggest that a reliance on student centred, self-directed learning and practical problem solving are common components. In light of this, they argue that PBL strategies are well suited to nursing education, with particular benefits in relation to the development of decision-making and in the accruing of problem-solving skills.

Undoubtedly adopting PBL as a teaching strategy is attracting wide interest within nurse education. It is advocated by Margetson (1997) who suggests that PBL is 'a conception of knowledge, understanding and education that is profoundly different from the more usual concept underlying subject based leaning'. Creedy and Alvi (2003) suggest that PBL prepares students very well for professional work because the processes of learning mirror those required in practice. On this they acknowledge that PBL is a well-established and effective method for the teaching of clinical reasoning.

A word of caution from Gibbon (2005) is that the move into higher education has meant a greater numbers of students within each cohort than previously experienced. Indeed, it is the case that two cohorts a year are enrolled. Nursing with its skill-base is not an easy subject to be taught in large classes, therefore innovative strategies of delivery may need to be fostered.

The specific aim of the study

The overall aim of the study, it will be recalled is to generate substantive theory about how nurse educators who have not previously taught a locally-developed PBL curriculum 'deal with' such a curriculum in undergraduate nurse education in their first year of involvement. Because capturing patterns which emerge in participants perspectives at various stages throughout the year and their actions in light of their perspectives are central to realising such an aim, a qualitative research approach will be utilised. On this Strauss and Corbin (1990) suggest that qualitative research broadly means 'any kind of research that produces findings not arrived at by statistical procedures or other means of quantification'. In addition, the work of Strauss and Corbin (1990) suggests that qualitative research attempts to uncover the nature of a person's experience. Grounded theory research methods, which will be used within an interpretivist framework, are consistent with such a position.

Substantial and original contribution to knowledge

The proposed study will make several substantial and original contributions to knowledge:

- It will generate substantive theory in this area where no such theory presently exists.
- The theory generated will lead to an understanding of how nurse educators deal with the introduction of a locally-developed PBL curriculum and the strategies they use to assist in dealing with the change.
- The theory will be instructive for facilitators seeking to develop the nurse education curriculum.
- The theory will prompt other studies into the under researched area of the use of PBL in nurse education, particularly in terms of the process utilised.

The research plan

Theoretical framework

The proposed study will be conducted within the interpretivist paradigm drawing, in particular, on symbolic interactionism as the theoretical perspective. The interpretevist paradigm places primary importance on the social meanings people attach to the world around them, and how they respond to them (Taylor and Bogdan 1998). One of the most well-known theoretical frameworks within this paradigm, symbolic interactionism is a theory as well as an approach to the study of human action. It examines the symbolic and the interactive together, as they are experienced and organised in everyday situations.

Blumer (1969) proposes three central principles of symbolic interactionism. First, people act towards things and other people, on the basis of the meanings these things and people have for them. Second, this attribution of meanings to things and people through symbols is a continuous process (symbols are defined by Blumer as signs, language, gestures, or anything that conveys meaning and the meaning is constructed in social interaction). Third, the meanings of objects and situations result from the interpretations individuals give them. Thus, people attribute meanings through a process of social interaction.

For the symbolic interactionist, therefore, the meaning of each thing, rather than being fixed, is constantly adjusted and shaped by new information. Meaning is derived from our experience of situations, and is constantly modified. It can even be totally changed because we are in continual engagement with the world around us (Woods 1992a). Thus, social inquiry must be grounded in the empirical world which is being studied; 'the minute-by-minute, day-to-day social life of individuals as they interact together, as they develop understandings and meanings, as they engage in "joint action" and respond to each other as they adapt to situations, and as they encounter and move to resolve problems that arise through their circumstances' (Woods 1992b: 338).

Grounded theory research methods, in keeping with these principles, are concerned with investigating situations involving the interaction of individuals and society. They seek to discover patterns of 'action and interaction between and among various types of social units' or actors (Strauss and Corbin, 1994: 278). These methods will be used in the analysis of data generated in the guiding questions for the study outlined in this proposal.

It will be recalled that the central aim of this study is to generate theory about how nurse educators who have not previously taught a locally developed PBL curriculum 'deal with' such a curriculum in undergraduate nurse education in their first year of involvement. The term 'deal with' is central to the aim of this proposed study.

O'Donoghue (2007) suggests that when looking at the notion of 'deal with' we are asking a particular question in 'shorthand form' and that to phrase the same question in its extended form is really to ask a number of interrelated questions. In other words, in 'symbolic interaction' by posing the question 'how do participants deal with' something, we are interested in detecting patterns over a particular period of time by examining participants perspectives, their actions in light of their perspectives and changes if any which take place in perspectives as a result of actions.

Consequently, it is essential to determine at the outset the perspectives of the participants by asking guiding questions in a systematic way. Adopting such an approach for the proposed study will be carried out by asking the following guiding questions:

1 What are nurse educators' intentions prior to the implementation of a locally developed PBL curriculum in their first year of involvement?
2 What strategies will nurse educators develop in the implementation of a locally developed PBL curriculum in their first year of involvement?
3 What is the significance which nurse educators attach to their intentions and strategies and the reasons they give for this?
4 What outcomes do nurse educators expect to result from their actions and the reasons they give for this?

These in turn will be broken down into data collecting questions.

At the commencement of the interview process, participants will be asked about their 'intentions' prior to the implementation of a locally developed PBL curriculum, as well as what strategies they intend to use and what is their significance for them. Subsequent interviews will be conducted asking participants the above questions with particular reference to their new perspectives (if any). Since part of the questioning involves asking participants why they say what they say and asking them to give reasons for their answers. As a result of engaging in the process at three-monthly intervals, it will be possible to detect patterns over a period of time.

The selection of the participants

In a qualitative study individuals are selected to participate in the research based on their first-hand experience with a culture, social interaction, or phenomenon of interest. Therefore the eight participants would be nurse educators currently teaching using the recently introduced PBL curriculum. Macnee and McCabe (2008) advocate that participant selection strategies in qualitative research seek to identify participants who have experience with the phenomena of interest, and with a small number of participants the goal remains to have as much depth and detail as possible. With this in mind, all of the eight individuals who will participate in this proposed study are currently working as nurse educators in an undergraduate nursing programme within a large tertiary nursing school. This university has been chosen as it will be delivering a hybrid locally developed PBL curriculum commencing in 2008. Streubert and Carpenter (1994) suggest that the participants in the study be 'active participants in the enquiry and help to inform with the purpose of helping those interested to better understand their lives and social interactions'.

Data collection

The collection and analysis of data will go hand in hand, in keeping with grounded theory methods (Punch 1998). Fontana and Frey (1994: 361) identify that 'asking questions and getting answers is a much harder task than it may seem at first'. Therefore interviewing for research purposes may not be as easy as it first seems. Awareness of the role of interviewer is seen as pivotal to ensure success. When looking at the meaning of 'an interview' Burns and Grove (2004) suggest that interviews involve verbal communication between the researcher and the subject, during which information is provided to the researcher. Interviews are important in gaining perspectives on how others understand and interpret their reality. Interviewing assumes a skill in listening and a non-threatening manner when asking questions.

Interviews can be open ended, the questionnaire type or directed interview. Glesne (2006) suggests that in qualitative research the things you see and hear about the people and circumstances become the 'nuggets' around which you construct your questions. Maxwell (1996: 74) states that, although there should be a relationship between research and interview questions, interview questions tend to be more contextual and specific than research questions and their development requires creativity and insight rather than a translation of the research question.

The interviews will take place in a setting where participants will feel comfortable in responding to the questions (Taylor and Bogdan 1998: 101). With their permission, the responses will be audio-recorded and transcribed verbatim. In addition, notes will be recorded for further clarification. Transcripts will be brought back to participants until agreement is reached on their substance.

Data analysis

Bogdan and Biklen (1982: 145) define qualitative data analysis as 'working with data, organizing it, breaking it into manageable units, synthesizing it, searching for patterns, discovering what is important and what is to be learned and deciding what you will tell others'. Flint (2005) identifies the notion of the constant comparative method of coding and analysing to generate an inductive theory which describes the actions of the substantive group.

Glaser (1978: 55) acknowledges that the purpose of coding data is to move on from having a set of data to generating a theory and Strauss and Corbin (1990: 61) state that coding is the process of analysing data. The process involves first fracturing the data then conceptually grouping it into codes that become the basis for generating the data (Glaser 1978). The process involves the fracturing of the data.

The literature suggests that to analyse using grounded theory methods involves three major types of coding: open coding, axial coding, and selective coding.

Open coding

Analysis begins with identification of the themes that emerge from the raw data. This initial coding of data is called open coding and starts when collection begins. Flint (2005) and Strauss and Corbin (1990) suggest that without this first basic analytical step the rest of the analysis and communication that follows could not take place. Flint (2005) also identifies that the analyst does not wait to engage in open coding until all the data has been collected. Rather, gathering and coding is an iterative process.

The analyst codes the incidents into categories (a group of codes) and while looking at the data the analyser has three types of questions in mind (Glaser 1998).

1. What is the data a study of?
2. What category does this incident indicate?
3. What is actually happening with the data, or what is the chief concern or problem for the people?

The basics defining rule of the constant comparative method of grounded theory (Glaser and Strauss, 1967: 106) is applied: 'while coding an incident for a category compares it with the previous incidents in the same and different groups coded in the same category'. Flint suggests that open coding initially happens very quickly, with the creation of an enormous amount of codes. As they are compared and as it is determined whether they fit, they are eventually saturated. This results in theoretical properties of a category being generated and eventually possibly even the generation of a core category.

Axial coding

The next stage of the process involves the re-examination of the categories identified to determine how they are linked, a complex process known as axial coding (Strauss and Corbin 1990: 57). The discrete categories identified in open coding are compared and combined in new ways as the researcher begins to assemble the 'big picture'. During axial coding the researcher is responsible for building a conceptual framework and for determining whether sufficient data exists to support that interpretation.

Once the analyst has found a variable that meets the criteria of a core category, selective coding begins.

Selective coding

'To selectively code for a core variable ... that means that the analyst delimits his coding to only those variables that relate to the core variable in sufficiently significant ways to be used in a parsimonious theory‘ (Glaser 1978: 61). The researcher in selective coding looks for the conditions and consequences that relate to the core process. The writing of memos is useful in this process. Memos are the theorising write-up of ideas about substantive codes and their theoretical coded relationships (Glaser 1998: 93). Memos can:

- raise the data to a conceptualisation level;
- develop the properties of each category which begins to define it operationally;
- present hypotheses about connections with clusters of other categories to generate the theory;
- begin to locate the emerging theory with other theories potentially more or less relevant.

Memos are the 'vehicle by which concepts and ideas pour out, are saved, and grow' (Glaser 1998: 178).

Glaser and Strauss (1967) state that the goal of grounded theory inquiry is to explain the underlying social processes that occur within a substantive area. When generated, these processes must meet the criteria of 'fit', 'work', and 'relevance'. Glaser (1998) suggests that if a grounded theory is carefully induced from the substantive area its categories and their properties will fit the realities under study in the eyes of the participants, practitioners, and researchers in the area. This means that a theorist does not begin with preconceived concepts and impose the data onto those concepts. Glaser (1992: 15) states that 'if it fits and works the grounded theory has achieved the relevance'.

Ensuring the trustworthiness of the study

Credibility

Credibility is enhanced when researchers describe and interpret their experiences as researchers. Guba and Lincoln (1994) refer to credibility instead of truth values and internal validity. Self awareness for a researcher is essential. One way to address this issue is for the researcher to keep a journal of the contents, and the process of interactions including reactions to various events. Guba and Lincoln (1994) suggest that using a journal encourages the recording of those relationships and this material may provide useful reflection.

Transferability

Sandelowski (1986) suggests the term 'fittingness' for evaluation of qualitative research and states that:

> A study meets the criterion for fittingness when its findings can fit into contexts outside the study situation and when its audience views its findings as meaningful and applicable in terms of its their own experience.

It is this fittingness the researchers aims to provide following the study.

Dependability

To meet the criteria for dependability the researcher will aim to ensure a clear audit trail. This will consist of discussing explicitly decisions taken about the theoretical, methodological, and analytical choices throughout the study.

Confidentiality and intellectual property

Throughout this study conscious efforts will be made to maintain confidentiality. All information provided by the participants will be used solely for the purpose of the research and will be stored securely in the researcher's university. Pseudonyms will be used to protect privacy.

Chapter 9

A proposal for a policy study

In recent years there has been a burgeoning of research in such specific fields as educational leadership, educational management, educational administration, curriculum studies, and teaching and learning studies. Concurrently, there has been an increasing recognition that these areas do not exist in a vacuum. Rather, they are located within a context which is shaped by historical and cultural conditions. Major lenses for studying this context have been provided by a number of research approaches. Prominent among these are those approaches centred on policy-analysis frameworks. The outcome has been a growth in educational policy studies. Furthermore, regardless of the underlying definition of policy and the nature of the frameworks utilised, these policy-analysis studies are all concept-driven, the central concept being that of 'policy' itself.

At the same time, the concept of policy is not a straightforward one. Indeed, its contested nature has led to a myriad of definitions. It is because of this that there are various approaches to policy analysis. Ozga (2000) describes three approaches that have developed over time. The first approach is the 'social administration project', where the researcher is concerned with the needs of the clients of the policy. This is well summarised by Majchrzak (1984: 12) where he states that policy research 'is defined as the process of conducting research on, or analysis of, a fundamental social problem to provide policy-makers with pragmatic, action-oriented recommendations for alleviating the problem'.

The second approach is the 'policy analysis project', which is concerned with the 'efficient and effective delivery of social policies irrespective of their content' (Ozga 2000: 39). This approach is therefore preoccupied with the outcomes of policy. Ozga's third approach is the 'social science project' and here the concern is to 'find out how things work, rather than putting them to work' (Ozga 2000: 40). In adopting this position Ozga would appear to be at one with Ham and Hill (1993: 2–5) in highlighting a traditional distinction between analysis *of* policy and analysis *for* policy.

The remainder of this chapter outlines a proposal to conduct a research project conceptualised as an 'analysis of policy' project, illustrating that one useful approach to such a policy analysis is where it is viewed as being closely aligned to the interpretivist paradigm. The proposal is also informed by a conceptualisation of policy analysis as a 'trajectory study' (Ball 1994), which involves a definition of policy as a cyclical, freewheeling, dialectical process. For Ball, the process has three dimensions or contexts: the context of influence, the context of text and the context of consequences. It was concepts such as these which constituted the major influences on the thinking of Ms. Victoria Valdebenito McFarlane when she began to prepare her Doctor of Education thesis proposal with myself and Professor Lesley Vidovich in 2016 in the Graduate School of Education, The University of Western Australia. Her particular interest centred on the changes taking place in curriculum policy and practice in universities in Chile. The proposal which was eventually developed and which will now be outlined was based on a realisation of the need to anchor the informing concepts and the emerging methodology in a paradigm's base, and the paradigm chosen as being most appropriate was that of interpretivism.

Title

Transforming university curriculum policies for a global knowledge society: A study of the situation in Chile

Aim

The aim of the study is to conduct an analysis of transforming university curriculum policies in Chile.

Background

University curriculum transformations are moving to centre stage in the higher education reform agendas of many countries as they strive to strengthen their position in a competitive global knowledge society (Organisation for Economic Cooperation and Development (OECD 2008)). Consequently, development of quality university curricula to attract the 'best and brightest' students in a mobile world will be a significant feature of the next decade (de Wit 2009). These international trends are evident in Chile, although specific curriculum transformations are shaped within the unique contexts of localised university settings in Chile (Marginson 2007). A number of the nation's universities are prominent in their engagement with curriculum policies which resonate strongly with those in Europe and the United States (US). Particularly influential is the European Higher Education Area promulgated by the Bologna Agreement (1999) to forge harmonization of university curriculum policy and increased student mobility across 45 European countries (Amaral and Neave 2008; Ravinet 2009). Such international reforms pose challenges for higher education in Chile (OECD 2008). Rising to these challenges requires a strong evidence base to support curriculum policy development in universities in Chile in a competitive knowledge era.

This project will focus on curriculum policy transformations at three research-intensive universities in Chile. At each of these institutions the emphasis at the undergraduate level is on developing their 'whole curriculum' (definition in 'Research background') on general education principles of a liberal-humanist nature, while specialist and professional university education are reconceptualised as being the province of postgraduate courses. These transformations, when viewed historically, are radical and unprecedented within Chile, while at the same time carrying extensive costs and risks for the universities themselves, as well as for national positioning within the international scene. Therefore, they offer particularly rich and fruitful possibilities for detailed study in the national interest.

Common features can be identified in the curriculum policy texts and discussions at the three universities. A number of these resonate with the European Bologna model and the US emphasis on liberal general undergraduate education and community engagement. They are:

- a shift from proliferation of degrees and courses, to fewer 'generic' undergraduate degrees;
- an articulation of bachelor, professional masters and doctorate degrees ('3+2 +3 years' model);
- a consequent lengthening of student time at university for those proceeding through all levels;
- an increase in curriculum breadth and depth through a stronger emphasis on research,
- communication skills, community service, and study abroad components;
- a greater emphasis on integrating knowledge across different disciplines; and
- a focus on internationalisation of the curriculum.

These curriculum policy transformations now warrant scholarly investigation based on the approach outlined in this proposal, which marries both historical and contemporary policy analysis.

Elaboration on the research aim

The project aims to provide an in-depth analysis of contemporary radical curriculum policies and practices at three universities, considering wider global and national contextual influences, as well as wider national and global outcomes in the competitive higher education landscape. More specifically, it aims to:

1 identify key influences from global and national level contexts which have an impact on university curriculum transformations in Chile;
2 analyse local level curriculum policy texts and practices in the three universities;

3 explore how the curriculum policies and practices in the universities compare with each other and with wider trends over time and place (especially Europe, the US, and Australia);
4 determine the outcomes of new curriculum policies for the universities in Chile and for changing higher education landscapes nationally and globally.

The project will inform university curriculum policies and practices for a global knowledge society in an area of research not addressed to date. In particular, it will contribute to significant and timely policy learning (Vidovich 2009) at local (university), national, and global levels.

Background literature

There are two main bodies of literature from which this project draws, and to which this study can make further significant contributions. The first is an international corpus of scholarly work on curriculum policy in education. For many years, this centred mainly on the schooling sector (Elmore and Sykes 1992), although more recently it has expanded to focus on such key higher education issues as contestations over core knowledge in particular disciplines, the establishment of US-style graduate schools in a number of European countries (Powell and Green 2007), the spread of the strongly-embedded US civic engagement practice to universities further afield (McIlrath and Mac Labhrainn 2007; Watson 2007), and initiatives on internationalising the curriculum (Jones and Killick 2007; Knight 2004; OECD 2008). What associated policies have in common is a focus on introducing curriculum innovations within existing university curriculum structures and content. Ten years ago, however, Bridges (2000) also drew attention to policies being adopted right across the academy, such as the deconstruction of the traditional university subject through modularisation, the cross-curricular key skills movement, and competence-based developments. These highlight issues of 'whole curriculum' change as promoted by educational theorists such as Scott (2003) and Gleeson (2010). They relate to such matters as the total range of curriculum objectives sought by an institution; the nature of the associated underlying values and beliefs; the extent to which the various objectives are prescribed for some, or for all, students; the pattern of components into which the 'whole' curriculum is divided and how lecturers and students are grouped in relation to this pattern; the nature of the content, the pedagogical approaches and the modes of assessment outlined; and the methods used to evaluate the success of the work.

The second body of informing literature is that on globalization, internationalisation, and educational policy borrowing/learning. For this project, I will draw on literature which examines contemporary higher education policy development in terms of dynamic interactions playing out simultaneously between global, national, and local (university) levels (Marginson 2007; Marginson and

Rhoades 2002; Vidovich 2004, 2009). Theories of globalisation form part of our conceptual framing and they are explicated further in the 'Approach and methodology'. Here, I highlight that the OECD has, for over well over a decade, been taking an increasingly powerful role as a key policy-actor in a globalised higher education policy community (Henry et al. 2001; Rizvi and Lingard 2010). I also clarify that, unlike some (Knight 2004) who prefer to see globalisation and internationalisation as distinct processes, I conceptualise them as increasingly interconnected. In relation to the 'internationalisation of higher education', the OECD (2008: 238) has defined it as 'the full spectrum of educational programmes and activities that contribute to internationalised learning, ranging from the internationalisation of programmes' content and delivery to the mobility of students and scholars'. More specifically, the OECD (2008: 257) has defined 'internationalising the curriculum' as 'strengthened foreign languages teaching and enhanced international perspectives in the substantive content of tertiary curricula'. Further, I highlight here that attenuated global and international interconnections have been accompanied by enhanced education policy borrowing across different jurisdictions (Phillips and Schweisfurth 2007), a phenomenon referred to both as cross-national attraction (Ertl 2006) and the cross-cultural transfer of educational concepts and practices (Tanako 2005). Much of this literature is concerned with the nature of educational theories, models, and methods transferred transnationally for academic or practical purposes, and the processes by which this takes place (Hoyler and Jons 2008).

The research plan

Conceptual frameworks

This is a study of radical transformations of curriculum policies and practices as universities increasingly engage with a global knowledge society. Theories of globalisation provide the overarching conceptual framework. While globalisation is a complex and contested phenomenon, Marginson and Rhoades (2002) have provided a useful tool for its analysis in higher education with their 'glo-na-cal' agency heuristic which distinguishes between 'global', 'national', and 'local' levels of policy processes. This heuristic is well recognised in the literature as a valuable device for analysing the processes of globalisation, especially in relation to the multiple levels of higher education policy activity (Cantwell and Maldonado-Maldonado 2009; Valimaa 2004), such as in the study being proposed here. Among its characteristics are that two-way interactions between policy-actors (organisations and individuals) are highlighted, as is the potential for the self-determining agency of these policy actors to negotiate policy relevant for their own specific settings (Marginson 2007). Equally, it constitutes a framework for identifying patterns of power and influence through the dimensions of 'reciprocity', 'strength', 'layers and conditions', and 'spheres'.

Within the overarching framework of globalisation, this study is an analysis of policy along the lines explicated by Simons et al. (2009); that is, it includes an analysis of 'policy determination and effects' as well as 'policy content'. They explain that these foci are concerned with 'how policy is made, why, when and for whom as well as the effects of policies (on groups) and its impact on a given problem' (p. 29), and 'values, assumptions and ideologies at stake in the policy process and content' (p. 29). To structure the empirical analysis, this project draws on the concept of a 'policy trajectory' (Ball 1994, 2006), which includes policy influences, texts, practices, and outcomes.

Research questions

The aims of the study have been translated into the following specific research questions which are structured around a global-national-local policy trajectory, including curriculum policy influences, policy texts, practices and outcomes:

1 What are the key influences from global and national level contexts which have an impact on university curriculum policy transformations in Chile?

- What have been the changing patterns of influences over time?
- What have been the relative influences from Europe, Australia, and the US on contemporary curriculum transformations in Chile?

2 What are the local level curriculum policy texts and practices in the three universities in Chile?
3 For each university:

- Where, when, and why have the changes occurred?
- Who are the key players, what are the key changes and how were the changes
- brought about?

4 How do curriculum policies and practices in the three universities compare with each other, and with wider trends over time (temporally/historically) and place (spatially)?
5 What are the likely outcomes of these new curriculum policies and practices for the universities and for changing higher education landscapes, nationally and globally?

The focus on the three universities in question as separate cases of curriculum policy transformations is in accord with growing calls for detailed 'situated case studies' (e.g. Marginson 2007) to better understand the dynamics of globalisation in higher education. This research strategy entails the investigation of 'a contemporary phenomenon within its real-life context, especially when the boundaries between phenomenon and context are not clearly evident' (Yin 2003: 13).

Data collection and analysis

Data will be collected and analysed in relation to the four main Research Questions (RQs) over the three years of the project. Three types of data – documents, interviews, and surveys – identifiable at the global (especially OECD, Europe, and the US), national (Chile), and local levels will be utilised. Reliance on documents will be heaviest at global and national levels, although selected interviews with key policy-players will also be used to probe curriculum policy transformations more deeply. Within the institutional case studies, curriculum policy will be examined through documents and interviews with key policy-actors, as well as surveys of larger numbers of 'grassroots' academics, to investigate policy-as-practice at the local (university) level. Given the global-to-local span of the research, study participants at this point will be limited to staff in universities, although future research could logically extend to other major stakeholder groups, especially students and employers.

Documents will be collected from global to local (university) levels. Examples of documents include OECD reports which map global trends; regional and national reports, discussion papers, policy statements, and major speeches by the policy elite (such as ministers); university policies; and newspaper articles.

Interviews will be conducted the three universities, interview participants (approximately 10 in each) will include vice-chancellors; at least two other senior executives; presidents of the staff unions; chairs of academic boards; chancellors; key middle managers having curriculum policy responsibilities; and any consultants appointed for the construction and implementation of new curriculum policy. Altogether, approximately 45 participants will be interviewed. Pilot interviews will trial a semi-structured interview schedule. While interview schedules will be adapted differently for interviews at global, national, and local (university) levels, there will be a common core to enhance triangulation of findings across the different levels. Written consent will be obtained prior to interviews of approximately 45 minutes duration. Interviews will be taped and transcripts returned to participants to check for accuracy, and then assigned a number to ensure participant anonymity.

Given their ongoing development of curriculum policy, personnel at the three universities will be contacted again towards the end of Year 3 of the study to ascertain any new dimensions to their transformations. Key informants will be followed up by email if significant changes have occurred.

For purposes of analysis, both policy documents and transcripts of interviews are viewed as texts, albeit created in different social contexts. Both will be analysed using critical discourse analysis which examines the relationships between textual content and the social conditions in which it was produced and interpreted; it focuses on the way power manifests itself through language (Considine 2005; Fairclough 2006).

Chapter 10

A proposal for a life history study

I became interested in the possibility of relating interpretivism to life history studies through a major research project in which I was involved with my colleague, Professor Clive Dimmock. Our specific focus of research was on trying to account for why some high school principals were successful managers of change within the context of the educational restructuring movement taking place in Australia in the 1990s. Exploring the concept of the 'life history' and associated life history research approaches presented fruitful avenues for pursuit in this regard.

We recognised that biographical and life history approaches in educational studies are not new. Thirty years ago, Abbs (1976) demonstrated the value of autobiographical approaches in teacher education. Later, Evetts (1989: 89) argued that life history accounts and biographies had become 'an increasingly popular source of sociological data'. She went on to highlight Plummer's (1983) contention that in sociology, research which highlights the actual human subject must provide the necessary counterbalance to positivistic emphases on structure and systems.

Having canvassed the field, we settled on the edited topical life history approach as holding out much potential for the study of principals who were promoting restructuring initiatives in the areas of curriculum, teaching, and learning. This, as we saw it, could allow us to take one step further the proposal by Ribbins and Sherratt (1992: 153) that studies of the principalship can benefit from adopting a biographical and autobiographical approach. What we sought was not only to develop accounts of schools and the role of the principals within them which integrate the perspectives of both the principals and the researchers, but also to examine the socialising influences relevant to the formation of the principal over the full life experience. Such an approach, as Sikes et al. (1985: 13) put it, 'is holistic, that is to say, concerned with a teacher's total life and career, and not just a segment or aspect of it'. These authors concluded by arguing that 'for a full understanding of teacher interests and motives, we need as complete a biographical picture as we can acquire' (Sikes et al. 1985: 13).

A number of cases for adopting this approach in studying the lives of teachers have been made over the past 25 years. Waring (1979) argued that an understanding of curriculum innovation is not possible without a history of context and she alerted us to the importance of considering the extent to which the interpretation and execution of curriculum briefs reflect the background and personalities of the curriculum organisers chosen. Goodson (1992: 6), in examining the literature on teacher socialisation, also made a convincing case by highlighting the fact that the period of pre-service training and early in-service teaching has been designated as the most formative socialising influence. An alternative tradition, he argued, has insisted that the situation is far more complicated than this:

> Many studies in the 1970s and 1980s have focused on the teachers' own experience as pupils, which is seen not only as important as the training period but in many cases more important. One way to follow up on this alternative tradition in teacher socialization research requires that we examine those socializing influences relevant to the formation of the teacher over the full life experience.

Elsewhere Goodson (1991: 144) has also argued as follows: 'There are critical incidents in the teachers' lives and specifically in their work which may crucially affect perception and practice'. More recently, he again articulated this position in a major work published with Sikes (Goodson and Sikes 2001).

In conclusion, a consideration of such positions led us to develop the following proposal where an explicit link is established between the symbolic interactionist theoretical position within the interpretivist paradigm and the concept of life history in order to develop a specific life history research approach appropriate for investigating our substantive area of interest. The outcome was a book entitled *Innovative School Principals and Restructuring: Life History Portraits of Successful Managers of Change* (Dimmock and O'Donoghue 1997).

Title

School restructuring initiatives and principals' biographies: An edited topical life history study

Research aim

Restructuring of school systems has been taking place in much of the world. It is widely acknowledged that the part which the school principal can play in managing associated processes is a crucial factor in ensuring their successful implementation. At the same time, however, research on the principalship has failed to keep pace with this changing context. Accordingly, there is a need for studies aimed at understanding the various aspects of principals' work as part of current restructuring.

The focus of restructuring has largely been on the administrative dimension of the phenomenon rather than on initiatives aimed at improving teaching and learning, the core activities of schooling. There is a growing acceptance internationally that there is a need to address this imbalance. Such research also needs to take cognisance of various contextual conditions. Thus, while the proposed research will focus on the principalship within the unique Western Australian (WA) context, it will also complement the research of those who are examining other contexts and make a contribution to studies aimed at illuminating similarities and differences on the wider international stage.

The specific aim of the proposed study is to adopt the edited topical life history research approach to generate theory regarding the relationship between innovative WA principals' activities aimed at improving teaching and learning and their life histories. A number of cases have been made for adopting this approach in studying the lives of teachers (Goodson 1992). These cases can also be made for the study of school principals.

Significance

In the immediate post-Second World War period, leadership studies focused on searching for traits which apparently successful leaders, including principals, displayed. The value in this research was that it led in the 1960s and 1970s to the emergence and widespread acceptance of two dimensions of leadership recognised by Blake and Mouton (1964), namely, task- and person-orientations. From this was spawned a host of theories about leadership styles. Most of these theories were developed with corporate leaders in mind, but they soon proved a rich source of ideas for application to the school principalship. Concurrently, the 1960s and 1970s witnessed an expansive literature, largely of a sociological nature, which focused on the roles that principals were expected to play. The research agenda of the 1980s shifted again, focusing strongly on the conception of the principal as instructional leader. This thrust of principal leadership research aligned closely with the emergence in the late 1970s and early 1980s of the school effectiveness movement (Purkey and Smith 1985). Principals who were instructional leaders were recognised as crucial agents in the effectiveness of their schools.

In Australia, the work of Chapman (1987) has been noteworthy in highlighting the relationship between the changing nature of the principalship and the restructuring context. As the 1980s drew to a close, two further developments in research on the principalship were discernible, both of which aligned with a shift in research emphasis from school effectiveness to school improvement and restructuring. One was the distinction between transactional and transformational leadership which highlighted the growing importance of leaders as managers of change, itself an endemic feature of improvement and restructuring; the other was the emergence of a socio-psychological oriented approach exemplified in cognitive studies of principals (Hallinger et al. 1993).

In evaluating the body of literature on the principalship at least four major trends are identifiable. First, much of it is prescriptive with surprisingly few sound empirical studies of principals. Second, a significant amount of the empirical work which exists has been generated using research methods and conceptual frameworks in the positivist tradition. Third, the studies tend to be of a general statistical nature dealing with samples of populations rather than being individual case studies. Fourthly, research on the principalship has tended to ignore both particular contextual conditions and the holistic standpoint which would take cognisance of the dynamic between the principal and the particular environment.

The background

The phenomenon of educational restructuring is taking place in much of the world, with deregulated, decentralised systems replacing central planning, control and supervision. This change is placing expectations on schools either to become self-managed, or to function under devolved authority from their central offices. These conditions have led to the development of the notions of school-based management, school-based budgeting, and the community management of schools. The process can assume different forms in different contexts, having been enacted at the national level in the United Kingdom and New Zealand, at the state level in Australia and at the district level in Canada. It has also involved significant curriculum changes in some countries.

Two related policy initiatives have been shaping change in Australian schools. The first centres on the restructuring of school systems and involves a shift from centralised governance to decentralised school-based management. The focus is on change at the whole-school level, primarily affecting governance, management and administration, rather than classroom activities of teaching and learning (Chadbourne and Clarke 1994). In the early stages of restructuring in Australia it was argued that such macro initiatives which involve a shift from centralised governance of decentralised school-based management would, on their own, lead to the achievement of enhanced learning for all students. However, while changes in the administrative and organisational contexts were targeted to create an environment conducive to improving teaching and learning, micro reforms were also necessary to bring about such improvement. Accordingly, the second policy initiative shaping change in Australian schools concerns school restructuring aimed at introducing more flexible, responsive, and student-oriented service delivery by targeting change in work organization, pedagogical practices, and learning processes.

The National Project on the Quality Teaching and Learning (NPQTL 1993) was launched by the Federal government in February 1991 to restructure the teaching profession, deal with low teacher morale, and improve the quality of teaching and learning. The National Schools Project, whose aim was to investigate how changes to work organization could lead to improved outcomes in student learning and school leadership, was initiated in association with the NPQTL. This project recognised the crucial part principals have to play in school restructuring aimed at the improvement of teaching and learning. At the same time, while there is no shortage of advice to principals on the role they should play in this regard, relatively little of it has been based on contemporary studies. This is not to deny the existence of a significant body of literature on the principalship. Rather, research on the principalship has failed to keep pace with the changing restructuring context.

Ribbins and Sherratt (1992: 160) pointed to one way forward in outlining a research agenda involving an in-depth longitudinal study of the headship. This was close to being an action research project, with the role of the experienced researcher approximating that of a consultant. A challenge now for other researchers is not only to adopt the approach of Ribbins and Sherratt, but also to adopt other approaches in a range of leadership and other contexts. The work of Leithwood et al. (1994) can be seen as an attempt to meet the challenge through their pioneering research on principals' problem-solving capacities.

This research proposal details a plan to meet the challenge of Ribbins and Sherratt in two respects. First, the approach is that of the edited topical life history. Second, the project focuses on principals who are considered by educational administrators, peers and staff to be undertaking adventurous change programmes to improve the quality of teaching and learning in their schools. Finally, the context of the project is Western Australia (WA).

The research plan

The aim of the study proposed here is to contribute to the existing knowledge base by using the edited topical life history approach to generate theory regarding the relationship between principals' life histories and the initiatives they are taking to improve curriculum, teaching, and learning in their schools. The theoretical framework underpinning such a research approach is now outlined.

This proposal highlights the need at a time of educational restructuring to develop in the case of principals a tradition which owes its origins in educational research to a movement of the late 1970s which 'fully opened up the question of how teachers saw their work and their lives' (Goodson 1992: 3–4). Accordingly, when initially deciding to study the work and effect of a number of principals in WA who are undertaking change programmes to improve the quality of curriculum, teaching, and learning in their schools, particular consideration was given to the need to generate a richness of data. This, it was felt, would be necessary so that patterns which exhibited the interaction between the creativity of the principals as agents and the structure within which they operated could, if they existed, be identified. Thus, the study will take its theoretical impetus from that stream of qualitative research known as symbolic interactionism.

Meltzer et al. (1975: 1) summarise symbolic interactionism as being:

> the interaction that takes place among the various minds and meanings that characterize human societies. It refers to the fact that social interaction rests

> upon a taking of oneself (self-objectification) and others (taking the role of the other) into account.

They go on to argue that the most basic element in this image of human beings is the idea that the individual and society are inseparable units; that while it may be possible to separate the units analytically, the underlying assumption is that a complete understanding of either one demands a complete understanding of the other. They then highlight the following:

> In the interactionist image, the behaviour of men and women is 'caused' not so much by forces within themselves (instincts, drives, needs, etc) but by what lies in between, a reflective and socially derived interpretation of the internal and external stimuli that are present.
>
> (Meltzer et al. 1975: 2)

Ritzer (1983: 301) developed the position of Blumer, one of the originators of modern symbolic interactionism, as follows:

> To Blumer, behaviorism and structural functionalism both tended to focus on factors (for example, external stimuli and norms) that cause behavior. As far as Blumer was concerned, both ignored the crucial process by which actors endow the forces acting upon them, as well as their own behaviors, with meaning. In addition to behaviorism, several other types of psychological reductionism troubled Blumer. For example, he criticised those who seek to explain human action by relying on conventional notions of the concept of 'attitude' ... what is important is not the attitude as an internalised tendency, but the defining process through which the actor comes to define his act. Blumer also singled out for criticism those who focus on conscious and unconscious motives. He was particularly irked by their view that actors are impelled by independent, mentalistic impulses over which they are supposed to have no control.

Ritzer concluded by arguing that Blumer was also opposed to sociologistic theories that view individual behaviour as determined by large-scale external forces. In short, he was opposed to any theory that ignores the processes by which actors construct meaning.

We find an illustration of what this means in Aspinwall's (1992: 254) account of her study of one teacher's professional life:

> It was impossible for Sarah to speak of her professional life without referring to her personal experiences. Significant figures and incidents from her childhood, her time at university studying politics, her children's own unhappy time starting school were all deeply influential in her decision to enter teaching and to her image of the kind of teacher she aspired to be. Her life

> experiences and her personality combined to give her an idealistic and demanding vision of teaching and teachers. This made her present colleagues particularly hard for her to understand and work with.

Minichiello et al. (1995: 152) highlight the arguments of Schwartz and Jacobs (1979) and Plummer (1983) that there is 'a fundamental affinity between the central tenets of symbolic interactionism and life history research'. Drawing from these arguments, they go on to state that there are three theoretical assumptions which are common to both traditions. The first assumption is that life is viewed as concrete experience. In other words, there is no point in studying abstractions of individuals or of social life. As Cooley (1956: 67) has put it, it is important to recognise that 'a separate individual is an abstraction unknown to experience, and so likewise is society when regarded as something apart from individuals'. Minichiello et al. (1995: 152) go on to argue that the central consequence of being concerned with life as concrete experience is that, as Plummer (1983: 54) has put it, 'in every case of study, we must acknowledge that experiencing individuals can never be isolated from their functioning bodies and their constraining social worlds'.

The second assumption highlighted by Minichiello et al. (1995) is that life is regarded as an ever-emerging relativistic perspective. In other words, human beings experience the world through their definitions of it. They quote Plummer (1983: 56) as follows: 'The reality shifts with a person's life and people act towards things on the basis of their understandings, irrespective of the "objective" nature of those things'. They conclude that if one accepts this theoretical assumption, then the most central and fundamental source of knowledge is the personal document, the life history which elicits 'the sense of reality' that human beings hold about their own worlds (Minichiello et al. 1995: 153).

The third assumption highlighted by Minichiello et al. (1995: 152) as being common to the symbolic interactionist and life history research traditions is that life is viewed as inherently marginal and ambiguous. This is tied to the two previous assumptions. They continue as follows:

> If we have taken one person's subjective reality seriously in a life history, and then considered it in relation to another person's, then there is always the possibility that ambiguity and incongruity will become evident in their definitions of the same situations.

They conclude that the message to the life history researcher is to move away from studying abstractions and get at the particular, the detailed, and the experiential, thus allowing one to grasp the ambiguities and inevitability of different perspectives.

At this point it is instructive to outline Goodson's (1992: 6) crucial distinction between the life story and the life history. He elaborates on the distinction thus:

> The life story is the 'story we tell about our life'; the life history is a collaborative venture, reviewing a wider range of evidence. The life story teller and

> another (or others) collaborate in developing this wider account by interviews and discussions and by scrutiny of texts and contexts. The life history is the life story located within its historical context.

He concludes by reminding us that while a great deal of valuable work on teachers' stories or narratives was carried out in the 1980s by academics, much of it did not embrace contextual or intercontextual analysis.

With regards to the life history, as distinct from the life story, Allport (1944) and Denzin (1989) distinguished between the complete or comprehensive life history and the topical life history. The complete or comprehensive life history is concerned with all aspects of the individual's life from birth. It is usually a long and complex account which focuses on the overall flow of life of an individual. In contrast, the topical life history focuses on only one phase, aspect or issue of the individual's life. Also, the life history, whether a complete or comprehensive life history or a topical life history, may be edited with comments and analysis by the researcher, either interspersed with the narrative, or in a combination which includes introductory passages and analytical commentary after the narrative, or incorporated in a combined form. At the same time, as Denzin (1989: 217) points out, all three forms contain three central elements: the person's own story of his or her life; the social and cultural situation to which the subject and others see the subject responding; and the sequence of past experiences and situations in the subject's life.

The life histories to be developed in relation to the case studies proposed here will be edited topical life histories. The decision that they should be 'edited' was made in the light of the advice given by Allport (1944: 78) that while unique styles of expression, including argot and colloquial phrasing, should remain unedited, editing for the sake of clarity or to remove repetitious material would seem justified. The 'topic' is the interaction between current restructuring initiatives and the principals' innovations in curriculum, the teaching and learning taking place in their schools. The participants to be selected and forms of data collection and analysis to be utilised in the study in order to construct such edited topical life histories will now be considered.

The selection of participants

An initial list of principals to be considered as possible participants in the study was drawn up on the basis of their reputations for attempting to promote adventurous change programmes to improve the quality of curriculum, teaching, and learning in their schools. The present researchers became aware of these reputations over the period of a year through the consistency of reporting by district superintendents and central office administrators, and through evaluation reports by academics, informal contacts with consultants, and hearsay from teachers and parents in the schools. Over a period of time, corroborative evidence from these multiple sources emerged to facilitate the construction of a final list of principals.

Following this, volunteers to participate were sought. In this regard, cognisance was taken of procedures outlined by Woods (1985). He argued that in seeking volunteers for life history studies there is always an element of pressure, no matter how courteous and non-committal, in the direct approach. He then recommended that one set out a market-stall to groups of teachers and invite offers; 'there is an immediate sense of negotiation in the "offer", for, in the interests of motivation, they should be allowed to work their personal interests into the general framework of the research' (Woods 1985: 14–15). The 'market-stall' would detail the broad aims of the research; the principles of the method; possible outcomes for education; possible outcomes for the teacher personally, 'such as greater understanding of self and career, and an aid to morale'. The latter, he says:

> may derive from knowledge of varieties of careers and career planning, and the general contextualising of one's own, which might touch on feelings of success and failure, and general job satisfaction. Above all, such a study promises to promote knowledge of self. As Stenhouse (1975: 144) argues, 'The outstanding characteristic of the extended professional is a capacity for autonomous professional self-development through systematic self-study'.
>
> (Woods 1985: 15)

Finally, the 'market-stall' would also detail possible outcomes for the researcher and a statement of guarantees, such as anonymity at all times, respect and protection of privacy, and a teacher's right to correct or withhold transcripts.

From the principals who volunteered, six participants, three males and three females, have already been selected for this study. The selection was influenced by a desire to cast widely for a variety of perspectives, rather than to select a random sample, or choose a sample that would be representative of a total population. At the same time, a gender balance is reflected in the selection. Diversity is also to be found in the school catchment areas, whose socioeconomic status ranges from middle and higher income urban populations to lower income urban and rural communities.

Data collection and analysis

Data will be gathered and analysed concurrently in three stages.

Stage 1

In this stage, descriptive data will be gathered about each school, including its location, its history, and the social background of its pupils. The purpose in generating such data is to assist in portraying the context within which each principal is working. Interviews will then be conducted with each principal separately. These interviews will be aimed at uncovering the principals' perspectives on what they have been doing to improve the quality of curriculum, teaching and learning in their schools, how they have been going about promoting such innovations, and why they feel they have been promoting them.

The semi-structured in-depth interview method (Taylor and Bogdan 1998: 76) will be utilised because it is concerned with creating the environment to encourage participants to discuss their lives and experiences in free-flowing, open-ended discussions. Also, it enables the researcher to interpret their views. In conducting the interviews, general principles as outlined by Spradley (1979) and Measor (1985: 63–73) will be followed. These include the following: having a clear purpose, which is made apparent to the participant; explaining why particular questions are being asked; using clear meaningful language; asking descriptive, structural, and contrast questions; using open-ended questions to elicit rich qualitative responses; avoiding leading questions; framing the same questions in different time dimensions; using effective probing to obtain further elaboration, explanation, and clarification; using cross-checks to investigate possible exaggerations and distortions; allowing the participant to do most of the talking; being non-judgemental and being sensitive to the participant's situation.

The initial interview with each participant is likely to last approximately two hours. An *aide-memoire* (Burgess 1982), or semi-structured interview guide, will be developed around the following headings to enable the participants to frame their thoughts on the improvement of the quality of curriculum, teaching, and learning in their schools as part of current restructuring: goals and objectives; enabling factors; constraining factors; dilemmas; stresses and stressors; actions taken; future directions; and feelings in retrospect about the whole process. However, neither the wording nor the ordering of the questions will be fixed. Furthermore, the participants will be given the *aide-memoire* prior to the interview in order to give them sufficient time to reflect on the headings. The adoption of such a procedure, it is felt, will facilitate the generation of both a quantity and quality of data which would be unlikely to emerge if reliance was to be placed on more immediate responses. Furthermore, because school restructuring matters are complex, it is felt that the principals will need time to give due consideration to the questions they will be asked. In this way, the subtleties of events and meanings can be explored and captured.

Cognisant of the argument made by Le Compte and Goetz (1982: 41) that 'the optimum guard against threats to internal reliability' may be the presence of more than one researcher, the interviews with five of the six principals will be conducted jointly by two experienced interviewers so that later, during analysis, they can discuss the meaning of the participants' words until agreement is achieved. As themes arise, they will be pursued with the participants in a lengthy conversation piece. In fact, the term 'conversation' is probably a much more appropriate term for the process than 'interview'. As Aspinwall (1992: 251) argues, the term 'interview' cannot convey the empathy and interest necessary to the process.

The conversations will be tape-recorded with the participants' consent. While tape-recording, the interviewers will also take notes. Woods (1985: 20) has described the purpose of such note-taking as follows:

> These are rather like the rough notes made during ethnographic fieldwork, when one is being assailed by a torrent of data. The cryptic jottings made at the time are sufficient to stir the memory later, when one can record the full data or impression at length. Now the tape recorder may capture what is said. But it cannot capture fleeting thoughts and impressions, as something the teacher says prompts first this thought and then that – the second invariably displacing the first from memory. The briefest of notes can aid recall.

In reading over one's notes along with the transcribed interviews one should be able to identify points on which one wishes the participant to elaborate and points which one wishes the participant to clarify. This elaboration and clarification will take place with the participants for modification until they become accepted by them as representative of their position (Lincoln and Guba 1985: 314–316). Again, this process will be guided by a procedure outlined by Woods (1985: 21):

> Initial conversations have to be followed up. In general, the points to look out for are of three kinds. (a) Corrective: These include inconsistencies, non sequiturs, omissions, lack of balance, implausibility, a too 'cut and dried' or 'black and white' account ... (b) Checking and in-filling: a copy of the transcript is returned to the teacher and he is asked to comment. Is he happy with it? Does it adequately represent his views? Does it say what he means to say? ... (c) Progressive: these are hints that are let fall of possible richness of data in areas according with the themes of the research.

In some cases, this will mean follow-up interviews after the initial one. Each of these interviews is likely to last approximately two hours.

Throughout all of the interviews in this and subsequent phases, cognisance will be taken of Langness and Frank's (1981: 34) contention that 'the key to successful anthropological fieldwork and also to successful life history taking is rapport'. At all times, the aim of the interviewers will be to be friendly and objective outsiders and to be cautious, diplomatic, persevering, and patient. They will also seek to be good listeners, trying not to interrupt and using body language and short expressions to indicate that they are 'interestedly quiet' (Burgess 1982). The conversations will be conducted, where possible, in 'ordinary' teacher discourse. At the end of Stage 1 of the research, the total set of transcribed material will be analysed following the procedures outlined by Marton (1985: 155), with utterances in the transcripts being brought together into categories on the basis of their similarities and categories being differentiated from one another in terms of their variance.

Stage 2

The next stage in the research is to conduct semi-structured interviews with the participants on their life histories. The decision to engage in this aspect of the research following Stage 1, rather than the other way around, has been influenced by Langness and Frank's (1981: 39) argument that the taking of an adequate and reliable life history 'involves a degree of intimacy with the informant and a knowledge of the community as well, that comes only with exceptionally good rapport'. They go on to advise not to attempt a life history until one has known the person and been in the field for some time. The nature of the data gathering undertaken in Stage 1 will facilitate such a development.

Three weeks before the first life history interview the participants will each be given another *aide-memoire* so that they can have time to reflect on the themes, begin the process of recall, and organise their recollections in a chronological sequence. The *aide-memoire* which will be developed for this occasion will be strongly influenced by Lancy's (1993: 204) suggestions. It will centre on the participants' family life, including their role as spouse and parent; personal school history, especially details of their professional training; their relationship with significant others, parents, and favourite teachers; their higher education, including institutions attended, subjects taken, likes and dislikes, influential lecturers, and significant events at college; a sense of their daily routines and life-styles; the nature of the schools and the classroom environments in which they taught; the characteristics and backgrounds of the students they taught, especially regarding class and ethnicity; a sense of the climate of the schools within which they taught and the prevailing teaching ethos; classroom routines in which they engaged, including the use of prepared curricula, grouping arrangements, management strategies, and the predominant instructional mode; professional development activities undertaken and recreational activities.

The adoption of a set of headings for the *aide-memoire* reflects the approach of Lemert (1955: 445–6) in his study of the life history of deviants. The contention is that those headings proposed by Lancy (1993: 204) are broad enough to be appropriate in investigating the lives of individual school principals. However, they will also be accompanied by a consideration of such factors as social class, religion, and social and political climate. As Pollard (1980) argues, sensitively handled and portrayed, the influences of these can be seen in the acted-out life and the formulating self. The intention overall is to generate data sufficiently rich to construct the sort of portrait which, as Plummer (1983: 69) puts it, would enable us 'to perceive the intersection of the life history of human beings with the history of their society'. The headings of the *aide-memoire*, along with the broader headings of social class, religion, and social and political climate, can also be seen as constituting a set of uniform standards so that as each new case is developed comparisons can be made across them.

Woods (1985: 19) makes the same point when he argues that the 'danger of reductionism and atomism should be guarded against from the beginning'.

Quoting Dollard (1935), he states that this can be done in a number of ways, notably by situating personal and career developments within relevant frameworks, such as social class, ethnicity, gender or generation, and within the prevailing socioeconomic circumstances; and by focusing upon the culture of the primary groups within an individual's biography. In order to probe these issues it will be necessary for the researchers to familiarise themselves with the general history of WA over the past 40 years, as well as with the history of education in the state over the same period.

Finally, when exploring each individual's life history, attention will be given to the point of Sikes et al. (1985: 20) that not all teachers necessarily experience smooth career progression; rather, 'a typical career is marked by critical incidents or phases'. Goodson and Walker (1991: 147) make the same point as follows:

> The new work on teachers' careers points to the fact that there are critical incidents in teachers' lives and specifically in their work which may crucially affect perception and practice. Certainly work on beginning teachers has pointed to the importance of certain incidents in moulding teachers' styles and practices.

Furthermore, cognisance will be taken of the contention by Sikes et al. (1985: 20) that, while such incidents can give one's career and one's life 'a beneficial boost', they can also 'deal it a savage blow, or both at the same time'.

Stage 3

The final stage of the research involves further analysis of the life history data generated from the first interview with each participant. The aim is to explore those life history details that might explain both the manner in which and the reasons why he or she undertook adventurous programmes in the area of curriculum, teaching, and learning. The decision to have this third stage of analysis was influenced particularly by the argument of Woods (1992: 374) that because the participants' memories, thoughts, and perceptions are of unknown scope and depth, even to themselves, accounts should be built up through successive discussions over a period of time. Accordingly, the previous conversations will be reviewed for accuracy and completeness.

Cognisance will also be taken of Mandelbaum's (1973) scheme for the analysis of life histories. Briefly, Mandelbaum has suggested that when analysing a life history we need to consider the dimensions of a person's life, the principal turnings, and the person's characteristic means of adaptation. A dimension is 'made up of experiences that stem from a similar base and are linked in their effects on the person's subsequent actions' (Mandelbaum 1973: 180). They are biological, cultural, social, and psychosocial. With regards to the first two, Mandelbaum states:

> The biological factors set the basic conditions for a life course; cultural factors mould the shape and content of a person's career. The cultural dimension lies

> in the mutual expectations, understandings and behavior patterns held by the people among whom a person grows up and in whose society he becomes a participant. Each culture provides a general scenario for the life course that indicates the main divisions, tells when transitions should be made, and imputes a social meaning to biological events from birth through death. Each scenario interprets and affects the biological dimension in its own way; each provides its own chart for the progress of a life.

The social dimension, in turn, consists of the social relations the person encounters during his or her life, the roles required of the person, the acts of personal choice characteristic of the group, and the commonly understood ways of working out recurrent conflicts. The psychosocial dimension refers to the individual's feelings, attitudes, and subjective world in general. Mandelbaum recognises that, while each of these is individually experienced, each individual's experiences are also likely to be similar in important ways to others in the same culture.

Turnings are the major transitions that an individual makes during the course of a life. These are accomplished when 'the person takes on a new set of roles, enters into fresh relations with a new set of people and acquires a new self conception' (Mandelbaum 1973: 181). A turning can take place gradually, or it can be a single event. Also, it may be either improvised or in some way prescribed.

Finally, adaptations 'are changes that have a major effect on a person's life and on one's basic relations with others' (Mandelbaum 1973: 181). Mandelbaum goes on to argue that individuals change their ways: 'Each person changes his ways in order to maintain continuity whether of group participation or social expectation or self-image or simply survival.' He concludes that while some of these new conditions are imposed by the individual's own physical development, others arise from changing external conditions, whether of custom or climate, family, or society.

Chapter 11

A proposal for an interactionist historical study

The potential for engaging in particular types of historical studies using the symbolic interactionist theoretical approach within the interpretivist paradigm suggested itself to me a number of years ago. I had, as an educational historian, been struggling for a long period with how to go about research aimed at trying to understand how teachers in previous eras understood various aspects of their lives. I was particularly interested in this research agenda as it applied to lay people who taught alongside priests, brothers, and nuns in Catholic schools in Australia. I got some early indications as to a way forward from the work of Silver (1980: 267) when he argued for 'the history of opinion'. This he defined as 'the history of how people, groups of people, people in action, have interpreted and reinterpreted their world'.

To pursue Silver's line of inquiry, it seemed to me, was to argue for the application of the 'hermeneutic' mode of historical research to the study of teachers' lives. It has been argued that such a mode is appropriate where there is an aspiration 'to explain events by referring to the motives, reasoning, meanings and intentions of the actors' (Fairburn 1999: 31). It is also a mode which relates very closely to the 'intentional explanation mode', where the investigator 'looks closely at the conscious desires, values, aims and purposes' of the members of the group being studied and relates these to their 'conscious beliefs about how the desired ends could be brought about' (Fairburn 1999: 26).

At the same time, I sought an approach that would be explicit in terms of clarifying and spelling out theoretical assumptions. The following proposal to investigate the experience of being a lay teacher in Western Australian Catholic schools during the period 1940–1980, indicates how I responded to this. At the same time, I deemed it important to state that I recognised that this was not the only valid approach to engaging in research on the substantive area of interest under consideration here. Rather, the position taken was that it had a very significant part to play alongside other approaches. In particular, I held that it could lead to the development of the micro-perspectives necessary for those interested in investigating the area through research projects based on other frameworks, including structuralism, feminist theory, and critical theory.

Title

From periphery to centre: An historical analysis of lay teachers' experiences in Australian Catholic schools from 1940 to 1980

Aim

The central aim of this project is to provide an historical analysis of the experience of being a lay teacher in Australian Catholic schools during the period 1940–1980. The project is based on three principal research questions:

a What were the perspectives of lay teachers in Australian Catholic schools during the period 1940–1980 regarding what it meant to be a teacher?
b How did the lay teachers carry out their work in light of those perspectives?
c What was the relationship between the perspectives of the lay teachers and the wider socio-historical structure?

The background

The broad background is the increasing interest over the past 25 years in the history of teachers and teaching, with researchers drawing on a range of theoretical and methodological approaches (McCulloch and Woodin 2010). In particular, educational historians have been undertaking explorations on 'the daily interactions of teachers with pupils, colleagues and the public at large, and teachers' own experiences of their pedagogy and work' (McCulloch 2011: 90). A major challenge in developing this research agenda is to focus on different 'types' of teachers for different periods and in different contexts. Catholic lay teachers in Australia for the period 1940–1980 constitute a particularly rich group in this regard.

A trend in recent years in the study of Catholic education, both internationally and nationally, is to conceptualise it within the parameters of 'faith-based schooling'. The history of such schooling in much of the Western world from the middle of the nineteenth century up to the present day is one of Christian-based institutions being gradually replaced by state-run ones. Nevertheless, throughout the period, Christian-based schools continued to constitute a relatively strong minority group, with various religious denominations reaching different accommodations with the state in different countries in terms of receiving support, including financial assistance, though sometimes not without controversy, and even conflict. The nature of the campaigns undertaken was the focus of interest for many researchers in the first half of the twentieth century.

By the 1960s, however, academic interest in Christian schooling waned, influenced partly by the analyses of sociologists of religion whose view generally was that such educational provision would soon disappear because, as they saw it, the world was in the grip of an irreversible process of secularisation (Bruce 2003: 42). The apparent decline was accompanied by secular marginalisation, with religion being subtly ignored as unimportant in the academic and media worlds. Recently, however, it has become apparent that the gradual retreat of religion from public space which was meant to eventuate in many European countries, has not become a reality, with religion being very much at the forefront of debate and activity. This, as Jackson (2007: 27) put it, is partly due to the global attention it has received as a result of the September 11, 2001 event. Equally, he recognised that positive events involving religion have had 'an impact on public consciousness in relation to issues within civil society' (Jackson 2007: 27).

It is against such a background that the renewed focus on religious-based schooling, now more usually referred to as 'faith-based' schooling, needs to be considered. One area of interest has been the expansion of 'fundamental' Christian schools. Minority non-Christian schools have also received much attention, in part because they are viewed as somewhat exotic in terms of what they see as being non-negotiable in a number of areas, including school dress, pedagogical approaches, and curriculum content. Equally, the resilience and growth of schools and school systems provided by the 'traditional' 'mainline' Christian churches merit scholarly investigation.

What characterises faith-based schools is that they 'reflect a particular religious worldview in the way they are organised, in what they teach, and in the integration of faith and learning' (Sullivan 2006: 937). The media has become especially interested in the phenomenon. Concurrently, there have been calls for a renewed scholarly emphasis on a wide variety of contemporary issues in the field, including those of a curricular, pedagogical, management and leadership nature (Lawton and Cairns 2005; Shah 2006; Luckcock 2007), while not overlooking a number of related scholarly works that have appeared over the past two decades. For example, among the seminal works that have resulted in the case of Catholic schooling (the oldest tradition in Christian schooling) are those of Bryk et al. (1993) on the USA, Grace (2002) on England, and Sweetman (2002) on New Zealand. However, they need to be accompanied by studies where the focus is very much on the historical background in order to provide an understanding of the broader contexts out of which the current situation has emerged. Such studies, as Weisse (2007: 9) has put it, can then be drawn upon to facilitate dialogue aimed at preventing conflict and supporting peaceful coexistence in a multi-religious society.

The latter argument holds for Australia, as for elsewhere. While a range of issues on Catholic education within the country need to be investigated, that of lay teachers in Catholic schools for the period 1940–1980 is a particularly rich area upon which to focus. This was an era of great change within the Catholic Church which impacted significantly on Catholic education in many countries, including

Australia. The middle of the period, the 1960s, was characterised not only by challenges to the 'traditional' Catholic 'mind-set' and religious practices arising from the activities of the Second Vatican Council, but also by a major reduction in vocations to religious life and, consequently, a major reduction in nuns, brothers, and priests as teachers in Catholic schools. The period also includes the year 1973, which ushered in 'the Whitlam era' in Australia, with promises of massive Federal Government aid to education, including Catholic schools, and this at a time when Catholic schools were being staffed more and more by lay teachers.

To focus on the period 1940–1980 is not to dismiss previous or subsequent periods as unworthy of attention. Rather, these periods merit major projects in themselves. The general background is the situation whereby the Catholic community in Australia was successful in maintaining and developing a substantial education sector independent of state education systems from the advent of legislation on education in all states in the latter half of the nineteenth century (O'Donoghue 2001: 19–21). Since the early decades of that century the teachers who worked in the Catholic education sector were categorised into the 'teaching religious' (members of religious teaching orders of priests, brothers, and nuns), who constituted the great majority, and the lay teachers who led what the Church viewed as the 'ordinary', unconsecrated life of being married, or single (O'Donoghue 2001: 101–112). Relatively little is known about the perspectives and activities of those in the latter category. This project will make one contribution to the deficit by studying the experience of being a lay teacher in Catholic schools in Australia during the period 1940–1980.

The project is proposed at a time when, as was pointed out at the beginning of this proposal, the history of teachers' lives is beginning to receive much increased attention not only nationally, but internationally. During the 1980s and early 1990s, educational historians in the USA (Altenbaugh 1992; Finkelstein 1989, 1998) began to open up the field, particularly in relation to the lives of teachers in government schools. This tradition is continued in work like that recently undertaken by Rousmaniere (2009). As the research output developed in both quality and extent, however, Silver (1994) argued that, apart from similar work in Canada, the remainder of the English-speaking world was not quite as active on the same front. Three years later, in 1997, attention was drawn to the situation whereby teachers in the United Kingdom (UK) constituted an occupational group whose lives historically were under-researched (Gardner and Cunningham 1997: 331). It is only very recently, with work like that of Goodman and Martin (2002), Robinson (2004), Cunningham and Gardner (2004) and Burke and Dudek (2010), that the situation has begun to be addressed for this context.

Historians in Australia have been more productive in the field. The early research of Spaull and colleagues on teaching and teacher unionisation (Spaull 1985; Spaull and Sullivan 1989) has provided essential historical views on the pressures under which teachers work today. Feminist historians (Kyle 1989; Mackinnon 1984; Theobald 1996) have also been major contributors and associated work on the gendered nature of women in teaching continues through works like that of Trimingham-Jack (2003) Trotman (2008) and Whitehead (2003). Research has also been undertaken on the role that teachers have played historically in the construction of masculinity (Brice 1995; Crotty 2001) and femininity (Theobald 1994; Whitehead 2007).

Some scholarly works also emerged on teachers and teaching in Catholic schools in Australia. Burley (1997 2001) opened up the complexity of the area by drawing attention to the various categories of Catholic teachers; female teachers in Catholic schools included, for example, 'choir nuns', 'lay nuns', and 'lay teachers'. The work of both 'types' of nuns as teachers in Australian schools has been examined by O'Brien (2005) and Trimingham-Jack (1998, 2003). Such contributions, while extremely valuable, also highlight the need for a much greater research project regarding the experience of what it meant to be a teacher in a Catholic school, a point also recently made forcefully by (Hellinckx et al. 2009) in relation to the situation internationally. This is not to overlook the extensive number of histories on Catholic educational institutions undertaken in various Australian states. These are admirable as attempts to provide some record of the activities of the teaching religious. In general, however, they tend to be hagiographic. Also, they present the work of the religious orders as divinely inspired Catholic altruism and ignore the more secular perspective which would view their undertakings as the result of a complex interaction of political, social, and economic forces. Furthermore, they tend to completely ignore the lay teachers who taught in Catholic schools. Thus, they perpetuate a practice of the Catholic Church in previous decades of viewing lay people in general as being of a lesser status than the *virtuoso*, those who were priests, brothers, and nuns (Burley and O'Donoghue 2006; O'Donoghue and Potts 2004).

A major consequence of the dominance of the latter view in the past was that lay teachers tended to be employed in Catholic schools in Australia only when no teaching religious were available and they were excluded from school policy development. The teaching religious promoted the notion that lay teachers were of inferior rank. In particular, there was no consideration of the possibility that married life, or living as a single person outside of religious life, might enhance one's qualities as a teacher and a school manager. However, while these and related lenses through which the Catholic hierarchy and the religious orders viewed the lay teachers are reasonably well understood (O'Donoghue 2004), there are hardly any studies on how the lay teachers viewed themselves. An investigation of this and associated issues would lead to a deeper knowledge of the history of the role and status of the lay teacher in Catholic education, and thus contribute to the growing knowledge-base on the history of the lives of teachers of all types both nationally and internationally.

Significance

The project will concentrate on the experience of being a lay teacher in Catholic schools in Australia during the period 1940–1980. It was during the middle of this period that major reforms took place within the Catholic Church (the Church) internationally (Hornsby-Smith 2000). These led to changes in the composition of the Catholic teaching force in many countries, including Australia. A major consequence is that nowadays young people being educated in Catholic schools in Australia are usually taught by lay teachers, the principals in their schools are lay women and men, and lay people predominate on their school boards. Equally, the presence of members of religious orders of nuns, religious brothers, and priests as teachers and administrators in the schools, is minimal (O'Donoghue 2004: 123–146). Yet, when many of the parents of those currently attending Catholic schools were themselves in schools the Catholic teaching force was dominated by the teaching religious. The turning point was the mid-1960s and the opening up of the Church to the modern world as a result of the Second Vatican Council (1962–1965). This coincided with large numbers leaving the orders, a major drop off in new recruits, and a consequent need to employ ever-greater numbers of lay teachers (Grace 2002).

The impact of the change on the lay teachers in Australian Catholic schools has not been the subject of much research. Certainly, there has been some work on the official perspective of the Church and of the teaching religious on the role and status of the lay teacher both before and after the Second Vatican Council (O'Donoghue 2004: 123–146). This work, however, has not been complemented by research projects aimed at investigating the lay teachers' own perspectives on their lives in the last years of the heyday of the teaching religious and the early years when they were being rapidly replaced, how the lay teachers carried out their work in light of those perspectives, and the relationship between their perspectives and the wider socio-historical structure. In seeking to address this deficit, the project proposed here is also influenced by the great lack of work on the social history of teaching in Australia more generally and by a belief that the most comprehensive way to begin to develop the field is to proceed on a state-by-state basis, concentrating on various categories of teachers in the different educational systems within each state through various historical periods.

The proposed study is also innovative in adopting symbolic interactionism as the theoretical position underpinning the methodology. While it is a position that has been used for many decades (and not without controversy) within the sociology of education, it has rarely been used in studies in the history of education. Educational historians have argued for conducting studies similar to this project by using 'hermeneutic' and 'intentional explanation' research approaches (Gardner 2010). However, symbolic interactionism has the advantage of being much more explicit in terms of clarifying theoretical assumptions and indicating how the project's principal research questions can be translated into a set of detailed data-gathering questions. As this will be the first time this particular social theory has been appropriated for a project in the history of Catholic education of the type proposed here, the outcome will constitute an exemplar for other social science educational historians interested in engaging in similar projects. Furthermore, the systematic use of 'inductive analysis' as a technical approach for analysing oral history testimony will be instructive for educational historians of 'insider' perspectives who tend not to lay bare their modes of data analysis with the same degree of precision as do those working from various structuralist perspectives, or those utilising various modes of statistical analysis.

The research plan

Lancy (1993: 253) has distinguished between the 'narrative tradition' in historical research in which arguments about causation are implicit for the most part, and 'social science history' where theories, assumptions, and methods of analyses are explicit. This project is conceptualised within the latter tradition. In particular, the principal research questions, in which the concept of 'perspective' is central, are derived from 'symbolic interactionism', a social theory which constitutes an appropriate theoretical framework for projects aimed at generating rich data of the type sought here. This long-established research tradition, which has been prominent at least during two periods in the last one hundred years (Ritzer 1994), has over the last 15 years been reinstated once again as a central position within contemporary social theory (Prus 1996; Charon 2001, O'Donoghue 2007). While it has taken on various nuances, symbolic interactionism is still underpinned by three central principles made explicit by Blumer in 1969:

1. human beings act towards 'things' on the basis of the meanings that the 'things' have for them;
2. this attribution of meaning to objects through symbols is a continuous process. The symbols are gestures, signs, language and anything else that may convey meanings;
3. the meanings are handled in, and modified through, an interpretative process used by the person in dealing with the things he or she encounters. (Blumer 1969: 2)

It is on the basis of actions taken in accordance with these principles that 'perspectives' or 'frameworks through which people make sense of the world' are formed.

Blumer's principles of symbolic interactionism are fundamental to the three major research questions of this proposal. His concept of 'perspectives' is central to the first research question, namely, what were the 'perspectives' of lay teachers in Australian Catholic schools during the period 1940–1980 regarding what it meant to be a teacher? Also, his principle that human beings act towards 'things' on the basis of the meanings that the 'things' have for them, is central to the second research question, namely, how did the lay teachers carry out their work in light of those perspectives?; 'things' covers a range of phenomena, from the concrete (people, material objects and institutions) to the abstract, which includes the situations in which people find themselves and the principles that guide human life. The third research question, namely, what was the relationship between the perspectives of the lay teachers and the wider socio-historical structure? is based on the notion that such conditions as 'time, space, culture, economic status, technological status, career history and individual biography' (Strauss and Corbin 1990: 103) can act to either facilitate, or constrain the action/interactional strategies taken within a specific context by an individual or a group. Coupled with this is the assumption within symbolic interactionism that where these conditions do act to facilitate action/interactional strategies they have to be managed by the individual or group. Thus, while not totally in harmony with the notion of Giddens (2004) of 'structuration', 'structure is not neglected in symbolic interactionism even though the emphasis is primarily on 'agency'.

From considerations so far, it is clear that the approach to be used in this project is heavily theory-laden. In this regard, some have argued for the application of the 'hermeneutic' mode of historical inquiry as utilised by Thompson (1965) to the study of teachers' lives. Such a mode is appropriate where there is an aspiration 'to explain events by referring to the motives, reasoning, meanings and intentions of the actors' (Fairburn 1999: 31). At the same time, the specific approach being advocated here is much more explicit in terms of clarifying theoretical assumptions, thus reflecting contemporary trends in the writing of educational biography. Finally, it is recognised that this is not the only valid approach to engaging in research on the substantive area of interest here. Rather, the position taken is that it has a very significant part to play alongside other approaches. In particular, it can lead to the development of the micro-perspectives necessary for those interested in investigating the area through research projects based on other frameworks, including structuralism, feminist theory, and critical theory.

The research will be undertaken in three stages:

Stage 1: The aim of this largely descriptive stage is to portray the context within which Catholic teachers in Australia taught during the period under examination. This portrayal will be based on such documentary evidence as annual reports on Catholic education in Australia, the 'rules and constitutions' and 'acts of chapter' of religious orders, school annuals and year books, and reports on education in the Australian Catholic newspaper. This evidence will be supplemented by descriptive data yielded through the individual oral histories of lay teachers to be conducted in 'Stage 2'.

Stage 2: This stage of the study will involve the use of semi-structured interviews to investigate the 'life stories' of 48 teachers who taught in Australian Catholic schools during the period 1940–1980 regarding how they understood and negotiated their working lives.

Cunningham and Gardner (2004: 6) have argued that one of the inherent and inevitable difficulties of any oral history project must be that it involves very small numbers of respondents in relation to the size of the original target group. Leaning heavily on both the position and experience of Foot (1998) and Thompson (2000), they conclude that, as a function of the natural mortality of potential respondents from that group, 'scientific sampling is simply not possible in this kind of work, even if it were seen as desirable'. Taking account of this position, the stance taken here is that participants can best be selected through having a 'purposive selection plan' (Punch 2005: 193).

The purposive approach to be adopted, while aiming to balance participants for gender, seeks to enhance the possibility of gaining access to as wide a variety of perspectives as possible. Thus, the research will be conducted within the metropolitan areas of four geographically disparate centres, namely, Perth, Melbourne, Sydney, and Brisbane.

In the first year of the project 24 participants will be interviewed at two sites, and another 12 will be interviewed at the remaining two sites in the second year. Each participant will be interviewed for approximately 2 hours, as experience shows that this is around the length of time required to elicit extensive and in-depth accounts. The interviews will be tape-recorded provided that consent will be received from the participants. Where consent is not forthcoming field notes will be made. Transcribed interviews will be 'checked back' with the participants until they become accepted as representative of their positions.

The participants will be given an *aide memoire* or semi-structured interview guide 2 weeks prior to the interviews to allow them to reflect on the headings.

Table 11.1 The interviews

	Perth		*Melbourne*		*Brisbane*		*Sydney*	
	Males	*Females*	*Males*	*Females*	*Males*	*Females*	*Males*	*Females*
Participants who ceased teaching in Catholic schools prior to 2nd Vatican Council	2	2	2	2	2	2	2	2
Participants who commenced teaching during the 2nd Vatican Council	2	2	2	2	2	2	2	2
Participants who commenced teaching after the 2nd Vatican Council	2	2	2	2	2	2	2	2

This will consist of conversation questions based on headings suggested by Lancy (1993: 204) for life history work and will be focused on eliciting data regarding the perspectives which the participants held and how they carried out their work in light of these perspectives.

The conversation questions will relate to:

- 'personal school and college history'; 'higher education experiences', 'professional training';
- a sense of daily routines and life-styles;
- the nature of the schools and the classroom environments in which they taught;
- classroom routines, preparation, and marking of school work, management strategies, instructional modes;
- professional development activities.

The exact wording and order of the questions are likely to change in the interview situation. This will enable the researcher to respond to the situation at hand and to gain new ideas on the topic.

The researcher is alert to issues raised in oral history research regarding problems of memory and will safeguard for them along lines proposed in Lumis (1987) and Perks and Thomson (1998). It will also be necessary to keep in mind Thomson's (1998: 585) point that one of the most significant shifts in oral history in recent times has been the recognition that 'the so-called unreliability of memory might be a resource, rather than a problem, for historical interpretation and reconstruction'. Primarily what is being referred to here is that memory can alert us to 'those aspects of one's past which become sedimented through regular repetition in life narratives' (Cunningham and Gardner 2004: 5). Equally, one needs to be alert to the dangers of approaching research of the type proposed here with various historical questions arising out of other research agendas of interest to the researcher. It will be necessary to 'bracket', or temporarily set aside, such questions in order to identify the issues of importance to the participants at the time. In the same way, various 'outsider' constructs such as the 'industrial-relations' and 'teachers-work' models of teachers and teaching which are regularly used in studies on the history of teachers' unions and the sociology of 'teaching as an occupation', need to be eschewed so that what emerges are the 'insider' constructs of the participants themselves, as opposed to frameworks generated by filtering their 'voices' through pre-chosen constructs.

Stage 3: This stage is concerned with the development of case studies of each of the three major groups of lay teachers already outlined: those who ceased teaching in Catholic schools prior to the meeting of the Second Vatican Council (1962–1965), those who taught in Catholic schools both before and after the Council, and those who commenced employment in Catholic schools after the Council ceased to function. Such an approach is based on the symbolic interactionist notion that group perspectives may occur 'when people see themselves as being in the same boat', but it also recognises that certain perspectives may not be shared by all and may be informed by individuals who see things differently.

Data analysis

Each of the transcripts from the individual case studies will be sorted into one of the three major groups of teachers noted above. Each group of transcripts will then be analysed using the 'inductive analysis' procedure outlined by Corbin and Strauss (2007). Also, the analysis will account for 'change-over-time', particularly through use of the notion of 'turnings' as the major transitions that an individual makes during the course of a life, and 'adaptations' as changes that have a major effect on a person's life and on one's basic relations with others.

Expected outcomes

The project will result in the following:

a an outline of the Australian Catholic educational world during the period 1940–1980, including a profile of the number of teaching religious and lay teachers classified according to non-religious order and religious order-managed schools (with the latter sub-classified according to order-type), the location of the schools, the physical and social environments of the locations, the school curricula imparted and the pedagogical practices adopted;

b (b)
48 individual oral histories based on the 'life stories' (Kotre 1984) of lay teachers who taught in Australian Catholic schools during the period 1940–1980 regarding how they understood and negotiated their working lives;

c an overall synthesis in the form of an historical analysis of the lives of lay teachers who taught in Australian Catholic schools during the period 1940–1980. The synthesis will be concerned with exploring not only whether the perspectives of the lay teachers changed, but also whether such change was influenced by their geographical, economic, social, and cultural working environments.

Benefit

Overall, the project will make a major contribution to understanding our region within the overlapping contexts of the Catholic and the educational world internationally. As well as filling a void in the literature on the social history of teaching in Catholic schools for the period in question, it will be of national benefit by:

1 developing an account of the impact of the professional and personal lives of lay teachers on shaping Catholic schools, the largest non-Government education sector in Australia;

2 providing insights into the ways of thinking of Catholic lay teachers, who have replaced teaching religious in the operation of Catholic education nationally;
3 contributing to understanding how changes in the Catholic Church internationally laid the foundations upon which contemporary thinking on Australian Catholic education takes place;
4 demonstrating Australia's capacity to respond to religious change of a global nature where it is not seen to undermine the pluralist state;
5 demonstrating how differences between the Catholic Church and the State were surmounted in the provision of lay-led denominational schooling, thus contributing to Australia's case aimed at highlighting its tradition of tolerance of 'difference', and facilitating the maintenance of security and harmony;
6 indicating that change in the personnel providing Catholic education over the period involved a replacement of the 'traditional' Catholic mind set of the religious with the post-Vatican 2 mind-set of Catholic lay personnel, and thus was not part of what some consider to have been a continuing secularisation of Australian society;
7 opening up the field for similar studies on other periods, and on teachers in State educational sectors, as well as on teachers in schools of other religious denominations.

Chapter 12

Research based on problem-focused proposals: Proposal no. 1

The previous chapters were concerned with research based upon 'concept-driven' ideas. The central concern in this chapter is with outlining a research proposal to illustrate how a symbolic interactionist theoretical position within the interpretivist paradigm can also be utilised to underpin research of the 'problem-focused' variety. Before examining the research proposal, however, it needs to be recognised that interpretivist research cannot accommodate research questions where one is searching for 'sure-fired' solutions to specific problems. The latter search tends to be the domain of those working within a positivist paradigm, particularly those who adopt an experimental methodology.

At the same time, it is arguable that the interpretivist paradigm has a crucial role to play in problem solving in a broader sense. Indeed, some would hold that the first task one needs to engage in when one sets out to consider how to approach what one perceives to be a problem, or set of related problems, is to develop a deeper understanding of the area. Broudy (1967) took up this point back in the 1960s in relation to problems which he characterised as belonging to the domain of education, although the position has applicability across the whole range of social issues and associated professions. His argument was that educationists should know not only how to do their job, but should also be conditioned by reflection. Sutherland (1985) argued along similar lines when she stated that society demands, and has a legitimate interest in demanding, that individuals who are working in the field of education should have their practical action properly conditioned by reflection. This was consistent with the rejection by Stanley (1968) of what he termed the 'craft mentality' in education when he contested the notion that educationists are mere practitioners operating within a system and according to procedures dictated by others. It was also consistent with Broudy's case for what he termed the 'interpretive use of knowledge'; a use that enables one to conceptualise and understand a problem or issue. Another way of stating the latter point specifically with regards to the field of education is that one should engage in studies of educational problems with the aim of coming to understand them within a framework which 'utilises the relationship of the school to the social order, and the aims, and the organisation, and the curriculum of the school of a particular society' (Broudy 1967: iv).

Overall, what one can distill from the arguments of those in sympathy with the position of educationists like Broudy is that there is a great need to engage in studies which allow one to gain a broad overview on educational problems. To hold this position is to be open to the possibility that what one considers in the initial stages to be a problem may strike one later on as not being a problem at all, while at this later stage also unforeseen problems may present themselves unexpectedly as being the 'real' ones in need of solutions. This was the nature of the thinking brought to bear by Dr Thida Kheang he embarked on preparing his PhD thesis proposal with myself and Professor Simon Clarke in the Graduate School of Education, The University of Western Australia.

Title

Leadership at the primary school level in post-conflict Cambodia: A study of the historical background, recent developments, and current concerns of school leaders

Project summary

The proposed study seeks to generate theory on leadership at the primary school level in post-conflict Cambodia. It will focus on three aspects of primary school leadership in Cambodia that are closely interrelated, namely, historical background, recent developments, and issues of current concern for primary school leaders.

Little is known about the nature of the context within which school leaders work in post-new war societies and in developing countries (Oplatka 2004). This study will be one contribution to filling the gap existing in the literature on educational leadership in those contexts. The study will also contribute to an understanding of the importance of considering context and its influence on leadership practices more generally, an area which has been largely neglected by scholars (Vroom and Jago 2007).

The proposed study will be interpretive in nature. It will employ qualitative methods of data collection and grounded theory methods of data analysis. Data collection methods will include semi-structured interviews, document analysis, and observations. Maximum variation selection and purposive selection are the strategies that will be used for the selection of schools and interview participants. Participants will comprise principals, deputy principals, and representatives of parent-teacher associations. Data will be analysed using grounded theory approaches.

The research aim

The proposed study seeks to generate theory on leadership at the primary school level in post-conflict Cambodia. It has three main aims:

1. To generate theory on the historical background to leadership at the primary school level in Cambodia from colonial times until 1998.

The reason behind the pursuit of this aim is that it is not easy to understand current school leadership in Cambodia without a clear understanding of how education in the nation has evolved over the years. A description and analysis of the background to primary school leadership during colonial times, and from independence until 1998, will be undertaken to achieve this aim.

2. To generate theory on the developments that have taken place in relation to leadership at the primary school level from the latest post-conflict era to the present.

Developments in relation to primary school leadership were set in train by the current political regime in Cambodia, which has been in power since 1998. As education reconstruction is one of the main priorities of a number of societies emerging from the identity-based conflict (Weldon 2010) that took place in the country, it is instructive to know what the Cambodia government has done in its efforts to develop education and, in particular, to shape primary school leadership.

3. To generate theory on the issues which are of current concern to primary school leaders and to investigate strategies adopted by them in order to deal with these issues.

Understanding issues which are of current concern to primary school leaders in Cambodia and investigating strategies adopted by them in order to deal with those issues can be of help in influencing education policy and guiding decision-making in Cambodia. Such understanding can be particularly helpful in developing professional development programmes for educational leaders in Cambodia. It can also be instructive to those working in other countries affected by conflict. This is not to say that this study will claim generalisability as in the case of research conducted within the positivist paradigm. Rather, it will lead to 'reader or user generalisability' (O'Donoghue 2007: 66). That is, readers will be able to relate to the study in order to understand their own and others' situations.

The study will also contribute to the body of knowledge on school leadership more broadly in post-conflict societies. The knowledge emanating from the study will help to inform future research on school leadership in post-conflict environments. It will also help to provide insights to guide and refine educational leadership practices (Watson 2009). This aligns with the point expressed by Harber and Dadey (1993) over 20 years ago when they argued that it is desirable to understand the issues and problems faced by school leaders operating in different contexts in order to design leadership development programmes to meet their real, rather than imagined, needs.

Particularly in relation to Cambodia, the proposed study has the potential to contribute substantially to knowledge in the field of educational leadership in the following ways:

- it can provide a broad historical background to primary school leadership in Cambodia;
- it can develop an understanding of the nature of the context within which school leaders work in post-conflict Cambodia and the strategies they use for dealing with the complexities of their work;
- it can inform school leadership preparation, development and support in Cambodia;
- it can provide a valuable framework for researchers wishing to engage in related studies on other levels within the education system of Cambodia and suggest developments for the future.

The research context

The terms 'post-conflict' and 'post-new war' are used interchangeably in this research proposal. While we often come across the term 'conflict' in popular media, or elsewhere, the term 'new war' is less widely used. This section distinguishes between 'new wars' and 'old wars'. Also, as the study will be undertaken in post-conflict Cambodia, it is important to understand why Cambodia qualifies as a post-new war society. An overview of the context within which education takes place in post-new war societies is also presented.

Old wars versus new wars

The terms 'old wars' and 'new wars' have been used in different ways by a number of political scientists. As a result, only the meaning assigned to these terms by Kaldor (2005) will be considered because it aligns with the context of the proposed study. 'Old war' refers to 'an idealised version of war that characterised Europe between the late eighteenth and the middle of the twentieth century'. An 'old war' is a war between states fought by armed forces in uniform, where the decisive encounter was battle (Kaldor 2005: 1). In addition, 'old wars' were state-building and contributed to the rise of the modern nation-state because states monopolised planned violence and eliminated private armies, or brigands, and established professional forces to subserve them. During 'old wars', the motto of the state was *protecto ergo obligo* (I protect therefore I am obeyed). Thus, the task of the state was to defend its people and territory against others in order to acquire legitimacy (Kaldor 2005). Furthermore, 'old wars', according to Kaldor (2005), followed, at least in theory, the rules set in the late nineteenth and early twentieth centuries at the Geneva and Hague Conventions. For example, the purpose of the Geneva rules was to minimise civilian casualties and to treat prisoners well. These rules were critical to establishing the wars' legitimacy. 'Old wars' reached their apex in the middle of the twentieth century. Since 1945, these wars have been rare (Kaldor 2005).

On the other hand, 'new wars' are wars that began in the second half of the twentieth century. In these wars, incumbents with economic superiority faced extremely persistent insurgents who sought to break their enemies' political will through demoralising and consistent attacks. 'New wars', Kaldor (2005: 2) adds, exacerbate the 'disintegration of the state through declines in GDP, loss of tax revenue, and loss of legitimacy'. They also build new sectarian identities (religious, ethnic, or tribal) that weaken the sense of a shared political community.

Although Kaldor's understanding of 'old wars' and 'new wars' received criticism related to the historical efficacy of her definitions, there is a need to understand that the distinction between them is not meant to be historically accurate in every detail. Rather, it helps our understanding of the context of what has been happening in post-new war societies and what we need to do about it (Kaldor 2005).

Cambodia as a post-new war society

Cambodia is an example of a post-new war society. Cambodia has been a country relying on foreign aid since the late 1960s when the Vietnam War affected the country and its influence led the country to pervasive civil war and brutal genocide (Phy 2009). The civil war and genocide taking place in the country can be understood within Kaldor's 'new war' theory. As earlier noted, Kaldor (2005) asserts that new wars occur in the context of the disintegration of authoritarian states under the impact of globalisation. The civil wars and genocide that happened in the late 1960s to 1980s in Cambodia depended greatly on transnational networks for support, finance and mobilisation. These transnational networks can be viewed as globalised forces which influenced the civil war and genocide in Cambodia. A coup d'etat against King Sihanouk by Commander Lon Nol was backed by the USA (Fergusson and Masson 1997). The Lon Nol government which was mainly dependent on the support from the USA continued to fight against the Viet Cong in early 1970s.

In 1975, the Khmer Rouge led by Pol Pot with strong financial and military support from China assumed power and the regime, strongly influenced by Maoist ideology, became the darkest page of Cambodian history in which millions of lives were claimed. It was assumed that in addition to military support, China provided USD100 million dollars to the Khmer Rouge. Phy (2009) concluded that civil war in Cambodia was indirectly caused by foreign aid, especially loans, which partly created corruption, particularly 'political corruption'. The author emphasised that corruption strongly affects the effectiveness of aid, leading to inequality of economic growth and chronic poverty, gradually making the country more fragile and prone to civil war. The intervention of those foreign supports indicates the role that globalisation played in the Cambodian crisis.

Kaldor (2005) points out that new wars may construct new sectarian identities leading to the loss of a shared political community. In Cambodia, the civil war intensified divisions between the Khmer Rouge and the Cambodian military supported by Vietnamese troop. Moreover, in the Cambodian conflict, civilian victimisation was deliberate instead of being a peripheral side effect of war. This is also a characteristic feature of new wars (Kaldor 2005).

Education in post-new war societies

According to the World Bank (2005: 13), conflict has a 'devastating impact on education, both in terms of the suffering and psychological impact on the pupils, teachers, and communities, and in the degradation of the education system and its infrastructure'. Yet, as the World Bank (2005) also holds, schools and education systems exhibit surprising resilience, and the perturbation caused by conflict provides opportunities as well as challenges for social and educational reconstruction.

Problems hampering the provision of education in post-new war societies may depend heavily on the extent of the damages and ravages caused by war. Nevertheless, there seem to be problems that are common to many post-conflict settings. These include the destruction of educational infrastructure and buildings, chronic shortages of qualified teachers, oversupply of under-qualified or unqualified teachers, and a good number of war-affected youth (World Bank 2005). Such problems call for a quick intervention by post-conflict governments aimed at reconstructing education (Weldon 2010). On this, the literature indicates that intervention aimed at reconstructing an education system in post-new war societies should target three broad areas that need special attention. The first area is that of physical reconstruction of school buildings (including emergency repair strategies, the needs of refugee education, and landmine safety issues). The second area that needs special attention is that of ideological reconstruction. This refers to democratisation of the education system and retraining of teachers. The third area that needs special attention is that of psychological reconstruction that responds to issues of 'demoralisation, loss of confidence and health-related issues of stress and depression' (Smith 2005: 384). Education for reconciliation, social repair and peace building, which is also a priority in post-conflict societies, should be reflected in the ideological and psychological reconstruction initiatives. Moreover, the psychological and ideological reconstruction areas are the most problematic and thus necessitate a much more thoughtful and careful intervention, than does the physical reconstruction process (Weinstein et al. 2007).

Notwithstanding the above call for intervention, some scholars argue that the voices of those most affected by conflict (including children, parents, teachers, and school leaders) are rarely heard in the education reconstruction process (Weinstein et al. 2007). Also, school policies and curriculum reforms devised by government officials and international agencies in post-conflict societies have often lacked sensitivity to the local school context. On this, Weinstein *et al.* (2007: 42) go on to say that 'educational change after mass violence suffers from untested assumptions, a dearth of focused research, a gap between broad concepts and practice in the field'. This situation suggests that education in post-new war societies is mainly informed by theoretical assumptions rather than by practices based on rigorous research evidence. This observation is especially pertinent to educational leadership in post-conflict settings.

Overview of the literature

In the past 20 years, most of the educational leadership research has been conducted in highly and/or relatively stable societies and has provided insights into school culture and change management (Fullan 2001; Hargreaves and Fullan 1992), the impact of school leadership on student achievement (Leithwood et al. 2004), and the extremely important role of the principal in the overall running of the school (Huber and West 2002). However, educational leadership at the individual school level in post-conflict societies has largely been ignored as a subject of academic research. A review of the literature on educational leadership in post-conflict settings indicates that very little empirical research has been undertaken at an international level into how school leaders in such contexts conceptualise their work.

The lack of attention devoted to school leadership in post-conflict situations is partly attributable to the neglect by scholars of the importance of considering context and its influence on leadership practices. Indeed, the role of contextual influences in informing leadership practice has seldom been taken into account. As Vroom and Jago (2007: 22) have argued, 'the field of leadership has identified more closely with the field of individual differences and has largely ignored the way the behavior of leaders is influenced by the situations they encounter'.

The premise underpinning the proposed study is that leadership is context-bound (Clarke and Wildy 2004). It is also assumed that the benefit of viewing leadership within this framework lies in its response to the diversity of school contexts and the unique circumstantial challenges and problems which schools face (O'Donoghue and Clarke 2010).

Even though the literature specifically connected with school leadership in post-conflict societies is scarce, some work has been undertaken that focuses on the relationship between education and conflict. Indeed, this is an emerging and pressing area of inquiry (Paulson and Rappleye 2007; Smith 2005) which bears various names, such as 'education and fragility', and 'education and insecurity' (Paulson 2011). Scholars and practitioners in the area have highlighted the role of education in contributing to, and fuelling, violent conflict (Hilker 2011; King 2005), as well as the importance of quality education for peacebuilding, reconciliation, and post-conflict reconstruction and development (Acedo 2011; Hodgkin 2006; Paulson 2011). At the same time, some scholars argue that work being undertaken in the field lacks rigorous research evidence as insights simply emerge from the delivery and evaluation of educational programmes in societies ruined by conflict (Paulson 2011). Consequently, there is a call for more critically informed and policy relevant research in this emerging area of inquiry (Novelli and Lopez Cardizo 2008).

In the specific literature on Cambodia, there exist very few empirical studies focused specifically on educational leadership in the post-conflict era. Pellini (2005) conducted a study entitled *Decentralization of Education in Cambodia: searching for spaces between tradition and modernity* which analysed participation of community in Cambodian schools, putting emphasis on the room for participation and school cluster approach adopted as a means of decentralisation of education in Cambodia. The thesis by Lim (2008), *Analysis of Principals' Instructional Leadership Behaviours in Selected Cambodian Secondary Schools*, analysed the instructional leadership behaviours of secondary school principals in Phnom Penh to see the extent to which they apply instructional practices in their daily work, looking from the perspectives of teachers and principals. The comparison between the actual practice and those suggested by the Ministry of Education, Youth and Sport was also made. Another study is that of Kheang (2011) entitled *Exploring the Implementation of School-Based Management in Cambodia: A Multiple Case Study*. It investigated the implementation of school-based management at primary level and examined how leadership influences the implementation process of school-based management. A more focused school leadership study is of Sam (2011) who conducted a study entitled *Leadership Capacities and Development of Effective Primary School Principals in Cambodia: A Case Study of Kampong Chhnang Province*. The study basically was designed to address the challenges confronted by the effective principals; leadership capacities considered most important for their performance and resources and strategies considered most effective for capacity building.

Notwithstanding the lack of empirical research on educational leadership in post-conflict Cambodia, some empirical studies that have focused on education more broadly in this context do exist. Dy and Ninomiya (2003) examined the process of development and change in basic education in Cambodia. This study, which was particularly focused on the review of educational policies and strategies initiated and implemented in the 1990s and the exploration of the impacts of UNESCO in basic education as well as the study of success and failure of the education reform in Cambodia, revealed that the government policies and strategies aimed at restructuring education and contributions from UNESCO made significant impacts on the improvement of basic education. Dy (2004) studied the development of education in Cambodia from historical perspectives. He concluded that social and political factors in the past decades greatly impacted the education system and the Sihanouk Regime was considered as the most glorious period for education development in Cambodian history whereas the Khmer Rouge took the education system down to zero. Similarly, Chin and Dy (2009) investigated the education reform context and process in Cambodia and noted the significant progress made by the government in improving the education sector, in particular physical infrastructures and access to education. However, the study observed a lack of the political will and commitment to adequately allocate budget funds for the education development, which has left the quality of education suffering. A similar finding on the failure of the government to take account of comprehensive education reform in order to improve quality of education is affirmed by Keng (2009) who examined the quality and equity of basic education in Cambodia. However, no research project has investigated the historical background to primary school leadership in Cambodia from colonial times until 1998, developments in primary school leadership there since then, and the concerns of primary school leaders and the strategies they use to deal with those concerns in post-conflict Cambodia.

The research plan

The following central research questions have been developed from the three aims of the study and they have also guided the choice of the research methodology:

- What is the historical background to primary school leadership in Cambodia from colonial times until 1998?
- What developments have taken place in relation to primary school leadership from the latest post-conflict era to the present?
- What issues are currently of concern to primary school leaders, and how do they deal with them?

Theoretical framework

The nature of the research questions requires a method of inquiry that enables interpretation of social phenomena (O'Donoghue 2007). In order to meet this requirement, the interpretivist paradigm has been selected to underpin the proposed study. The term paradigm here refers to a set of assumptions about the world, and what constitute proper methods for investigating that world (Punch 2009).

The proposed study falls within the interpretivist paradigm because it seeks to reveal the meanings people assign to situations and behaviour, and which they use to understand their world (O'Donoghue 2007). Interpretivists believe that human and social actions have meanings and have to be interpreted and understood within the context of social practices. Understanding these meanings that are constructed through interaction between human beings facilitates an understanding of social reality and phenomena (O'Donoghue 2007). Adopting an interpretivist paradigm necessitates that the researcher will be interested in subjective meanings of reality, namely, the way in which individuals make sense of their world and the way in which they attribute meanings to it (Sarantakos 2005).

Within the overall paradigm of interpretivism, symbolic interactionism is the specific theoretical position that will inform the study. Blumer (1969: 2, 5) identifies five principles of symbolic interactionism:

1 Human beings act towards things on the basis of the meanings that these things have for them.
2 The meanings of such things are derived from, and arise out of, the social interaction that one has with one's fellows.
3 These meanings are handled in, and modified through, an interpretive process used by the person in dealing with the things he [*sic*] encounters.
4 The actor selects, checks, suspends, regroups, and transforms the meanings in light of the situation, in which he [*sic*] is placed at the direction of his action.
5 Meanings are used and revised as instruments for the guidance and formation of the action.

The symbolic interactionist theoretical approach is appropriate for the proposed study because it will allow the researcher to uncover meanings that individuals (school leaders) attach to such 'things' as people, institutions, concepts, policies, and how these meanings influence their actions (O'Donoghue 2007). Considered in terms of the specific focus of the study, school leaders, according to symbolic interactionist principles, acquire meaning from their own experience of leading schools. Furthermore, because they are constantly interacting with the world that meaning may be confirmed, transformed, reinforced, or changed in light of the school context (O'Donoghue 2007).

Elaboration on the central research questions

The proposed study will focus on three aspects of primary school leadership in Cambodia that are closely interrelated, namely, historical background, recent developments, and issues of current concern for primary school leaders.

The study will be informed by the following three research questions.

The first research question

WHAT IS THE HISTORICAL BACKGROUND TO PRIMARY SCHOOL LEADERSHIP IN CAMBODIA FROM COLONIAL TIMES UNTIL 1998?

This first research question of the proposed study is aimed at generating theory on the historical background to leadership at the primary school level in Cambodia. It will be primarily addressed through an analysis of sources contained in a wide range of public and private records and documents. The interpretivist research paradigm will be used to guide the work of the researcher in reviewing these sources.

As the study is exploratory in nature, it would be impossible to determine ahead of the empirical work the total specific research questions needed to guide the research in relation to this first research question. The following questions, however, have been designed to guide the initial collection of data.

Guiding research questions

1 What policies and practices did the Cambodia education authorities implement to establish primary school leadership from colonial times until 1998?
2 What were the influences that shaped primary school leadership in Cambodia from colonial times until 1998?
3 What are the continuities and changes that can be perceived to have existed in primary school leadership in Cambodia from colonial times until 1998?
4 When and why did changes occur in primary school leadership up to 1998, and who/what influenced these changes?
5 Under what conditions were primary schools led in Cambodia from colonial times until 1998?
6 What were the perceived advantages and disadvantages between different approaches to primary school leadership from colonial times until 1998?

The second research question

WHAT DEVELOPMENTS HAVE TAKEN PLACE IN RELATION TO PRIMARY SCHOOL LEADERSHIP FROM THE LATEST POST-CONFLICT ERA TO THE PRESENT?

The second research question of the proposed study is aimed at generating theory on the developments that have taken place in relation to primary school leadership in Cambodia since 1998. This question will be also addressed through the analysis of a wide range of contemporary documents and public records, supplemented by individual interviews.

Again, as the study is exploratory, it is impossible to outline at this early stage an exhaustive list of specific research questions to be answered. However, the following guiding questions, derived from the second central research question, will inform the initial data collection process.

Guiding research questions

1 What policies and practices has post-conflict Cambodia implemented that have led to the current situation regarding primary school leadership?
2 What have been the reasons behind, and influences on, the policies and practices implemented to establish current primary school leadership?
3 What continuities can be perceived to exist between pre-conflict primary school leadership and current primary school leadership in Cambodia?
4 What are the changes that can be perceived to exist between pre-conflict primary school leadership and current primary school leadership in Cambodia?
5 When and why did changes occur in primary school leadership from the latest post-conflict era to the present, and who/what influenced these changes?
6 What are the advantages and disadvantages that key stakeholders have identified between pre-conflict primary school leadership and current primary school leadership in Cambodia?

The third research question

WHAT ISSUES ARE CURRENTLY OF CONCERN TO PRIMARY SCHOOL LEADERS, AND HOW DO THEY DEAL WITH THEM?

The third research question of the proposed study is aimed at generating theory on the issues that are of current concern to primary school leaders in Cambodia. The strategies adopted by these leaders to deal with those issues will also be investigated. Issues are taken as matters affecting, or having an impact on, people in their everyday lives; they are matters that interest individuals, or capture their attention, because they are important or affect them.

In addressing the third research question, individual and group interviews will be conducted. The following guiding questions, linked to the third research question, will guide the data collection process:

1 What aims do school leaders have in their performing of their work? What reasons do they give for having these aims? What challenges do they face in trying to realise their aims?
2 What are the strategies that school leaders adopt in trying to realise their aims? What reasons do they give for adopting these strategies? What challenges do they face in adopting them?
3 What significance to the principals attach to their aims and strategies? What reasons do they give for their position on this? What challenges do they face in trying to maintain this position?
4 What outcomes do the principals expect from pursuing their aims and strategies? What reasons do they give for expecting these outcomes? What challenges do they face in trying to realise them?
5 What is the nature of the context within which the principals work which influence them in their work and which provide them with challenges?

Selecting participants

Purposive selection will be used for the selection of participants for interviewing in relation to research questions two and three. Purposive selection is selection with a specific purpose in mind (Punch 2009). The participants will consist of principals, deputy principals, and representatives of School Support Committee (SSC) from eight schools. Principals and deputy principals will be interviewed because they are in the best position to report on the current concerns of school leaders. They are also in the best position to communicate the developments that have taken place in relation to primary school leadership. SSC representatives will be selected because of their pivotal role in collaborating with schools and because of their role in representing the views of the community and parents about the education of their children. Various concerned representatives at district, provincial, and ministerial level will also interviewed to gain wider views on the development of school leadership. They are selected because they are in a good position to inform the development related to primary school leadership taking place.

Three participants (the principal, deputy principal, and a SSC representative) will be selected from each school and one respondent from district, provincial, and ministerial level. Thus, the total number of participants will be 27. To ensure for diversity in participants' perspectives, selection will ensure that a broad range of characteristics is represented, such as the experience and gender of the principal, deputy principal, SSC representative, and education officers at all levels.

Selection of schools

The selection of schools will also be purposive (Punch, 2009). This means that schools will be selected with a specific purpose in mind. Size and location of the school are significant. Having a variety of locations and school sizes will enable the researcher to uncover as wide a scope of perspectives as possible.

Consistent with the maximum variation selection strategy (Punch 2009), four schools will be selected from the capital city and provincial town and four other schools will be selected from a rural/remote area within the country. With regards to the school size, both small and large schools in the urban and rural schools will be selected. The categorisation of schools as small or large will be based on the number of students in the school (Anderson et al. 2010).

Data collection

Data collection methods will include semi-structured interviews, document analysis, and observations. These data-gathering methods are most appropriate for a study adopting a symbolic interactionist theoretical approach within the interpretivist paradigm (O'Donoghue 2007). Data will largely be obtained by means of a thorough document analysis for the first research question and by means of document analysis supplemented by interviews for the second research question. The third research question will be investigated exclusively by means of interviews with principals, deputy principals, and SSC representatives. On-site observations will also be used as another source of data for the study.

Interviews

An interview is an appropriate data-collection method for the proposed study because it enables researchers to gain access to 'people's perceptions, meaning, definitions of situations and constructions of reality' (Punch 2009: 144). Semi-structured in-depth interviews will be used as tools of data collection for research questions two and three. A semi-structured interview is the most suitable data-gathering tool for a study aimed at investigating the perspectives of people on a phenomenon (O'Donoghue 2007). This type of interview is flexible and focuses on how the interviewees understand events and issues (Bryman 2004).

Semi-structured interviews will be conducted with each of the three participants in each school. As eight schools will be selected the total number of individual interviews will be 24. Individual interviews will be followed by eight group interviews; that is, one group interview with three participants (principal, deputy principal, and a SSC representative) at each school. Also, separate semi-interview will be applied to the three officers from district, provincial, and ministerial levels. The purpose of group interview is to search for further insights to supplement data obtained through individual interviews. Each interview will be tape-recorded. The tape will then be transcribed to begin data analysis. Where recording will not be authorised by participants, field notes will be made. An *aide memoire*, or interview guide, will be developed to assist with interviews and will be given to participants a week before the actual interview in order to gain greater 'flexibility in the conduct of interview' (Bryman 2004: 324).

Document study

Researchers 'study documents as much as, if not more than, people' (Sarantakos 2005: 293). On this, Punch (2009) supports the study of documents by explaining that 'documents, both historical and contemporary, are a rich source of data for education and social research' (p. 158). The researcher will study relevant documents in order to know what is going on, or what has taken place. The documents that will be analysed include public records such as Ministry of Education, Youth and Sport documents, governmental and non-governmental documents, school-related documents in districts, and minutes of school meetings. Academic papers, conference papers, newspapers, and any other document containing information about the historical background to, and recent developments in, primary school leadership in Cambodia will also be analysed.

Unstructured non-participant observation

In a non-participant observation, the researcher studies participants, or settings, from the 'outside' (Sarantakos 2005), while in an unstructured observation, the researcher does not use pre-specified categories and explores the setting or participants' perspectives and actions in a natural open-ended way (Punch 2009). Unstructured non-participant observation will be employed as a means to check, or verify, interview data, and to stimulate further data-gathering questions.

Data analysis

Grounded theory methods of data analysis will be employed in the study. Grounded theory analysis emphasises 'the conceptualisation of the data, and the generation of conceptually abstract categories grounded in the data' (Punch 1998: 218). It is undertaken by reducing raw data into concepts that are designated to stand for categories (Punch 2000). The concepts are inductively inferred from the data.

This inductive inference is referred to as the process of abstraction (Punch 1998). The outcome of grounded theory analysis is a set of propositions showing connections between concepts which are more abstract than the data themselves (Punch 1998).

In accordance with the interpretivist research approach, data collection and analysis will be undertaken concurrently (Strauss and Corbin 1990). Conducting data analysis during data collection helps the researcher ensure that one undertakes an effective coverage of the research topic (Sarantakos 2005). Analysis will begin immediately after the collection of the first set of data and after transcribing the first interview. The interview transcripts will be supplemented by observer notes and comments in order to analyse the context within which primary school leaders work.

Grounded theory analysis uses three coding methods, namely, open coding, axial coding, and selective coding (Punch 2009). It is planned that the first stage of grounded theory analysis, open coding, will be used to commence data analysis. Then, the 'open-coded' data will be further analysed using the 'analytic induction' technique.

Open coding

Open coding is concerned with 'fracturing', or 'breaking open', the data to generate conceptual labels and categories for use in theory building. The purpose is to use data to 'generate conceptual categories in the data, at a first level of abstraction' (Punch 2009: 183). These categories are called substantive codes and are more abstract than the data they describe (Punch 2009). At the beginning of analysis, different pieces of data will be constantly compared with each other to help generate abstract categories. This comparison will be done concurrently with 'asking questions about which more abstract concept the piece of empirical data indicates' (Punch 2009: 184). This questioning will enable the researcher to find the theoretical possibilities that are suggested by the data. The developed categories will be tested against the data to ensure they are empirically grounded (Punch 2009; Sarantakos 2005). The relationship between concepts and categories emerging from the data will be illustrated using codes, memos, and diagrams.

After completing open coding, a mode of data analysis called analytic induction will be used. Analytic induction is aimed at producing 'complete and universal statements about social phenomenon' (Sarantakos 2005: 351). The analytic induction technique will therefore lead to the formulation of general statements or propositions in relation to the three research questions.

Chapter 13

Research based on problem-focused proposals: Proposal no. 2

This chapter presents the second proposal illustrating how a symbolic interactionist theoretical position within the interpretivist paradigm can also be utilised to underpin research of the 'problem-focused' variety. This time, the proposal relates to recent changes in the education system in Serbia. It was prepared by Dr. Jelena Rakovic when she embarked on preparing for her PhD studies with myself and Professor Simon Clarke in the Graduate School of Education, The University of Western Australia.

Title

Primary school leadership in a society in transition: A study of the historical background, recent developments, and current concerns of primary school leaders in Serbia

Project summary

Serbia is a post-communist country in Southeast Europe. It is in transition from communism to democracy and working towards integration into the European Union (EU). Furthermore, since 2001, the education system in Serbia has been undergoing change based on the principles of decentralisation and democratisation. This requires a move away from the inherited education system which was based on centralisation and the communist ideology.

When it comes to Serbia's education change, school leaders are in a particularly challenging position, since they are the ones who need to both understand and implement what is required. They are, on the one hand, influenced by the requirements of the education policy and, on the other hand, by school practices from the communist era. The study being proposed here is a response to this observation. It aims to investigate the historical background to primary school leadership in Serbia from the days of the communist era up to the recent embracement of democracy, the developments which have taken place in relation to primary school leadership during the current stage of transition, and the issues that are currently of concern to primary school leaders in Serbia, and how they deal with them.

The study is conceptualised within the interpretivist paradigm, using grounded theory approaches to data gathering and analysis. Documents will be the primary sources of data for studying the historical and contemporary context, and interview transcripts will constitute the main data for analysing the perspective of school leaders on issues of concern. The research findings will be used to inform Serbian school leadership policy, as well as principal preparation and development, and will also provide a basis for further research projects to be conducted on educational leadership in Serbia.

The background

Major changes have occurred throughout human history that have significantly transformed the economic, cultural, and political systems in society. Some important European examples in the last three hundred years include the French Revolution (1789–1799), the Spanish Civil War (1936–1939), and the Russian Revolution of 1917. More recently, after the fall of the Berlin Wall in 1989, post-communist European societies have been transitioning from communism to democracies during what some term as a 'return to Europe'. Among the most challenging and violent transformations that have been taking place in this regard have been those of the Former Yugoslavia, which have been influenced by nationalism, ethnic conflict, and economic hardship.

Serbia is one of the successor countries of the Socialist Federal Republic of Yugoslavia (SFRY) that is seeking to restructure its political, social, and economic systems in order to eventually become a part of the EU. Indeed, the quest for membership of the EU has been the single most important factor in driving change within the country (Bideleux and Jeffries 2007). EU accession requires a transformation from the former communist societal organisation to a democratic one. More specifically, the process of joining the EU is based on meeting a number of prerequisites associated with the economy, trade, education, environment, quality indicators, effectiveness and efficiency (Nicolaidou 2008). By accepting to pursue the changes required by the EU accession criteria, Serbia is attempting to participate in the global and European knowledge economy and society.

Since the collapse of the Berlin Wall in 1989, the processes of globalisation and regionalisation have become major forces in Europe as it responds to the developments in knowledge, learning, new communication technologies, and social inclusion (Dale 2009a). In order to keep up with associated trends, economic competitiveness is seen as being essential; Europe's relatively poor level of competitiveness is perceived to be a major threat to its future success (Dale 2009b). This is an important reason why the EU strives to become competitive enough to thrive in the global economy. It is also the reason Serbia strives to become competitive enough to join the EU.

Across the EU, as well as in individual member and aspiring countries, development of education is seen as one of the crucial elements in attaining the desired level of competiveness. On this, education, training, and research are regarded as the driving forces for economic development and social cohesion for the creation of a knowledge society (Nicolaidou 2008). Indeed, education is thought to have the potential to make the EU the most competitive knowledge society in the world (Clarke and Wildy 2009). This attitude contributed to a recently renewed emphasis on changing education systems in Europe, as exemplified in the European Commission's 'Europe 2020' policy, which features education prominently as a priority for developing an economy based on knowledge and innovation (Alexiadou 2014).

As a country aspiring to join the EU, Serbia has responded to these trends with an education 2020 policy of its own. This policy points to the need to develop and improve the country's education system in order to boost employment and create conditions for the development of the knowledge society (MoE/RS 2012). The policy also emphasises that failing to harmonise the education system in Serbia with EU requirements will marginalise the country, as it will not be competitive enough to attract foreign capital, and not be able to develop a democratic social structure (MoE/RS 2012).

The EU-inspired education changes are being implemented in a system inherited from communist Yugoslavia that was largely based on the Soviet model of education. This model taught the existence of a single universal truth and addressed the importance of having the same curricula and textbooks for everyone (Bîrsea 1994). The acquisition of factual information and its practical application in predetermined settings was emphasised. The argument was that when the economy is planned, the objective is to train the work force for a predetermined set of skills the society anticipates it will need (Heyneman 1998). In contrast, democratic models of education were seen as promoting cultural, political ideological, and religious pluralism through tailor-made curricula and textbooks (Bîrsea 1994), the objective being to train individuals to adapt to changing conditions because, in market economies, the future is uncertain (Heyneman 1998).

In making the change from one system to the other, a main problem for Serbia has been in overcoming the inherited system. This is not surprising since education change can be a complicated and challenging task. For one thing, the meaning of 'education' can vary considerably across countries and peoples, and can be tightly linked to notions of identity, ethnicity, history, civilisation, and culture (Nicolaidou 2008). Thus, people who are implementing change need to be both objects and agents of change in order for the change to happen.

Specifically, for the Serbian education context, school leaders, and particularly, school principals, are the ones who have to deal with the clash between the two systems, and implement the changes in practice. They are positioned between pressures from current education policy and inherited education practice. In other words, attempting to understand and implement changes within a context that is shifting constantly, school leaders are located in a challenging position between two opposing views of society, while also being positioned between the rhetoric on education and the school realities.

This posits various challenges for education researchers. The study proposed here is one response to these challenges. It seeks to better understand the position of school leaders in the Serbian education system by studying the historical background of the Yugoslav communist education system, recent education developments, and current concerns of education leaders at the school level in times of EU-inspired education changes. The intention is that an understanding of the inherited education context, contemporary influences and concerns of school leaders will prove valuable in inferring policies and plans for future directions.

Research aim

The research problem identified points to the main aim of the research which is to generate theory on leadership at the primary school level in Serbia, a country transitioning from communism to democracy. In order to accomplish this main research aim, it is necessary to generate theory on:

a. The historical background to primary school leadership in Serbia from the days of the communist era up to the recent embracement of democracy.

Generating theory on the historical background to primary school leadership in the Serbian context will facilitate understanding of the previous education system. This is important as it informs the current context. The understanding generated will point to related areas of tension that current school leaders may be experiencing.

b. The developments which have taken place in relation to primary school leadership during the current stage of transition.

Generating theory on the recent developments in primary school leadership in Serbia will provide a description and an explanation of the EU-inspired changes that are being implemented in the country. By understanding the elements of the current changes that are shaping primary school leadership in transition, it should be possible to uncover influences on current school leaders as they implement the changes.

c. The issues that are currently of concern to primary school leaders in Serbia, and how they deal with them.

Generating theory on the current concerns of primary school leaders in Serbia will uncover the issues and challenges they face in moving from one system to another, as well as the strategies they use to deal with various pressures and their own changing roles.

Central research questions

The concerns addressed by the aims of the study point to the following central research questions:

- What is the historical background to primary school leadership in Serbia from the days of the communist era up to the recent embracement of democracy?
- What developments have taken place in relation to primary school leadership during the current stage of transition?
- What issues are currently of concern to primary school leaders in Serbia, and how do they deal with them?

Significance of the research

The focus of the research is on school leadership at the primary school level because of its important position in the implementation of education changes in Serbia and because of its potential to positively affect students' learning through improved classroom practice. More specifically, education policy and decision-making in Serbia will benefit from being informed on the issues that are of current concern to primary school leaders, as well as on the strategies adopted by them in order to deal with those issues. Moreover, such understanding can also be of help in creating programmes for preparation, professional development, and support of primary school leaders in Serbia resulting in the improvement of education practice at the school level. Finally, future research on school leadership in transitioning contexts can be informed by the findings of the proposed research to be carried out in the Serbian context.

Background literature

It is necessary to locate the three research questions within the scholarly literature, as well as in terms of context. A starting point is to recall that the two most important influences that currently act to shape the education context in Serbia are the EU-inspired democratic education changes and the previous communist education system.

As far as the EU-inspired changes are concerned, the concept of school leadership is undergoing change in the country as the Serbian education system moves from a communist-based one to a democratic-based one. The European concept of school leadership is democratic in nature and aligned with the democratic purposes guiding the work of the EU (Clarke and Wildy 2009). An important element in the European approach to educational leadership is the concept of distributed leadership (Clarke and Wildy 2009). It is a concept new to the Serbian education system and it is based on the European democratic values that are being adopted through the changes.

The underlying democratic values promoted through the concept of distributed school leadership are based on the values of a democratic society. Consequently, distributed leadership is characterised by individual autonomy, participation, collective engagement, and change and development (Jones 2014). It is a collective activity that blurs the boundaries between traditionally-defined organisational roles by redistributing power and responsibility towards those who hold expertise (Watson 2009). Distributed leadership enables a range of people to be acknowledged for their expertise and to influence change, and it contributes to functional change because it takes local contexts and cultures into account (Jones 2014). Also, the democratic values of individuality, engagement, participation, and context-bound development are promoted through the concept of distributed leadership.

Distributed leadership is not a separate leadership model and it cannot be developed into a model that is easily implementable. Rather, it is considered an addition to the formal leadership structures (Jones 2014). In particular, the concept is generally used to underpin various approaches to capacity-building in schools (Watson 2009). It focuses on the intellectual and social capital that leaders need to harness, focus, liberate and empower, while building and releasing capacity (O'Donoghue and Clarke 2010). In other words, distributed leadership is seen as a means to improve schools in their contexts, instead of prescribing a specific leadership model to follow.

A major challenge in implementing distributed leadership in schools is that the concept contradicts the hierarchical systems of school governance which dominate school education systems (Watson 2009). Decentralising school governance and transforming the way schools are run changes the roles and responsibilities of school leaders (Nicolaidou 2008). School leaders are suddenly not only responsible for running a school according to policy rules and regulations, they are also expected to motivate, develop, support, manage budgets and staff, and foster links with the broader community (Nicolaidou 2008). Associated shifts in education governance towards decentralisation seem to be making new professional demands on school leaders and placing more responsibility on them.

When it comes to post-communist contexts, changing the focus from centralisation to decentralisation may not be readily acceptable to leaders and practitioners due to the fact that education systems in such contexts are still heavily centralised. Certainly, school principals are well skilled in managing tasks set by the central authority and they place lower priority on relationship building and developing visions or strategic plans for their schools (Magno 2009). Moreover, school leaders are influenced by the past and find it difficult to break old habits (Goddard 2007), so the inherited practices can remain relatively stable over an extended period of time, even as change is occurring (Melville et al. 2014). On this, O'Donoghue and Clarke (2010) argue that, since the inherited practices are an essential part of the cultural context, it is of vital importance to consider context in attempting to implement Western models of thought and action.

In communist Yugoslavia, the position of school leaders depended on the social order that gradually changed over time. At first the education system was heavily centralised, but as the societal system changed from communism to self-management and market socialism, the education system became decentralised (Ristanović 1981; Tot 1966, 1974). Concurrently, the role of school leaders changed from that of being supervisors and controllers who represented the centralised government to becoming managers and facilitators who needed to respect the teachers' views in decision-making (Tot 1966). Since the inherited context in Serbia retains elements of decentralisation as well as centralisation, one might conclude that such a background has made it easier to change the system towards a democratic decentralised system in the process of current changes.

However, research on school leadership in Serbia shows this not to be the case. Rather, it shows school principals under pressure from the dramatic transitional changes that have brought more responsibility to the school than it used to have (Andevski 2004). It shows them struggling to understand and adapt to the tasks which go beyond traditional activities (Andevski and Dudjak 2011). It also shows that they are overwhelmed by responsibility and believe that change is not worth the effort, especially when taking into account the circumstances under which they work. The working conditions of school leaders in Serbia are often ruled by negative selection, corruption, nepotism, and political affiliation (Andevski and Arsenijević 2012). In such a context, it is required of them to create opportunities for school improvement and inspire staff to take responsibility and carry out change (Andevski and Dudjak 2011). The pressure induced by these change proposals has left school leaders struggling with additional responsibility and adapting to new professional demands in a changing and challenging context that relies on them for inspiring and leading the change.

The challenges in Serbian school leadership have also had an effect on education policy development in Serbia. It is recognised that school principals in the country are highly educated, but that the area in which they lack expertise is in the practical managerial skills needed by the modern school (Sajfert et al. 2009). In order to contribute to improvement in the quality of school management, the Ministry of Education has recently adopted competency standards of school principals which deal with leading the learning and teaching in schools, cooperation with parents, planning organisation and control, development and leading human resources, the law, and financial and administrative management (Manojlović et al. 2013). The perceived lack of managerial skills needed for school improvement within the current changes has also inspired research into how the characteristics of school leaders in Serbia match the characteristics required by the democratic education changes.

Research on school leadership in Serbia also indicates that school principals struggle with the democratic changes of the education system, as well as with the implementation of the concept of distributed leadership. On this, there have been a few quantitative studies looking at the ability of Serbian school employees to adapt to democratic educational structures and distribute leadership potential amongst their staff (Andevski and Arsenijević 2012; Andevski et al. 2012). The results show a lack of democratic orientation, especially when compared to school principals in Croatia, probably due to the fact that the Croatian system had been democratised to a higher degree than that in Serbia before it joined the EU (Andevski et al. 2012).

No empirical studies, however, have looked in depth at the issues school leaders face in implementing national policy, nor have they investigated the strategies school leaders use to deal with such issues. Similarly, no studies have examined the inherited communist system and analysed it in relation to the EU-inspired changes in order to try to understand school leaders' issues. The proposed research responds to this situation. It will deal with the complex position of the school leaders in Serbia that places them between two social systems (communism and democracy) and two levels of pressures in education (education policy and school practice). Additionally, comparing the current school leaders' position to that in the previous era, as well as to the one envisioned for them by the education changes, will also shed light on the issues they face and how they deal with them.

The research plan

Considering the nature of research problem, which is to seek to understand the position of the Serbian school leaders in times of education and societal changes, a qualitative research approach based on the interpretivist paradigm was deemed appropriate (O'Donoghue 2007). This is so because the emphasis in the study is on revealing the meanings people assign to situations and actions, and thus on understanding their world (O'Donoghue 2007). Basic assumption of interpretivism is that individuals seek understanding of the world in which they live and work and develop meanings regarding their experiences through interacting with others (Creswell 2013; Densin and Lincoln 2011; Schwandt 2003). In other words, knowledge is constructed by social interaction and mutual negotiation and it is specific to the situation being investigated (Lincoln and Guba 2003; O'Donoghue 2007). Understanding the meanings constructed through interaction facilitates an understanding of social reality and phenomena (O'Donoghue 2007).

The goal of interpretivist research is to make sense of, or interpret, the meanings others have about the world by focusing on the specific contexts and historical and cultural settings of the participants (Creswell 2013). The researcher uses his or her skills as a social being to try to understand how others understand their world (O'Donoghue 2007) in order to understand and explain human and social reality (Crotty 1998).

Within the overall paradigm of interpretivism, symbolic interactionism is the specific theoretical position that will make it possible to focus on the importance of reality as people perceive it (O'Donoghue 2007). The focus is on the participants' perspectives, the actions they take in the light of their perspectives, and the patterns which develop through the interaction of perspectives and actions over particular periods of time (O'Donoghue 2007). Not only by focusing on school leaders' perspectives, but also on their actions and patterns of action in response to their perspectives, it will be possible to uncover the issues they face as well as how they deal with them in times of education changes.

Symbolic interactionism is intimately related to the method of theory construction known as grounded theory, a process of inductive theory building based squarely on observation of data (Birks 2011; Crotty 1998; Oktay 2012). There is a major focus on trying to generate theory about process (O'Donoghue 2007). The inquirer generates a general explanation, a theory, from the data itself (Bryant 2007; Creswell 2013). Grounded theory is a strategy for engaging in both research and data analysis (Punch 2009). Grounded theory makes it possible to identify research problems from professional practice and from organisational and institutional contexts (Punch 2009).

Elaboration on the central research questions

The proposed research centres on the complex position of school leaders in Serbia being located between two social systems (communism and democracy) and two levels of pressures in education (education policy and school practice). In order to understand the issues school leaders' face and the strategies they develop for facing those issues, it is necessary to compare the current school leaders' position to the one in the previous era, as well as to the one currently envisioned for them by the education changes. Therefore, there are three interrelated aspects of the research area to be addressed, namely, the historical background, recent developments, and issues of current concern for primary school leaders.

The first research question

WHAT IS THE HISTORICAL BACKGROUND TO PRIMARY SCHOOL LEADERSHIP IN SERBIA FROM THE COMMUNIST ERA TO THE COMMENCEMENT OF THE ERA OF TRANSITION?

This research question will guide inquiry into the historical background to primary school leadership in Serbia in order to understand the previous education system that forms an important part of the current context and plays a part in shaping the way school leaders understand the education changes and their implementation. The following guiding questions have been designed to assist the research into the historical background to primary school leadership in Serbia:

1 What policies and practices did the Serbian education authorities implement to establish primary school leadership in the communist era?
2 What were the influences that shaped primary school leadership during this era?
3 What are the continuities and changes that can be perceived to have existed in primary school leadership in Serbia during this era?
4 When and why did changes occur in primary school leadership prior to the current phase of transition, and who/what influenced these changes?

5 Under what conditions were primary schools led in Serbia during the communist era?
6 What were the perceived advantages and disadvantages between different approaches to primary school leadership during the communist era?

The second research question

WHAT DEVELOPMENTS HAVE TAKEN PLACE IN RELATION TO PRIMARY SCHOOL LEADERSHIP FROM THE COMMENCEMENT OF THE ERA OF TRANSITION TO THE PRESENT?

This research question will guide the inquiry into the recent developments in primary schooling in Serbia in order to understand the way EU-inspired changes are being implemented. Key changes that are an important part of the current context will be identified in order to understand the issues with which primary school leaders have to deal. The following guiding questions have been designed to assist the research into the recent developments of the primary school leadership in Serbia:

1 What policies and practices has Serbia implemented that have led to the current situation regarding primary school leadership?
2 What have been the reasons behind, and influences on, the policies and practices implemented to establish current primary school leadership?
3 What continuities can be perceived to exist between pre-transition primary school leadership and current primary school leadership in Serbia?
4 What are the changes that can be perceived to exist between pre-transition primary school leadership and current primary school leadership in Serbia?
5 When and why did changes occur in primary school leadership during the current period of transition, and who/what influenced these changes?
6 What are the advantages and disadvantages that key stakeholders have identified between primary school leadership during the communist era and current primary school?

The third research question

WHAT ISSUES ARE CURRENTLY OF CONCERN TO PRIMARY SCHOOL LEADERS, AND HOW DO THEY DEAL WITH THEM?

In relation to the current education changes in the country, primary school leaders are required to be both the objects and the agents of change. The above research question will guide the inquiry on the issues primary school leaders in Serbia face, as well as on the strategies they use to deal with those issues. The following guiding questions on this have also been designed:

1 What aims do school leaders have when performing their work? What reasons do they give for having these aims? What challenges do they face in trying to realise their aims?
2 What are the strategies that school leaders adopt in trying to realise their aims? What reasons do they give for adopting these strategies? What challenges do they face in adopting them?
3 What significance do school leaders attach to their aims and strategies? What reasons do they give for their position on this? What challenges do they face in trying to maintain this position?
4 What outcomes do school leaders expect from pursuing their aims and strategies? What reasons do they give for expecting these outcomes? What challenges do they face in trying to realise them?
5 What is the nature of the context within which school leaders work which influences them in their work and which provides them with challenges?

Data collection

Each of the central research questions above requires a different set of data to be collected. The first two questions are similar in that they largely require data in the form of documents, and the third question largely requires data to be collected through interviews. The interpretivist research paradigm will inform the investigation based on both of these kinds of sources. Documents can be used in interpretivist studies, especially when other data gathering methods are unable to provide historical insights about the phenomenon (Bowen 2009). In this particular study, it is primarily documents that will be used to provide data for the historical and contemporary context, and interviews will be used to investigate the current perspectives of school principals. Combining such sets of data is possible in grounded theory studies, as documentary data may be collected in conjunction with interviews (Patton 2002). Both contemporary and historical documents are readily available, since the Serbian education system routinely produces a vast amount of them. These will be used as a rich source of data (Punch 2009). Special care will be taken to link historical documents to the contemporary ones, as well as to link documents in general to the interviews (Patton 2002).

The first question, which deals with the historical background to primary school leadership in Serbia, requires perusing documents published in communist Yugoslavia. Various public documents from the communist era will be analysed, including government reports, laws, policy texts, archival sources, as well as research reports from that period. Thus, document study will serve the purpose of providing a historical context surrounding the setting in question (Marshall and Rossman 2006).

The second question, which deals with the recent developments regarding primary school leadership in Serbia, requires perusing documents published in Serbia since the embracement of democracy and the start of education changes in 2001.

Such documents include public records, reports, and policy documents issued by the Ministry of Education, as well as school-related documents of various education boards at the district and provincial levels. EU policy documents that are used in Serbia to guide the changes will also be perused. Such documents will provide insight into the nature of the contemporary context in which primary school principals in Serbia work.

The third question, which deals with the current concerns of primary school leaders in Serbia about the nature of the current education changes, requires the collection of data by means of semi-structured, in-depth interviews. Such interviews are the most prominent data collection tool in qualitative research (Punch 2009) and they play a central role in the data collection in a grounded theory study (Creswell 2013). By constantly comparing data from participants with ideas about the emerging theory, the researcher will arrive at an understanding of how individuals experience the process in question (Creswell 2013).

The research will be conducted in six different schools in Serbia that will be chosen purposefully (Creswell 2013; Punch 2009). Diversity in the selection of schools will be maximised, since schools chosen will differ in size, length of operation, and location (city, town, rural area). By utilising purposeful maximum variation sampling, the researcher will be able to uncover as wide a range of perspectives as possible (Patton 2002).

The participants will include principals, deputy principals, representatives of the School Boards, and officers in charge of education at different levels of governance. As six public primary schools will be involved, the total number of individual interviews conducted in the schools will be 18. Three participants (the principal, deputy principal, and a representative of the School Board) will be chosen from each school, along with one participant from each level of education, namely, district, provincial, and ministerial levels. Thus, the total number of participants involved will be 21. Diversity will be obtained by choosing participants who differ from each other in terms of experience, gender, and the location of the school in which they work. Representatives of School Boards will be able to contribute to the research on primary school leadership in Serbia since they are involved in various aspects of school governance and decision-making. They include various education officers at district, provincial, and national levels, as they are involved in education change implementation, and are able to offer their own perspective on the development of primary school leadership in Serbia.

Data analysis

Grounded theory is both an overall approach to research and a set of procedures for developing theory through the analysis of data (Punch 2009). Grounded theory as analysis aims directly at the generating abstract theory to explain what is central in the data (Oktay 2012; Punch 2009). While the researcher collects data, she or he begins analysis; it is an iterative process between data collection and analysis (Creswell 2013). Data collection and data analysis occur in parallel and repeatedly. This process continues until data saturation is reached (Glaser and Strauss 1968; O'Donoghue 2007). First, the researcher reads the data in the textual form, makes margin notes, and writes down initial ideas (Creswell 2013). Second, in the process of open coding, information in the data is segmented through breaking raw data into words, lines, and segments which generate open coding categories – initial conceptual units of information to be used in theory building (Charmas 2006; Creswell 2013; Oktay 2012; Punch 2009). Third, in the process of axial coding, one open category is selected as the central phenomenon and relationships between categories are formed that show context, causal condition, consequences, strategies etc. (Charmas 2006; Creswell 2013; Oktay 2012; Punch 2009). Fourth, in the process of selective coding, data is interpreted through interrelated categories that develop a higher order conceptualisation or a theoretical model of the process in question (Charmas 2006; Creswell 2013; Oktay 2012; Punch 2009). Finally, propositions extracted from the data are represented in a theory or a visual model (Creswell 2013).

References

Abbs, P. (1976). *Root and Blossom*, London: Heinemann.

Acedo, C. (2011). Education and conflict: From emergency response to reconstruction and peacebuilding, *Prospects*, 41: 181–183.

Adelman, C., Jenkins, D. and Kemmis, S. (1976). Rethinking case study, *Cambridge Journal of Education*, 6(3): 139–150.

Adjukovic, M. and Adjukovic, D. (1993). Psychological well being of refugee children. *Child Abuse and Neglect*, 17: 843–854.

Alexiadou, N. (2014). Policy learning and Europeanisation in education: The governance of a field and the transfer of knowledge, in A. Nordin and D. Sundberg (eds.) *Transnational Policy Flows in European Education: The Making and Governing of Knowledge in the Education Policy Field*, Oxford: Symposium Books.

Allard, A.C. and Santoro, N. (2008). Experienced teachers' perspectives on cultural and social class diversity: Which differences matter? *Equity and Excellence in Education*, 41(2): 200–214.

Allen, R. (2002). Acquiring English: Schools seek ways to strengthen language learning, *Curriculum Update*, Fall, 1–8.

Allport, G.W. (1944). *The Use of Personal Documents in Psychological Research*, New York: Social Science Research Council.

Altenbaugh, R.J. (1992). *The Teacher's Voice*, London: Falmer Press.

Amaral, A. and Neave, G. (2008). On Bologna, weasels and creeping competence, in A. Amaral, G. Neave, P. Maassen and C. Musselin (eds.) *Bologna: Universities and Bureaucrats*, New York: Springer.

Anderson, M., Davis, M., Douglas, P., Lloyd, D., Niven, B., and Thiele, H. (2010). *A Collective Act: Leading a Small School*, Victoria, Australia: ACER Press.

Anderson, N. (1923). *The Hobo*, Chicago: University of Chicago Press.

Andevski, M. (2004). Management in school: Have principles finally accepted the challenge? *Pedagoška Stvarnost*, 50(3–4): 194–201.

Andevski, M. and Arsenijević, J. (2012). Leadership characteristics of schools' employees in Serbia. *Industrija*, 40(3): 146–148.

Andevski, M. and Dudjak, L. (2011). Director role in creating culture: Learning organization at school. Paper presented at the Proceedings of the XV International Scientific Conference on Industrial Systems, University of Skopje, Macedonia.

Andevski, M., Arsenijević, J. and Spajić, B. (2012). Leadership characteristics of employees in school systems in the Republic of Croatia and the Republic of Serbia, *Croatian Journal of Education – Hrvatski Casopis Za Odgoj i Obrazovanje*, 14(4): 881–915.

Anisef, P., Brown, R., Phythian, K., Sweet, R. and Walters, D. (2008). *Early School Leaving Among Immigrants in Toronto Secondary Schools*, Toronto: CERIS.

Appleyard, R. (2001). International migration policies: 1950–2000, *International Migration*, 39(6): 7–18.

Aran, R. (1967). *Main Currents in Sociological Thought*, New York: Basic Books.

Aspinwall, K. (1992). Biographical research: Searching for meaning, *Management Education and Development*, 23(3): 248–257.

Atkinson, P. and Housley, W. (2003) *Interactionism: An Essay in Sociological Amnesia*, London: Sage.

Atkinson, P., Coffey, A. and Delamont, S. (2003). *Key Themes in Qualitative Research: Continuities and Change*, Walnut Creek, CA: Altamira Press.

Australian Bureau of Statistics (ABS) (2008a). *Western Australian Statistical Indicators*, Canberra: Commonwealth of Australia.

Australian Bureau of Statistics (ABS) (2008b). *Year Book Australia*, Canberra: Commonwealth of Australia.

Ball, S. (1994). *Education Reform: A Critical and Post-structural Approach*, Buckingham, UK: Open University Press.

Ball, S. (2006). *Education Policy and Social Class: The Selected Works of Stephen J. Ball*, London: Routledge.

Barrows, H.S. and Tamblyn, R.M. (1980). *Problem Based Learning: An Approach to Medical Education*, New York: Springer.

Becker, H.S., Geer, B., Riesman, D. and Weiss, D. (eds.) (1968). *Institutions and the Person*, Chicago: Aldine.

Bevis, E.O. and Murray, J.P. (1990). The essence of the curriculum revolution: Emancipatory teaching. *Journal of Nurse Education*, 29(7): 326–331.

Bhattacharya, K. (2017). *Fundamentals of Qualitative Research: A Practical Guide*, London: Routledge.

Bideleux, R. and Jeffries, I. (2007). *A History of Eastern Europe: Crisis and Change*, London: Routledge.

Biley, F.C. and Smith, K.L. (1999). Making sense of problem-based learning: The perceptions and experiences of undergraduate nursing students, *Journal of Advanced Nursing*, 30(5): 1205–1212.

Birks, M. (2011). *Grounded Theory: A Practical Guide*, Los Angeles, CA: Sage Publications.

Bîrzea, C. (1994). *Educational Policies of the Countries in Transition*, Strasbourg: Council of Europe.

Blackledge, D. and Hunt, B. (1985). *Sociological Interpretations of Education*, London: Routledge.

Blair, M. (2002). Effective school leadership: The multi-ethnic context, *British Journal of Sociology of Education*, 23(2): 179–191.

Blake, R.R. and Mouton, J.S. (1964). *The Managerial Grid*, Houston, TX: Gulf.

Blumer, H. (1969). *Symbolic Interactionism*, Englewood Cliffs, NJ: Prentice Hall.

Bogdan, R. (1974). *Being Different: The Autobiography of Jane Fry*, New York: John Wiley.

Bogdan, R. and Biklen, S. (1982). *Qualitative Research for Education: An Introduction to Theory and Methods*, Boston, MA: Allyn & Bacon.

Bogdan, R. and Biklen, S. (1992). *Qualitative Research for Education: An Introduction to Theory and Methods* (2nd edn), Boston, MA: Allyn & Bacon.

Borgatti, D. (2002). *Introduction to Grounded Theory*. Retrieved 22 May 2007, from www.analytictech.com/mb870/introtoGT.htm

Boud, D. and Feletti, G. (2003). *The Challenge of Problem Based Learning*, London: Kogan Page.

Bouma, G.D. (2000). *The Research Process*, Melbourne: Oxford University Press.

Bowen, G. A. (2009). Document analysis as a qualitative research method, *Qualitative Research Journal*, 9(2): 27–40.

Brice, I.D. (1995). Australian boys' schools and the historical constructions of masculinity, 24th Annual ANZHES Conference, Sydney: ANZHES.

Bridges, E. (2000). Back to the future, *Cambridge Journal of Education*, 30(1): 37–55.

Broudy, H.S. (1967) *Philosophy of Education: An Organisation of Topics and Selected Sources*, Chicago: University of Illinois Press.

Bruce, S. (2003). *God is Dead: Secularization in the West*, Oxford: Blackwell.

Bryant, A. (2007). *The SAGE Handbook of Grounded Theory*, London: Sage Publications.

Bryk, A., Lee, V. and Holland, P. (1993). *Catholic Schools and the Common Good*, Cambridge, MA: Harvard University Press.

Bryman, A. (2004). *Social Research Methods*, Oxford: Oxford University Press.

Burgess, R.G. (1982). The unstructured interview as a conversation, in R.G. Burgess (ed.) *Field Research: A Sourcebook and Field Manual*, London: Allen & Unwin.

Burke, C. and Dudek, M. (2010). Experiences of learning within a twentieth-century radical experiment in education, *Oxford Review of Education*, 36(2): 203–218.

Burley, S. (1997). Lost leaders from the convent and the classroom 1880–1925, in J. McMahon, H. Neidhart and J. Chapman (eds.) *Leading the Catholic School*, Richmond, Victoria: Spectrum.

Burley, S. (2001). Resurrecting the religious experiences of Catholic girls' schooling in South Australia in the 1920s, *Educational Research and Perspectives*, 28(1): 28–44.

Burley, S. and O'Donoghue, T.A. (2006). God's Antipodean teaching force: An historical exposition on Catholic teaching religious in Australia, *Teaching and Teacher Education*, 24(1): 180–189.

Burnley, I. (2001). *The Impact of Immigration on Australia: A Demographic Approach*, London: Oxford University Press.

Burns, N. and Grove, S.K. (2004). *The Practice of Nursing Research: Conduct, Critique and Utilisation*, Philadelphia, PA: W.B. Saunders.

Candy, P. (1989). Alternative paradigms in educational research, *Australian Educational Researcher*, 16(3): 1–11.

Cantwell, B. and Maldonado-Maldonado, A. (2009). Four stories: Confronting contemporary ideas about globalization and internationalisation in higher education, *Globalisation, Societies and Education*, 7(3): 289–306.

Cardno, C. (2002). Team learning opportunities and challenges for school leaders, *School Leadership and Management*, 22(2): 211–223.

Carspecken, P.F. (1996). *Critical Ethnography in Educational Research: A Theoretical and Practical Guide*, New York: Routledge.

Cassity, E. and Gow, G. (2005). Making up for lost time: The experiences of Southern Sudanese young refugees in high schools, *Youth Studies Australia*, 24(3): 51–55.

Castells, M. (2000). *The Rise of the Network Society*, Oxford: Blackwell.

Chadbourne, R. and Clarke, R. (1994). *Devolution: The Next Phase, Western Australian Secondary Principals' Association: A Response*, Perth: Secondary Principals' Association.

Chapman, J. (1987). Decentralization, devolution and the administration of schools, *Education Research and Perspectives*, 14(2): 62–75.

Charmaz, K. (1994). The grounded theory method: An explication and interpretation, in B. Glaser (ed.) *More Grounded Theory Methodology: A Reader*, Mill Valley, CA: Sociology Press.

Charmaz, K. (2002). Qualitative interviewing and grounded theory analysis, in J.F. Gubrium and J.A. Holstein (eds.) *Handbook of Interview Research: Context and Method*, London: Sage.

Charmaz, K. (2003). Grounded theory: Objectivist and constructivist methods, in N. Denzin and Y. Lincoln (eds.) *Strategies of Qualitative Inquiry*, London: Sage.

Charmaz, K. (2005). Grounded theory in the 21st century: Applications for advancing social justice studies, in N. Denzin and Y. Lincoln (eds.) *Handbook of Qualitative Research*, Thousand Oaks, CA: Sage.

Charmaz, K. (2006). *Constructing Grounded Theory: A Practical Guide through Qualitative Analysis*, London: Sage.

Charmaz, K. (2014). *Constructing Grounded Theory* (2nd edn), Los Angeles, CA: Sage.

Charon, J.M. (2001). *Symbolic Interactionism: An Introduction, an Interpretation, an Integration*, Upper Saddle River, NJ: Prentice Hall.

Cheek, J., Gillham, D. and Mills, P. (2007) Using a computerised clinical database to enhance problem based learning strategies for second year undergraduate nursing students, *International Journal of Medical Informatics*, 50(13): 1–20.

Chenitz, W. and Swanson, J. (eds.) (1986) Qualitative research using grounded theory, in *From Practice to Grounded Theory*, Menlo Park, CA: Addison-Wesley.

Chin, S. and Dy, S.S. (2009). Educational reform context and process in Cambodia, in Y. Hirosato and Y. Kitamura (eds.) *Education in the Asia-Pacific Region: Issues, Concerns and Prospects: Vol. 13. The Political Economy of Educational Reforms and Capacity Development in Southeast Asia*, Dordrecht: Springer.

Christie, P. and Sidhu, R. (2006). Governmentality and 'fearless speech': Framing the education of asylum seeker and refugee children in Australia, *Oxford Review of Education*, 32(4): 449–465.

Clancy, A. (2005). The design, development and implementation of a PBL curriculum in nurse education. Paper presented at the International Conference on Problem Based Learning, 12–14 June, Rovaniemi University of Applied Sciences, University of Lapland, Finland.

Clare, J., White, J., Edwards, H. and Van Loon, A. (2002). *Learning Outcomes and Curricular Development in Major Disciplines: Nursing*, Adelaide, South Australia: School of Nursing and Midwifery, Flinders University.

Clarke, S. and Wildy, H. (2004). Context counts: Viewing small school leadership from the inside out, *Journal of Educational Administration*, 42(5): 555–572.

Clarke, S. and Wildy, H. (2009). The Europeanisation of educational leadership: Much ado about nothing? *European Educational Research Journal*, 8(3): 352–358.

Cohen, L. and Manion, L. (1989) *Research Methods in Education*, London: Routledge.

Connole, H., Smith, B. and Wiseman, R. (1993). *Issues and Methods in Research: Study Guide*, Adelaide, South Australia: University of South Australia.

Considine, M. (2005). *Making Public Policy*, Cambridge: Polity Press.

Cooley, C.H. (1956). *Human Nature and the Social Order*, Glencoe, IL: Free Press.

Corbin, J. and Strauss, A. (2007). *Basics of Qualitative Research: Procedures for Developing Grounded Theory*, Newbury Park, CA: Sage.

Crabtree, B.F. and Miller, W.L. (eds.) (1992). *Doing Qualitative Research*, Newbury Park, CA: Sage.

Cranston, N. and Ehrich, L.C. (2005). Enhancing the effectiveness of senior management teams in schools, *International Studies in Educational Administration*, 33(1): 79–91.

Creedy, D. and Alvi, C. (2003). Problem-based learning in an integrated nursing curriculum, in D. Boud and G. Feletti (eds.) *The Challenge of Problem-Based Learning*, London: Kogan Page.

Cressey, P. (1932). *The Taxi Dance Hall*, Chicago: University of Chicago Press.

Creswell, J.W. (2005). *Educational Research: Planning, Conducting, and Evaluating Quantitative and Qualitative Research*, Columbus, OH: Pearson.

Creswell, J.W. (2013). *Qualitative Inquiry and Research Design: Choosing Among Five Approaches*, Los Angeles, CA: Sage.

Crotty, M. (1998). *The Foundations of Social Research: Meaning and Perspective in the Research Process*, St Leonards, NSW: Allen & Unwin.

Crotty, M. (2001). *Making the Australian Male: Middle-Class Masculinity 1870–1920*, Melbourne: Melbourne University Press.

Cunningham, P. and Gardner, P. (2004). *Becoming Teachers: Texts and Testimonies 1907–1950*, London: Woburn Press.

Dale, R. (2009a). Contexts, constraints and resources in the development of European education space and European education policy, in R. Dale and S.L. Robertson (eds.) *Globalisation and Europeanisation in Education*, Oxford: Symposium Books.

Dale, R. (2009b). Introduction, in R. Dale and S.L. Robertson (eds.) *Globalisation and Europeanisation in Education*, Oxford: Symposium Books.

de Wit, H. (2009). Internationalisation, teaching and learning and strategic partnerships. Keynote address at Internationalising Learning and Teaching in Academic Settings Conference, Sydney University, November. np.

Denzin, N.K. (1989a). *Interpretitive Interactionism*, Thousand Oaks, CA: Sage.

Denzin, N.K. (1989b). *The Research Act*, Englewood Cliffs, NJ: Prentice Hall.

Denzin, N.K. and Giardina, M.D. (2016). *Qualitative Inquiry Through a Critical Lens*, London: Routledge.

Denzin, N.K. and Lincoln, Y. (eds.) (2011). *The Sage Handbook of Qualitative Research*, Thousand Oaks, CA: Sage.

Department of Education and Training (DET). (2008). *Annual Report 2007–2008*, Perth, Western Australia: Department of Education and Training.

Department of Immigration and Multicultural and Indigenous Affairs (DIMIA). (2005). *Refugee and Humanitarian Issues: Australia's Response*, Canberra: Australian Government Publishing Service.

Deretchin, L.F. and Contant, C.F (1999). Learning behaviours in a mixed traditional and problem based learning curriculum, *Education for Health: Change in Training and Practice* 12: 169–180.

Derouet, J.L. (1991). Lower secondary education in France: From uniformity to institutional autonomy, *European Journal of Education*, 26(2): 119–132.

Diekelmann, N. (2002). Too much content…, epistemologies' grasp and nursing education, *Journal of Nursing Education*, 41: 469–470.

Diesing, P. (1972). *Pattterns of Discovery in the Social Sciences*, London: Routledge and Kegan Paul.

Dimmock, C. and O'Donoghue, T.A. (1997). The edited topical life history approach, *Leading and Managing*, 3(1): 48–70.

Dinham, S. (1994). The use of the telephone interview in educational research: One case study, *Education Research and Perspectives*, 21(2): 17–27.

Dollard, J. (1935). *Criteria for the Life History*, New York: Libraries Press.

Dove, L.A. (1986). *Teachers and Teacher Education in Developing Countries*, London: Croom Helm.

Drinan, J. (1991). The limits of problem-based learning, in D. Boud and G. Feletti (eds.) *The Challenge of Problem-based Learning*, London: Kogan Page.

Driver, C. and Beltran, R.O. (1998). Impact of refugee trauma on children's occupational role as students, *Australian Occupational Therapy Journal*, 45: 23–38.

Dy, S.S. (2004). Strategies and policies for basic education in Cambodia: Historical perspectives, *International Education Journal*, 5(1): 90–97.

Dy, S.S., and Ninomiya, A. (2003). Basic education in Cambodia: The impact of UNESCO on policies in the 1990s, *Education Policy Analysis Archives*, 11(48), np.

Earnest, J., Housen, T. and Gilleatt, S. (2007). *A New Cohort of Refugee Students in Perth: Challenges for Students and Educators*, Perth, Australia: Teaching and Learning Forum, Curtin University of Technology.

Eisenbruch, M. (1988). The mental health of refugee children and their cultural development, *International Migration Review*, 22: 282–300.

Eisner, E. (1983). The art and craft of teaching, *Educational Leadership*, January: 5–13.

Eisner, E. (1985). *The Art of Educational Evaluation*, London: Falmer Press.

Elmore, R. and Sykes, G. (1992). Curriculum policy, in P. Jackson (ed.) *Handbook of Research on Curriculum*, New York: Macmillan.

Emery, M. (1986). Introduction, in M. Emery (ed.) *Qualitative Research*, Canberra: Australian Association for Adult Education.

Engel, C.E. (1997). Not just a method but a way of learning, in D. Boud and G. Feletti (eds.) *The Challenge of Problem Based Learning* (2nd edn). London: Kogan Page.

Entwistle, H. (1971). The relationship between theory and practice, in J.S. Tibble (ed.) *An Introduction to the Study of Education*, London: Routledge and Kegan Paul.

Ertl, H. (2006). *Cross National Attraction in Education*, Oxford: Symposium.

Erwin, J.E. and Soodak, L.C. (1995). I never knew I could stand up to the system: Families' perspectives on pursuing inclusive education, *Journal of the Association of Persons with Severe Handicaps*, 17(4): 205–212.

Evenson, D.H. and Hmelo, C.E. (2000). *Problem-Based Learning: A Research Perspective on Learning Interactions*, Mahwah, NJ: Lawrence Erlbaum Associates.

Evetts, J. (1989). Married women and career: Career history accounts of primary head teachers, *Qualitative Studies in Education*, 2(2): 89–105.

Ezzy, D. (2002). *Qualitative Analysis: Practice and Innovation*, Crows Nest, New South Wales: Allen & Unwin.

Fairburn, M. (1999). *Social History: Problems, Strategies and Methods*, London: Macmillan Press.

Fairclough, N. (2006). *Language and Globalization*, London: Routledge.

Feiman-Nemser, S. and Floden, R.E. (1986). The cultures of teaching, in M.C. Wittrock (ed.) *Handbook of Research on Teaching*, New York: Macmillan.

Fergusson, L.C. and Masson, G. L. (1997). A culture under siege: Post-colonial higher education and teacher education in Cambodia from 1953 to 1979, *History of Education*, 26(1): 91–112.

Finch, J. (1986). *Research and Policy*, London: Falmer Press.

Finkelstein, B. (1989). *Governing the Young: Teacher Behaviour in Popular Primary Schools in Nineteenth Century United States*, London: Falmer Press.

Finkelstein, B. (1998). Classroom management in the United States, in N.K. Shimahara (ed.) *Politics of Classroom Life: Classroom Life in International Perspective*, New York: Garland.

Flint, N. (2005). *Methodological Conundrums: Confessions of a Latent Grounded Theorist*, Melbourne: Australian Association for Research in Education.

Floden, R.M. and Huberman, M. (1989). Teachers' professional lives: The state of the art, *International Journal of Educational Research*, 13: 455–466.

Fontana, A. and Frey, J. (1994). Interviewing: The art and science, in N.K. Denzin and Y.S. Lincoln (eds.) *Handbook of Qualitative Research*, Thousand Oaks, CA: Sage.

Foot, J.M. (1998). Words, songs and books: Oral history in Italy. A review and discussion, *Journal of Modern Italian Studies*, 3(2): 64–74.

Francis, S. (2007). *School's in for Refugees: Whole-School Guide to Refugee Readiness*, Brunswick, Victoria: Victorian Foundation for Survivors of Torture Inc.

Friedman, R. (2000). *Integration and Visibility*, Oslo: University of Oslo – Forum for University History.

Fullan, M. (1982) *The Meaning of Educational Change*, New York: Teachers College, Columbia University.

Fullan, M. (2001). *The New Meaning of Educational Change*, New York: Teachers College Press.

Galbally, F. (1978). *Review of Post Arrival Programs and Services to Migrants*, Canberra: AGPS.

Gardner, P. (2010). *Hermeneutics, History and Memory*, London: Routledge.

Gardner, P. and Cunningham, P. (1997). Oral history and teachers' professional practice, *Cambridge Journal of Education*, 27(3): 331–342.

Gardner, W. (1979). *Colonial Cap and Gown*, Christchurch, New Zealand: University of Canterbury.

Gibbon, C. (2005). *SONIC: A Reflective Account of a Learning and Teaching Journey*, Manchester, UK: The Higher Education Academy.

Giddens, A. (2004). *Sociology*, Cambridge: Polity Press.

Glaser, B. (1978). *Theoretical Sensitivity: Advances in the Methodology of Grounded Theory*, Mills Valley, CA: Sociology Press.

Glaser, B. (1992). *Basics of Grounded Theory Analysis: Emergence vs Forcing*, Mills Valley, CA: Sage.

Glaser, B. (1998). *Doing Grounded Theory Issues and Discussions*, Mills Valley, CA: Sociology Press.

Glaser, B. and Strauss, A. (1965). *Awareness of Dying*, Chicago: Aldine.

Glaser, B. and Strauss, A. (1967). *The Discovery of Grounded Theory: Strategies for Qualitative Research*, Chicago: Aldine.

Glaser, B. and Strauss, A. (1968). *Time for Dying*, Chicago: Aldine.

Gleeson, J. (2010). *Curriculum in Context*, New York: Peter Lang.

Glesne, C. (2006). *Becoming Qualitative Researchers: An Introduction*, Boston, MA: Pearson Education.

Goddard, T. J. (2007). The professional development needs of educational leaders in post-conflict Kosovo, *The Education Forum*, 71(3): 200–210.

Goetz, J. and Le Compte, M. (1984). *Ethnography and Qualitative Design in Education Research*, Orlando, FL: Academic Press.

Goodman, J. and Martin, J. (2002). (eds.) *Gender, Colonialism and Education: The Politics of Experience*, London: Woburn Press.

Goodson, I. (1991). Teachers' lives and educational research, in I.F. Goodson and R. Walker (eds.) *Biography, Identity and Schooling: Episodes in Educational Research*, London: Falmer Press.

Goodson, I. (1992). (ed.) *Studying Teachers' Lives*, London: Routledge.

Goodson, I. and Sikes, P. (2001). *Life History Research in Educational Settings: Learning from Lives*, Buckingham, UK: Open University Press.

Goodson, I. and Walker, R. (eds) (1991) *Biography, Identity and Schooling: Episodes in Educational Research*, London: Falmer Press.

Gordon, L. (1992). The state, devolution and educational reform in New Zealand, *Journal of Education Folio*, 7(2): 187–203.

Goulding, C. (2002). *Grounded Theory: A Practical Guide for Management, Business and Market Research*, London: Sage.

Grace, G. (2002). *Catholic Schools: Mission, Markets and Morality*, London: RoutledgeFalmer.

Gronn, P. (1998). Our playmates: The culture of teaming in a human resource development unit, *Leading and Managing*, 4(4): 294–318.

Gronn, P. (2003). *The New Work of Educational Leaders: Changing Leadership Practice in an Era of School Reform*, London: Sage.

Guba, E. and Lincoln, Y. (1994). Competing paradigms in qualitative research, in N. Denzin and Y. Lincoln (eds.) *Handbook of Qualitative Research*, Thousand Oaks, CA: Sage.

Habermas, J. (1972). *Knowledge and Human Interests*, London: Heinemann.

Hage, J. and Powers, C. (1992) *Post-Industrial Lives: Roles and Relationships in the 21st Century*, New York: Sage.

Haig, Y. and Oliver, R. (2007). *Waiting in Line: African Refugee Students in Western Australian Schools*, Bunbury, WA: Edith Cowan University.

Hakuta, K., Butler, Y.G. and Witt, D. (2000). *How Long Does It Take English Learners to Attain Proficiency?*Los Angeles, CA: The University of California Linguistic Minority Research Institute Policy Report.

Hallinger, P., Leithwood, K. and Murphy, J. (eds.) (1993). *Cognitive Perspectives on Educational Leadership*, New York: Teachers College Press.

Ham, C. and Hill, M.J. (1993). *The Policy Process in the Modern Capitalist State*, London: Harvester Wheatsheaf.

Hamilton, R. and Moore, D. (2004). Education of refugee children, in R. Hamilton and D. Moore (eds.) *Education Interventions for Refugee Children*, London: RoutledgeFalmer.

Hammersley, M. and Atkinson, P. (1983). *Ethnography: Principles in Practice*, London: Tavistock.

Harber, C. and Dadey, A. (1993). The job of the headteacher in Africa: Research and reality, *International Journal of Educational Development*, 13(2): 147–160.

Hardcastle, M.A., Holmes, C. and Usher, K. (2018) Carspecken's five-stage critical qualitative research method: An application to nursing research, *Qualitative Health Research*, 16(1): 151–161.

Hargreaves, A. and Fullan, M.G. (1992). Introduction, in A. Hargreaves and M.G. Fullan, (eds.) *Understanding Teacher Development*, London: Cassell Villiers House.

Heath, P. (2002). *Our duty of care: National review of nursing education*, Canberra: Department of Education Science and Training.

Hellinckx, B., Simon, F. and Depaepe, M. (2009). *The Forgotten Contribution of the Teaching Sisters*, Leuven: Leuven University Press.

Henry, M., Lingard, B., Rizvi, F. and Taylor, S. (2001). *The OECD, Globalization and Education Policy*, Amsterdam: Pergamon.

Heyneman, S.P. (1998). The transition from Party/State to open democracy: The role of education, *International Journal of Educational Development*, 18(1): 21–40.

Hilker, L.M. (2011). The role of education in driving conflict and building peace: The case of Rwanda, *Prospects*, 41: 267–282.

Hill, B. and Allen, R. (2001). Immigration policy, multicultural and anti-racist education in Australia: Charting the changes, in F. Salili and R. Hoosain (eds.) *Multicultural Education: Issues, Policies and Practices*, Charlotte, CT: Information Age Publishing.

Hill, B. and Allen, R. (2004). Multicultural education in Australia: Historical development and current status, in J.A. Banks and C.A. Banks (eds.) *Handbook of Research on Multicultural Education*, Seattle: University of Washington.

Hodder, I. (1994). The interpretation of documents and material culture, in N.K. Denzin and Y.S. Lincoln (eds.) *Handbook of Qualitative Research*, London: Sage.

Hodgkin, M. (2006). Reconciliation in Rwanda: Education, history and the state, *Journal of International Affairs*, 60(1): 199–210.

Hones, D.F. and Cha, C.S. (1999). *Educating New Americans: Immigrant Lives and Learning*, Mahwah, NJ: Lawrence Erlbaum Associates.

Hopkins, D. (1993). *A Teacher's Guide to Classroom Research*, Buckingham, UK: Open University Press.

Hornsby-Smith, M.P. (2000). Catholic schooling in England and Wales, in M. Eaton, J. Longmore and A. Naylor (eds.) *Commitment to Diversity: Catholics and Education in a Changing World*, London: Cassell.

Hosmer, D. and Lemeshow, S. (1989). *Applied Logistic Regression*, New York: John Wiley.

Hoyler, M. and Jons, H. (2008). Kampf um talente? *Geographische Rundschau*, 60(6): 60–64.

Huber, S.G. and West, M. (2002). Developing school leaders: A critical review of current practices, approaches and issues and some directions for the future, in K. Leithwood and P. Hallinger (eds.) *Second International Handbook of Educational Leadership and Administration*, Dordrecht: Kluwer.

Husén, T. (1988). Research paradigms in education, in J. Keeves (ed.) *Educational Research, Methodology, and Measurement: An International Handbook*, Oxford: Pergamon.

Iredale, R. and Fox, C. (1997). The impact of immigration on school education in New South Wales, Australia, *The International Migration Review*, 31(3): 655–669.

Jackson, R. (2007). European institutions and the contribution of studies of religious diversity to education for democratic citizenship, in R. Jackson, S.Miedema, W.Weisse and J.P. Willaime (eds.) *Religion and Education in Europe: Developments, Contexts and Debates*, Munster: Waxman Verlag.

James, W. (1958). *Talks to Teachers on Psychology: And to Students on Some of Life's Ideals*, New York: W.W. Norton.

Jones, E. and Killick, D. (2007). Internationalisation of the curriculum, in E. Jones and S. Brown (eds.) *Internationalising Higher Education*, London: Routledge.

Jones, S. (2014). Distributed leadership: A critical analysis, *Leadership*, 10(2): 129–141.

Kaldor, M. (2005). Old wars, cold wars, new wars, and the War on Terror, *International Politic*, 42(4): 491–498.

Keng, C.S. (2009). Basic education in Cambodia: Quality and equity, in Y. Hirosato and Y. Kitamura (eds.) *Education in the Asia-Pacific Region: Issues, Concerns and Prospects, Vol. 13: The Political Economy of Educational Reforms and Capacity Development in Southeast Asia*, Springer.

Kennedy, M.M. (1979). Generalizing from single case studies, *Evaluation Quarterly*, 3(4): 661–679.

Kheang, T. (2011). Exploring the implementation of school-based management in selected public schools in Cambodia: A multiple case study, Master Thesis, De La Salle University-Manila, Philippines.

Khoo, S. (2003). A greater diversity of origins, in S. Khoo and P. McDonald (eds.) *The Transformation of Australia's Population*, Sydney: University of New South Wales Press.

King, N. (2004). Using interviews in qualitative research, in C. Cassell and G. Symon (eds.) *Essential Guide to Qualitative Methods in Organisational Research*, London: Sage Publications.

King, E. (2005). Educating for conflict or peace: Challenges and dilemmas in post-conflict Rwanda, *International Journal*, 60(4): 904–918.

Kirk, J. and Miller, M. (1986). *Reliability, Validity and Qualitative Research*, Beverly Hills, CA: Sage.

Knight, J. (2004). Internationalization remodelled, *Journal of Studies in International Education*, 8(1): 5–31.

Kotre, J. (1984). *Outliving the Self: Generativity and the Interpretation of Lives*, Baltimore, MD: Johns Hopkins University Press.

Kuhn, T. (1970). *The Structure of Scientific Revolutions*, Chicago: University of Chicago Press.

Kvale, S. (1996). *Interviews: An Introduction to Qualitative Research Interviewing*, Thousand Oaks, CA: Sage.

Kyle, N.K. (ed.) (1989). *Women as Educators in 19th and 20th Century Australia*, Wollongong: University of Wollongong, School of Learning Studies.

Lancy, D.F. (1993). *Qualitative Research in Education*, New York: Longman.

Langness, L.L. and Frank, G. (1981) *Lives: An Anthropological Approach to Biography*, Novato, CA: Chandler & Sharp.

Lawton, D. and Cairns, J. (2005). Faith schools: Some political issues and an agenda for research, in R. Gardner, J. Cairns and D. Lawton (eds.) *Faith Schools: Consensus or Conflict*, London: Routledge Falmer.

Layder, D. (1995). *Understanding Social Theory*, Thousand Oaks, CA: Sage.

Le Compte, M. and Goetz, J. (1982). Problems of reliability and validity in ethnographic research, *Review of Educational Research*, 52(1): 31–60.

LeCompte, M. and Preissle, J. (1993). *Ethnography and Qualitative Design in Educational Research*, New York: Academic Press.

Leithwood, K., Begley, P.T. and Cousins, B. (1994) *Developing Expert Leadership for Future Schools*, London: Falmer Press.

Leithwood, K., Seashore, L.K., Anderson, S. and Wahlstrom, K. (2004). *How Leadership Influences Student Learning*, New York: Wallace Foundation.

Lemert, E.A. (1955). *Social Pathology*, New York: McGraw-Hill.

Lewins, F. (1992). *Social Science Methodology: A Brief but Critical Introduction*, Melbourne: Macmillan.

Lim, P. (2008). Analysis of principals' instructional leadership behaviours in selected Cambodian secondary schools, Master Thesis, De La Salle University-Manila, Philippines.

Lincoln, Y.S. and Guba, E. (1985). *Naturalistic Inquiry*, Beverly Hills, CA: Sage Publications.

Lincoln, Y.S. and Guba, E. (2003). Paradigmatic controversies, contradictions, and emerging confluences, in N.K. Denzin and Y.S. Lincoln (eds.) *The Landscape of Qualitative Research: Theories and Issues*, Thousand Oaks, CA: Sage Publications.

Locke, K. (2001). *Grounded Theory in Management Research*, London: Sage Publications.

Lofland, J. (1971). *Analyzing Social Settings: A Guide to Qualitative Observation and Analysis*, Belmont, CA: Wadsworth.

Luckcock, T. (2007). Faith in school leadership: Conceptualising the distinctiveness and inclusiveness of church school leadership, *Management in Education*, 21(15): 15–20.

Lumis, T. (1987). *Listening to History: The Authenticity of Oral Evidence*, London: Hutchinson.

Mackinnon, A. (1984). A new point of departure, *History of Education Review*, 13(2): 1–4.

Macnee, C. and McCabe, S. (2008). *Understanding Nursing Research Reading and using research and evidence based practice* (2nd ed.). Philadelphia, CA: Lippincott Williams & Wilkins.

Magno, C. (2009). Reimagining the school leadership paradigm in a postsocialist context, *European Education*, nv: np.

Majchrzak, A. (1984). *Methods for Policy Research*, Newbury Park, CA: Sage.

Mandelbaum, D.G. (1973). The study of life history: Ghandi, *Current Anthropology*, 14(3): 177–206.

Mann, C. and Stewart, F. (2002). Internet interviewing, in J.F. Gubrium and J.A. Holstein (eds.) *Handbook of Interview Research: Context and Method*, Thousand Oaks, CA: Sage: 603–627.

Manojlović, G., Arsovski, S., and Nikolić, I. (2013). Standardi direktora u funkciji kvaliteta škola. Paper presented at the Osma nacionalna konferencija o kvalitetu života, Kragujevac, June.

Mansouri, F. and Kamp, A. (2007). Structural deficiency or cultural racism: The educational and social experiences of Arab-Australian youth, *Australian Journal of Social Issues*, 42(1): 87–102.

Margetson, D. (1997). *Wholeness and educative learning: The question of problems in problem – based learning*. Paper presented at Changing to PBL Conference, 10–13 September, Brunel University. np.

Marginson, S. (2007). Global position and position taking: The case of Australia, *Journal of Studies in International Education*, 11(1): 5–32.

Marginson, S. and Rhoades, G. (2002). Beyond national states, markets, and systems of higher education, *Higher Education*, 43(3): 281–309.

Marks, G.N. (2005). Accounting for immigrant non-immigrant differences in reading and mathematics in twenty countries, *Ethnic and Racial Studies*, 28(5): 925–946.

Marshall, C. and Rossman, G.B. (2006). *Designing Qualitative Research*, Thousands Oaks, CA: Sage Publications.

Matza, D. (1969). *Becoming Deviant*, Englewood Cliffs, NJ: Prentice-Hall.

Maudsley, G. (1999). Roles and responsibilities for the problem based learning tutor in the undergraduate medical education curriculum, *British Medical Journal*, 318: 657–661.

Maxwell, J. (1996). *Qualitative Research Design: An Interactive Approach*, Thousand Oaks, CA: Sage.

McBrien, J.L. (2005). Educational needs and barriers for refugee students in the United States: A review of the literature, *Review of Educational Research*, 75(3): 329–364.

McCulloch, G. (2004). *Documentary Research in Education, History and the Social Sciences*, London: RoutledgeFalmer.

McCulloch, G. (2011). *The Struggle for the History of Education*, London: Routledge.

McCulloch, G. and Woodin, T. (2010). Towards a social history of learners and learning, *Oxford Review of Education*, 36(2): 133–140.

McHugh, J.D. (1994). The lords will be done interviewing the powerful in education, in G. Walford (ed.) *Researching the Powerful in Education*, London: Routledge.

McIlrath, L. and MacLabhrainn, I. (2007). *Higher Education and Civic Engagement: International Perspectives*, Aldershot, UK: Ashgate.

Mead, G.H. (1934). *Mind, Self and Society*, Chicago: University of Chicago Press.

Measor, L. (1985). Interviewing: A strategy in qualitative research, in G.R. Burgess (ed.) *Strategies of Educational Research*, London: Falmer Press.

Meighan, R. (1995). Home-based education effectiveness research and some of its implications, *Educational Review*, 47(3): 275–287.

Meltzer, B.B., Petras, J.W. and Reynolds, L.T. (1975). *Symbolic Interaction: Genesis, Varieties and Criticism*, London: Routledge and Kegan Paul.

Melville, W., Jones, D. and Campbell, T. (2014). Distributed leadership with the aim of 'reculturing': A departmental case study, *Formerly School Organisation*, 34(3): 237–254.

Merriam, S.B. (1988). *Case Study Research in Education*, San Francisco, CA: Jossey Bass.

Merton, R.K (1968). On sociological theories of the middle range, in R.K. Merton (ed.) *Social Theory and Social Structure*, New York: Free Press.

Miller, J., Mitchell, J. and Brown, J. (2005). African refugees with interrupted schooling in the high school mainstream: Dilemmas for teachers, *Prospect*, 20(2): 19–33.

Minichiello, V., Aroni, R., Timewell, E. and Alexander, L. (1995). *In-Depth Interviewing: Principles, Techniques and Analysis*, Melbourne: Longman.

MoE/RS. (2012). *Strategija razvoja obrazovanja u Srbiji do 2020. godine: Nacrt za diskusiju*, Belgrade: Government of the Republic of Serbia, the Ministry of Education and Science.

National League for Nursing. (1990). *Accreditation standards for baccalaureate degree programs and master's degree programs*, New York: National League for Nursing.

National Project on the Quality of Teaching and Learning (NPQTL). (1993). *National Schools Project: Report of the National External Review Panel*, Canberra: Australian Government Publishing Service.

Nicolai, S. and Triplehorn, C. (2003). *The Role of Education in Protecting Children in Conflict*, np: Humanitarian Practice Network, Overseas Development Institute.

Nicolaidou, M. (2008). Attempting a Europeanization of educational leadership: philosophical and ideological dimensions, *Theory and Practice*, 11(2): 211–223.

Novelli, M. and Lopez Cardizo, M.T.A. (2008). Conflict, education and the global south: New critical directions, *International Journal of Educational Development*, 28(4): 473–488.

O'Brien, A. (2005). *God's Willing Workers: Women and Religion in Australia*, Sydney: University of New South Wales Press.

O'Donoghue, T.A. (2001). *Upholding the Faith: The Process of Education in Catholic Schools in Australia, 1922–65*, New York: Peter Lang.

O'Donoghue, T.A. (2004). *Come Follow me and Forsake Temptation: Catholic Schooling and the Recruitment and Retention of Teachers for Religious Teaching Orders, 1922–1965*, Bern: Peter Lang.

O'Donoghue, T.A. (2007). *Planning your Qualitative Research Project*, London: Routledge.

O'Donoghue, T.A. and Clarke, S. (2010). *Leading Learning: Process, Themes and Issues in International Contexts*, London: Routledge.

O'Donoghue, T.A. and Potts, A. (2004). Researching the lives of Catholic teachers who were members of religious orders: Historiographical considerations, *History of Education*, 33(4): 469–482.

OECD. (2008). *Tertiary Education for a Knowledge Society*, Paris: OECD.

Oktay, J.S. (2012). *Grounded Theory*, Oxford: Oxford University Press.

Olliff, L. and Couch, J. (2005). Pathways and pitfalls, *Youth Studies Australia*, 24(3): 42–46.

Open University. (1972). *School and Society (Course E282)*, Milton Keynes, UK: Open University Press.

Oplatka, I. (2004). The principalship in developing countries: Context, characteristics and reality, *Comparative Education*, 40(3): 427–448.

Ozga, J. (2000). *Policy Research in Educational Settings: Contested Terrain*, Buckingham, UK: Open University Press.

Patton, M.Q. (2002). *Qualitative Evaluation and Research Methods*, Newbury Park, CA: Sage.

Paulson, J. (ed.). (2011). *Education, Conflict and Development*, Oxford: Symposium Books.

Paulson, J. and Rappleye, J. (2007). Education and conflict: Essay review, *International Journal of Educational Development*, 27: 340–347.

Pellini, A. (2005). Decentralization of education in Cambodia: Searching for spaces for participation between traditions and modernity, *Compare: A Journal of Comparative and International Education*, 35(2): 205–216.

Perks, R. and Thomson, A. (eds.) (1998). *The Oral History Reader*, London: Routledge.

Phillips, D. and Schweisfurth, M. (2007). *Comparative and International Education*, New York: Continuum.

Phy, S. (2010). *Foreign Aid–Corruption Nexus in Cambodia: Its Consequences on the Propensity of Civil War*, Munich: GRIN.

Plummer, K. (1983). *Documents of Life*, Sydney: Allen & Unwin.

Polit, D.F., Beck, C.T. and Hungler, B.P. (2001). *Essentials of Nursing Research: Methods, Appraisal and Utilization*, New York: Lippincott.

Pollard, A. (1980). Teacher interests and changing situations of survival threat in primary school classrooms, in P. Woods (ed.) *Teacher Strategies*, London: Croom Helm: 34–60.

Popkewitz, T. (1984). *Paradigm and Ideology in Educational Research: The Social Functions of Intellectuals*, London: Falmer Press.

Porter-O'Grady, T. (2003). A different age of leadership, *Journal of Nursing Administration* 33: 105–110.

Potts, A. (1997). *College Academics*, Charlestown, New South Wales: William Michael Press.

Powell, S. and Green, H. (2007). *The Doctorate Worldwide*, Maidenhead, UK: Open University Press.

Prus, R. (1996). *Symbolic Interaction and Ethnographic Research*, Albany, NY: State University of New York Press.

Punch, H. and Wildy, H. (1995). Grounded theory in educational administration: Leadership and change. Paper presented at The International Conference of the Australian Council for Educational Administration, Sydney, July.

Punch, K. (1988). *Introduction to Social Research: Quantitative and Qualitative Approaches*, London: Sage.
Punch, K. (2000). *Developing Effective Research Proposals*, London: Sage.
Punch, K. (2005). *Introduction to Social Research: Quantitative and Qualitative Approaches*, London: Sage.
Punch, K. (2009). *Introduction to Research Methods in Education*, London: Sage.
Purkey, S.C. and Smith, M.S. (1985). School reform: The district policy implications of the effective schools literature, *The Elementary School Journal*, 85: 353–389.
Ravinet, P. (2009). La construction européenne de l'enseignement supérieur, in R. Dehousse (ed.) *Politiques européennes*, Paris: Presses de Sciences Po.
Reid, J.C. (1994). *Nursing Education in Australian Universities. Report of the National Review of Nurse Education in the Higher Education Sector*, Australian Government, Department of Education, Science and Training, Canberra.
Ribbins, P. and Sherratt, B. (1992). Managing the secondary school in the 1990s: A new view of headship, *Educational Management and Administration*, 20(3): 151–160.
Rigg, S.M. (2017). *The Woman in the Principal's Office*. Unpublished Doctor of Education Thesis, Graduate School of Education, University of Pennsylvania.
Ristanović, S. (1981). *Samoupravljanje U Obrazovanju Od Partizanskih Skola Do Slobodne Razmene Rada*, Beograd: Naučna knjiga.
Ritzer, G. (1983). *Sociological Theory*, New York: Alfred A. Knopf.
Ritzer, G. (1994). *Sociological Beginnings: On the Origins of Key Ideas in Sociology*, New York: McGraw-Hill.
Rizvi, F. and Lingard, B. (2010). *Globalizing Education Policy*, London: Taylor & Francis.
Robinson, W. (2004). *Power to Teach: Learning through Practice*, London: Woburn.
Rose, A.M. (ed.) (1962). *Human Behaviour and Social Processes*, London: Routledge and Kegan Paul: 3–19.
Roth, L. (2007). *Multiculturalism*, Briefing Paper No. 9/07, Sydney, New South Wales: NSW Parliamentary Library Research Service.
Rousmaniere, K. (2009). The great divide: Principals, teachers and the long hallway between them, *History of Education Review*, 38(2): 17–27.
Rubin, H.J. and Rubin, I.S. (1995). *Qualitative Interviewing: The Art of Hearing Data*, London: Sage.
Rutter, J. (2003). *Supporting Refugee Children in 21st century Britain: A Compendium of Essential Information*, London: Trentham Books.
Sachs, J. and Logan, L. (1990). Control or development? A study of in service education, *Journal of Curriculum Studies*, 22(5): 473–481.
Sajfert, D., Cvijanović, S. and Atanasković, P. (2009). Organizing and managing in elementary schools in Serbia, *Industrija*, 37(4): 77–102.
Sam, S. (2011). Leadership capacities and development of effective primary school principals: A case study of Kampong Chhnang Province, Master Thesis, Northeast Normal University, P.R. China.
Sandelowski, M. (1986). The problem of rigor in qualitative research, *Advances in Nursing Science*, 8: 27–37.
Sarantakos, S. (2005). *Social Research* (3rd edn), New York: Palgrave MacMillan.
Schmid, C.L. (2001). Educational achievement, language-minority students, and the new second generation, *Sociology of Education*, 74: 71–87.

Schwandt, T. A. (2003). Three epistemological stances for qualitative enquiry, in N.K. Denzin and Y.S. Lincoln (eds.) *The Landscape of Qualitative Research: Theories and Issues*, Thousand Oaks, CA: Sage.

Schwartz, H. and Jacobs, J. (1979). *Qualitative Sociology: A Method to the Madness*, New York: The Free Press.

Schweitzer, R., Melville, F., Steel, Z. and Lacherez, P. (2006). Trauma, post-migration living difficulties, and social support as predictors of psychological adjustment in resettled Sudanese refugees, *Australian and New Zealand Journal of Psychiatry*, 40: 179–187.

Scott, D. (ed.) (2003). *Curriculum Studies*, London: Routledge.

Shah, S. (2006). Educational leadership: An Islamic perspective, *British Educational Research Journal*, 32(3): 363–385.

Shields, C.M. (2004). Dialogic leadership for social justice: Overcoming pathologies of silence, *Educational Administration Quarterly*, 40: 109–131.

Sikes, P.J., Measor, L. and Woods, P. (1985). *Teacher Careers: Crises and Continuities*, London: Falmer Press.

Silver, H. (1980). Nothing but the present, or nothing but the past, in P. Gordon (ed.) *The Study of Education: A Collection of Inaugural Lectures*, London: Woburn Press.

Silver, H. (1994). Historiography of education, in T. Husen and T.N. Postlethwaite (eds.) *The International Encyclopaedia of Education*, London: Pergamon.

Silverman, D. (2005). *Doing Qualitative Research*, London: Sage.

Simons, M., Olssen, M. and Peters, M. (2009). Re-reading education policies, in M. Simons, M. Olssen and M. Peters (eds.) *Re-Reading Education Policies: A Handbook Studying the Policy Agenda of the 21st Century*, Rotterdam, The Netherlands: Sense Publishers.

Sinclair, A. (2000). Women within diversity: Risks and possibilities, *Women in Management Review*, 15(5/6): 137–145.

Sindell, P.S. (1974). Some discontinuities in the enculturation of Mistassini children, in G.D. Spindler (ed.) *Education and Cultural Process: Towards an Anthropology of Education*, New York: Holt, Rinehart and Winston.

Skilbeck, M. (1975). *School Based Curriculum Development*, London: Harper & Row.

Smith, A. (2005). Education in the twenty-first century: Conflict, reconstruction and reconciliation, *Compare: A Journal of Comparative and International Education*, 35(4): 373–391.

Smith, D. and Lovatt, T. (1991). *Curriculum: Action on Reflection*, Wentworth Falls, New South Wales: Social Science Press.

Spaull, A. (1985). *A History of Federal Teachers' Unions in Australia, 1921–85*, Canbera: Australian Teachers' Federation.

Spaull, A. and Sullivan, M. (1989). *A History of the Queensland Teachers' Union*, Sydney: Allen and Unwin.

Spindler, G.D. (1974). *Education and Cultural Process: Towards an Anthropology of Education*, New York: Holt, Rinehart & Winston.

Spradley, J.P. (1979). *The Ethnographic Interview*, New York: Holt, Rinehart and Winston.

Stainback, W. and Stainback, S. (1984). A rationale for the merger of special and regular education, *Exceptional Children*, 51: 102–111.

Stake, R.E. (1978). The case study method in social inquiry, *Educational Researcher*, 7: 5–8.

Stanley, W.O. (1968). The social foundations subjects in the professional education of teachers, *Educational Theory*, 18(3): 224–236.

Stenhouse, L. (1975). *An Introduction to Curriculum Research and Development*, London: Heinemann.

Strauss, A. (1987). *Qualitative Analysis for Social Scientists*, Cambridge: Cambridge University Press.

Strauss, A. and Corbin, J. (1990). *Basics of Qualitative Research. Grounded Theory Procedures and Techniques*, Newbury Park, CA: Sage.

Strauss, A. and Corbin, J. (1994). Grounded theory methodology: An overview, in N. Denzin and Y. Lincoln (eds.) *Handbook of Qualitative Research*, Thousand Oaks, CA: Sage Publications.

Streubert, H. and Carpenter, D. (1994). *Qualitative Research in Nursing: Advancing the humanistic Imperative*, Philadelphia: Lippincott.

Sullivan, J. (2006). Faith schools: A culture within a culture in a changing world, in M. deSouza, G. Durka, K. Engerbretson, R. Jackson and A. McGrady (eds.) *International Handbook of the Religious, Moral and Spiritual Dimensions of Education*, Dordrecht: Springer.

Sultana, R. (1991). Social movements and the transformation of teachers' work: Case studies from New Zealand, *Research papers in Education*, 6(2): 113–152.

Sutherland, E. (1937). *The Professional Thief*, Chicago: University of Chicago Press.

Sutherland, M.B. (1985). The place of theory of education in teacher education, *British Journal of Educational Studies*, 33(1): 222–234.

Sweetman, R.A. (2002). *A Fair and Just Solution? A History of the Integration of Private-Schools in New Zealand*, Palmerston North, New Zealand: Dunmore Press.

Tanako, M. (2005). *Educational Policy Borrowing*, Oxford: Symposium.

Taylor, S.J. and Bogdan, R. (1998). *Introduction to Qualitative Research Methods*, New York: John Wiley & Sons.

Theobald, M. (1994). History of women's education in Australia, in T. Husen and T.N. Postlethwaite (eds.) *The International Encyclopaedia of Education*, London: Pergamon.

Theobald, M. (1996). *Knowing Women: Origins of Women's Education in Nineteenth-Century Australia*, Cambridge: Cambridge University Press.

Thomas, G. (1997). What's the use of theory, *Harvard Educational Review*, 67(1): 75–104.

Thomas, W.I. and Znaniecki, F. (1918–20). *The Polish Peasant in Europe and America*, New York: Dover.

Thompson, E.P. (1965). *The Making of the English Working Class*, London: Victor Gollancz.

Thompson, P. (2000). *The Voice of the Past: Oral History*, Oxford: Oxford University Press.

Thomson, A. (1998). Fifty years on: An international perspective on oral history, *Journal of American History*, 85(2): 581–595.

Thrasher, F. (1927). *The Gang*, Chicago: University of Chicago Press.

Tot, L. (1966). *Mesto I Uloga Direktora Skole U Uslovima Samoupravljanja: Zbornik Stručno-metodskih Radova*, Beograd: Mlado Pokolenje.

Tot, L. (1974). *Društveno-ekonomski Položaj, Funkcija i Savremena Organizacija Naše Samoupravne Osnovne Skole: Doktorska Disertacija*, Subotica: Univerzitet u Novom Sadu, Subotica.

Trimingham-Jack, C. (1998). The lay sister in educational history and memory. Proceedings of the ANZHES Annual Conference, Auckland: ANZHES.

Trimingham-Jack, C. (2003). *Growing Good Catholic Girls. Education and Convent Life in Australia*, Melbourne: Melbourne University Press.

Trotman, J. (2008). *Girls Becoming Teachers*, New York: Cambria Press.

Uhrmacher, P.B. (1993). Coming to know the world through Waldorf education, *Journal of Curriculum and Supervision*, 9(1): 87–104.

Uhrmacher, P.B., McConnell Moroye, C. and Flinders, D.J. (2017) *Using Educational Criticism and Connoiseurship for Qualitative Research*, London: Routledge.

United Nations High Commissioner for Refugees (UNHCR). (1992). *Convention and Protocol: Relating to The Status of Refugees*, New York: UNHCR.

Usher, R. (1996). A critique of the neglected epistemological assumptions of educational research, in D. Scott and R. Usher (eds.) *Understanding Educational Research*, London: Routledge.

Valimaa, J. (2004). Nationalisation, localization and globalization in Finnish higher education, *Higher Education*, 48: 27–54.

Vidovich, L. (2004). Global-national-local dynamics in policy processes: A case study of 'quality' policy in higher education, *British Journal of Sociology of Education*, 25(3): 341–354.

Vidovich, L. (2009). You don't fatten the pig by weighting it: contradictory tensions in the 'policy pandemic' of accountability infecting education, in M. Simons, M. Olssen and M. Peters (eds.) *Re-reading Education Policies: Studying the Policy Agenda of the 21st Century*, Rotterdam, The Netherlands: Sense Publishers.

Vroom, H.V. and Jago, G.A. (2007). The role of the situation in leadership, *American Psychologist*, 62(1): 17–24.

Wangmo, T. and Choden, K. (2011). The education system in Bhutan from 747 AD to the first decade of the twenty-first century, in Yong Zhao, Jing Lei, Guofang Li, Ming Fang He, Kaori Okano, Nagwa Megahed, David Gamage and Hema Ramanathan (eds.) *Handbook of Asian Education: A Cultural Perspective*, London: Routledge.

Walker, A. (2005). *Effective leadership in multi-ethnic schools. Part I: Priorities, strategies and challenges.* Unpublished paper.

Walker, J.T. and Lofton, S.P. (2003). Effect of a problem based learning curriculum, on students perceptions of self-directed learning, *Issues in Educational Research* 13.

Waring, M. (1979). *Social Pressure and Curriculum Innovations: A Study of the Nuffield Foundation Science Teaching Project*, London: Methuen.

Watson, D. (2007). *Managing Civic and Community Engagement*, Maidenhead, UK: Open University Press.

Watson, L. (2009). Issues in reinventing school leadership: Reviewing the OECD report on improving school leadership from an Australian perspective, *Leading and Managing*, 15(1): 1–13.

Weinstein, M.H., Freedman, W.S. and Hughson, H. (2007). School voices: Challenges facing education systems after identity-based conflicts , *Education, Citizenship and Social Justice*, 2(1): 41–71.

Weisse, W. (2007). The European project on religion and education: 'REDCo'. An introduction, in R. Jackson, S. Miedema, W. Weisse and J.P. Willaime (eds.) *Religion and Education in Europe: Developments, Contexts and Debates*, Munster: Waxman.

Weldon, G. (2010). Post-conflict teacher development: Facing the past in South Africa, *Journal of Moral Education*, 39(3): 353–364.

Whitehead, K. (2003). *The New Women Teachers Come Along*, ANZHES Monograph Series, Sydney: ANZHES.

Whitehead, K. (2007). The spinster teacher in Australia from the 1870s to the 1960s, *History of Education Review*, 36(1): 1–17.

Wirth, L. (1928). *The Ghetto*, Chicago: University of Chicago Press.

Wolcott, H.F. (1973). *The Man in the Principal's Office: An Ethnography*, New York: Holt, Rinehart & Winston.

Wolcott, H.F. (1992). Posturing in qualitative research, in M. LeCompte, W. Milroy and J. Preissle (eds.) *Handbook of Qualitative Research in Education*, San Diego, CA: Academic Press.

Woods, P. (1983). *Sociology and the School*, London: Routledge and Kegan Paul.

Woods, P. (1985). Conversations with teachers: A potential source of their professional growth, *Curriculum Inquiry*, 12(3): 239–255.

Woods, P. (1986). *Inside Schools: Ethnography in Educational Research*, London: Routledge and Kegan Paul.

Woods, P. (1992a). Symbolic interactionism, in J. Goetz (ed.) *A Handbook of Qualitative Research in Education*, London: Sage.

Woods, P. (1992b). Symbolic interactionism: Theory and method, in M. LeCompte, W. Milroy and J. Preissle (eds.) *Handbook of Qualitative Research in Education*, San Diego, CA: Academic Press.

Woods, P. (2005). *Successful Writing for Qualitative Researchers*, London: Routledge.

World Bank. (2005). *Reshaping the Future: Education and Post-conflict Reconstruction. The International Bank for Reconstruction and Development*, Washington, DC: World Bank.

Yin, R. (2003). *Case Study Research: Design and Methods*, Thousand Oaks, CA: Sage.

Young, M.F.D. (ed.) (1971). *Knowledge and Control: New Directions for the Sociology of Education*, London: Collier-Macmillan.

Index